THE WAY OF THE SPIRIT

A Bible Reading Guide and Commentary

THE WAY OF THE SPIRIT

A Bible Reading Guide and Commentary

Vol. 1

THE CALL AND THE CROSS

**The Pentateuch
(Genesis – Deuteronomy)
Mark's Gospel
Hebrews
Romans**

JOHN McKAY

Kingdom Faith

First published in Great Britain in 1988
by Marshall Morgan and Scott Publications Ltd.

Reprinted, with corrections, in 1993 & 1997
by Kingdom Faith Ministries.

Revised Edition published in 1999
by Kingdom Faith Ministries
Roffey Place, Old Crawley Road, Faygate,
Horsham, West Sussex RH12 4RU
Tel 01293 851543
Fax 01293 851330
E-mail: theway@kingdomfaith.com

Copyright © 1988 John McKay

All rights reserved. No part of this publication may be reproduced, stored in a retrieval system, or transmitted, in any form or by any means, electronic, mechanical, photocopying, recording or otherwise, without the permission in writing, of Kingdom Faith Ministries.

Scripture in all four volumes of
The Way of the Spirit taken from the
HOLY BIBLE, NEW INTERNATIONAL VERSION.
Copyright © 1973, 1978, 1984 by
International Bible Society. Used by
permission of Hodder and Stoughton Limited.

ISBN: 0 9522198 0 8

Printed by Indeprint, Guildford at Creative Print & Design

With gratitude to God for all who have
taught me in the faith of Christ,
encouraged me in his service,
and sustained me with their prayers.

But now we have been released from the law so that we serve in the new way of the Spirit, and not in the old way of the written code.
Thanks be to God—through Jesus Christ our Lord!
Rom. 7.6,25 – NIV

Contents

List of Maps, Charts and Diagrams   x
Acknowledgements   xiii
Preface   xv

Part One: INTRODUCTION   1
1. GOD'S HISTORY OF REDEMPTION   3
   When the Time had Fully Come …   4
   The Beginning of the Story   8
   Studying the Pentateuch   9
2. PARADISE LOST (Gen. 1–11)   14

Part Two: THE CALL OF FAITH   25
3. THE PROMISE AND THE PATRIARCHS
   (Gen. 12–50)   27
   The World in Patriarchal Times   28
   Abraham (Gen. 12–25)   33
   Isaac (Gen. 21–35)   40
   Jacob (Gen. 25–50)   42
   The Sons of Jacob/Israel (Gen. 37–50)   46
4. GOD'S GRACE IN SALVATION (Exod. 1–18)   52
   The World of the Exodus   53
   The Exodus, a Triumph of Faith (Exod. 1–18)   54

Part Three: THE CALL OF OBEDIENCE   69
5. GOD'S GRACE IN REVELATION AND
   DISCIPLINE (Exod. 9 – Num. 36)   71
   At Mt. Sinai: A New Beginning
   (Exod. 19 – Num. 10)   71

From Sinai to Kadesh (Num. 10–20)	81
From Kadesh to the Plains of Moab (Num. 20–36)	88
6. NOW CHOOSE LIFE (Deuteronomy)	95
The Message of History (chs. 1–11)	97
Applying the Message at the Heart of the Law (chs. 12–26)	100
Blessing, Curse and Repentance (chs. 27–30)	105
Moses' Last Days (chs. 31–34)	106
7. THE HEART OF THE LAW	109
What the Law Contains	109
What the Law Requires	111
What the Law Offers	113
Part Four: SACRIFICE AND THE CROSS	117
8. SACRIFICE AND PRIESTHOOD	119
The Tabernacle	121
Priests and Levites	123
The Sacrifices	124
The Festivals	128
The Atoning Power of the Blood	131
9. STUDYING THE NEW TESTAMENT SEQUEL	134
A Christian Approach to the Pentateuch	134
Palestine in Jesus' Time	136
The Messiah, the New Covenant and the Spirit	142
10. FAITH IN ACTION (St. Mark's Gospel)	146
Mark and his Portrait of Jesus	146
'The Beginning of the Gospel' (1.1-13)	149
Early Ministry by the Sea of Galilee (chs. 1–5)	154
Wider Ministry in Galilee and beyond (chs. 6–9)	157
On to Jerusalem (9.14 – 10.52)	161
Jesus' Last Week (chs. 11–15)	163
Part Five: CHRISTIAN INTERPRETATION	169
11. THE SHADOW AND THE REALITY (The Epistle to the Hebrews)	171
The Son is Superior to Angels (1.1 – 3.1)	172
The Son is Superior to Moses (3.2 – 4.2)	174
Jesus is the *Great* High Priest (4.14 – 6.20)	175

	Jesus' Priesthood is Superior to Aaron's (7.1 – 10.39)	177
	Jesus is the Author and Perfecter of our Faith (chs. 11–12)	181
12.	FAITH AND THE RIGHTEOUSNESS FROM GOD (Paul's Gospel in Romans)	183
	Introductory Summary of Paul's Gospel (1.16-17)	184
	The Wrath of God (1.18 – 3.20)	186
	The Righteousness of God (3.21 – 7.25)	187
	New Life in the Spirit, and the Hope of Glory (ch. 8)	193
	God's Plan and Purpose in History (chs. 9–11)	196
	The Heart of the New Law is Love (chs. 12–15)	200

Part Six: CONCLUSION — 205
13. FAITH MEANS FORWARD IN OBEDIENCE — 207

Chronology — 211
Glossary and Index — 217
Summary Outline and Reading Guide — 227
Home Study Course — 235

List of Maps

The Distribution of the Nations	22
The World of the Patriarchs	29
The Migration of the 'Sea Peoples'	31
Abraham's Journeys in Gen. 11–13	35
Main Sites in Canaan in Patriarchal Times	38
Jacob's Journey Home	45
The Journey from Egypt to Canaan	55
Possible Route of the Exodus and the Crossing of the Sea	63
From Sinai to Canaan	86
The Journey to Transjordan (Num. 21)	90
Where the Tribes are to Settle (Josh. 13–21)	93
Palestine in 30 AD	139
The Traditional Site of Jesus' Baptism (John 1.28)	151
Jesus' Galilean Ministry (Places mentioned in Mark 1–9)	155
The Journey to Jerusalem	162
Jerusalem	165

Charts and Diagrams

The Heritage of Cain and Seth	20
The Patriarchal Age	32
The Patriarchal Family	33
Dating the Exodus	54
Outline of the Sinai Story in Exod. 19–40	72
The Book of the Covenant	73
The Holiness Code	78
The Arrangement of the Tribes in Camp (Num. 2)	80
The Arrangement of the Tribes on the March (Num. 10.11-28)	82
The Tabernacle	122
Sacrifices and Offerings	127
Main Seasons and Festivals	129
From Moses to Christ—at a glance	137
Rulers of Palestine in New Testament Times	140
The Shadow and the Reality	180
'Through Christ Jesus the law of the Spirit of life set me free from the law of sin and death'	194
Paul's Doctrine of History (a free adaptation of a diagram in C.H. Dodd's *The Epistle of Paul to the Romans*, Hodder & Stoughton, 1932)	199

Acknowledgements

It would be impossible to list all the people who have contributed to the making of this book. Immediately it grew out of my lectures at Roffey Place Christian Training Centre, the faith college of the Bethany Fellowship in Sussex. It inevitably owes much to what I learned in my academic past as lecturer in Theology at Hull University, but many of the insights into the meaning of God's Word contained in it also came through the challenges of preaching and pastoral ministry and through conversation with other ministers of the Gospel. Above all I acknowledge an amazing unveiling of the mystery of the Scriptures that came when God filled me with his Holy Spirit, and I rejoice that something of the blessings I have been privileged to receive through his inspiration and share with my students can now be made more widely known through these pages.

My thanks also to the rest of the staff and students at Roffey Place, as well as the leaders and members of the Bethany Fellowship, who have had to bear with me while writing.

Most particularly I thank my wife, Marguerite, not only for reading my manuscripts and proofs and making many helpful suggestions, but for her patience, prayers and loving support, in which my sons, James and Iain, have also shared along with her. Without their constant help and encouragement, this work would certainly have been a great deal poorer.

John McKay
7th March, 1988.

Over the past eleven years this volume has been reprinted several times with small alterations and additions to produce greater clarity and incorporate further revelations. This time I have taken the opportunity afforded by reprinting to make some fairly major changes, to rewrite some passages and extend others, with the result that the page numbering does not always correspond exactly with the earlier printings, particularly after p. 119 where two extra pages have been added.

The unfolding of revelation never ceases. More extensive rewriting would certainly have been possible, but I have not altered the text more than I thought necessary, so that the Bible course is preserved as originally conceived.

Thank you to my son James for his patience in remaking all the maps and charts for computerised printing, and to David Stearns for redesigning the cover, with its illustration symbolising the fire of God's Spirit tracing its way over the pages of Bible-history.

16th May, 1999.

Preface

When I was young I loved Bible-stories. As I grew older I still loved them, but the Book they came from puzzled me. Somehow I could not grasp its plan; I could not find the key to unlock its mysteries.

Yet Jesus gave his disciples that key. After his resurrection he expounded it to the two on the road to Emmaus:

> *Beginning with Moses and all the Prophets, he explained to them what was said in all the Scriptures concerning himself.*
> (Luke 24.27)

Shortly after that he expounded it again to the Eleven and some others with them:

> *He said to them, 'This is what I told you while I was still with you: Everything must be fulfilled that is written about me in the Law of Moses, the Prophets and the Psalms.'*
>
> *Then he opened their minds so they could understand the Scriptures. He told them, 'This is what is written: The Christ will suffer and rise from the dead on the third day, and repentance and forgiveness of sins will be preached in his name to all nations. You are witnesses of these things. I am going to send you what my Father has promised; but stay in the city until you have been clothed with power from on high.'*
> (Luke 24.44-49)

Jesus clearly taught his disciples that the Bible had one consistent theme running right through it from the beginning, culminating in his own ministry, and preparing for the coming of the Spirit to his followers.

That central theme eluded me for a long time. I knew it must be there, but the more I searched and studied, the more complex the issue became—that is, until the Lord blessed me with the gift of his Holy Spirit. Almost immediately my Bible sprang to life and began to make excellent and coherent sense, page after page, book after book.

Naturally I was thrilled, though also amazed that, after many years of scholarly research, I had not understood earlier. Then I discovered that other Christians were experiencing the same illumination after baptism in the Holy Spirit and I began to recognise that, while there are many different ways of reading the Bible—the way of the historian, of the literary critic, of the theologian, and so forth—all ways I had explored fairly thoroughly in my academic career, what I had now discovered was another way, *the way of the Spirit*, and that gave me a satisfaction and enlightenment I had not hitherto known possible.

It is partly to share something of what I have learned on this way and partly to encourage others to enter on it that I now write.

The Overall Plan of Study.
This volume is the first in a series of four covering the whole Bible. Each deals with a successive period of Old Testament history, concentrates on the books of the Old Testament associated with that period and examines particular aspects of faith related to it. Each volume then traces the sequel to the story told in the Old Testament section through books of the New Testament that seem to provide an appropriate follow up, and in doing so separately examines one of the four well-known portraits of Jesus as Priest, King, Prophet and Lord.

The Purpose of the Series.
The purpose is to fill a gap by providing a commentary-guide to understanding the way of the Spirit through the Bible, not simply to produce yet another introduction to the Bible. There are plenty of these already, some giving far fuller coverage of many subjects than these four volumes do.

	VOL. 1 THE CALL AND THE CROSS	VOL. 2 TIMES OF REFRESHING	VOL. 3 HEIRS OF THE PROPHETS	VOL. 4 MY LORD AND MY GOD
OLD TESTAMENT	2000-1230 BC The Pentateuch Faith, obedience and sacrifice	1230-500 BC The Histories The Kingdom, revival and Messianic hope	1050-400 BC The Prophets Prophecy, revival and charismatic faith	600-0 BC The Writings The Lordship of God in history, worship and belief
NEW TESTAMENT	Mark Romans and Hebrews Jesus as Priest	Matthew Acts and Paul's mission letters Jesus as King	Luke Selections from Acts & various epistles, Revelation Jesus as Prophet	John 1-3 John, Paul's captivity & pastoral letters, James, Peter & Jude Jesus as Lord

For example, those who want to study archaeology, textual criticism, literary criticism, Biblical theology, Jewish culture and customs, and the like, will have to consult other works. Some of these fields are inevitably touched on in passing, but not studied in depth, for our concern lies elsewhere.

The gap to be filled is one recognised by many Christians who have been influenced over the past twenty to thirty years by the Charismatic Movement. Classical Pentecostalism never developed a total Biblical theology of its own, but tended to adopt already existing evangelical and fundamentalist systems of interpretation. Charismatics have mostly done the same, but with differing degrees of dissatisfaction since these theological systems, as well as the more liberal ones, usually fail to meet their need to learn more about the ways of the Spirit, the power of faith, revival, healing ministry, the dynamic of the word, etc.—in fact everything that relates to personal experience of God in the life of the believer. That is why we shall be endeavouring here, as we trace the Bible stories, to lay bare the heart that pulsates within giving them life, to tap their dynamic source, which is, of course, the Spirit of God himself.

As we study the history of Israel, we shall see how, unlike secular history, it is very much a story about God's dealings with men. When we trace the accounts of individual lives, we shall find they too are stories about the working of God's Spirit in transforming men. And throughout we shall also discover just how much the Bible does delight in the very things many Christians love to hear about in the Church today: the miraculous, the prophetic, the visionary, the love and fellowship of Spirit-filled believers, and so forth.

Our aim is therefore to provide a reasoned account of Christian faith, vision and experience as it is, or should be, grounded in Scripture. Hence, alongside and overarching the internal chronological and topical arrangement of each individual volume outlined above, there is a more comprehensive pattern relating to our overall purpose.

- Vol. 1 outlines the basic principles on which all Christian life and experience need to be founded: faith in God's promises, obedience to his call and acknowledgment of the saving power of Christ's sacrifice.
- Vol. 2 traces the main movements of revival in Biblical history, thus highlighting the principles by which God's kingdom operates and outlining the challenges and vision that inspire all men of the Spirit.
- Vol. 3 examines the experiences and teachings of prophets and other men of the Spirit in both Testaments more directly, demonstrating how their faith and vision are of the very essence of Biblical hope.
- Vol. 4 looks at the common approaches of Spirit-filled Christians and the Bible to worship, service, pastoral matters, the challenges of daily living, and the like.

How to approach the Way of the Spirit in the Bible.
These books are written as Bible-reading guides and so should be used in conjunction with the Bible.[1] As you read, pray that the Holy Spirit, whose work is to lead into all the truth, will take you behind all I have written here and show you his truth for yourself—and more than that, that he will

---

[1] A simple reading guide is provided on pp. 227-33. Workbooks and teaching tapes are also available for those who wish to use this book as the manual for a full home-study teaching course—see p. 235.

lead you to the very source of that truth in the life of God himself. Remember the warning of our Lord Jesus: 'You diligently study the Scriptures because you think that by them you possess eternal life. These are the Scriptures that testify about me, yet you refuse to come to me to have life.' (John 5.39f)

As you read your Bible with the aid of these notes, do not become too preoccupied with details, the precise interpretation of individual passages, words or phrases, complex historical or theological issues, etc., but rather allow yourself to walk on the stage of the ancient world, first with the men of Old Testament times, and then with Jesus and his disciples. Go with Jesus around Galilee, listen to him speaking, participate in the astonishment and excitement of the crowd, share in the puzzlement and the illumination of his disciples, get the feel of what you read. The information given in these pages is mainly intended to help you lay hold of that 'feel' for yourself, particularly as it relates to the vision, the power and the life of God these men of old knew.

The Bible can be read both for its information about the things of God and also for the enjoyment of its life. The first is theology, but on its own that can become the letter that kills, and so it needs to be coupled with the second, for 'the word of God is living and active ... it penetrates even to dividing soul and spirit ... it judges the thoughts and attitudes of the heart.' (Heb. 4.12) Our theology has to be living, and it is only the Spirit that gives life.

Paul also speaks about the difference between reading Scripture with and without the illumination of the Holy Spirit in 2 Cor. 3.14-18, where he says that Jews who read without the Spirit do so with a veil over their hearts. 'But,' he continues, 'whenever anyone turns to the Lord, the veil is taken away.' Then he adds, 'Now the Lord is the Spirit ...' and this 'comes form the Lord, who is the Spirit'. This removal of a veil is something Christians commonly experience after baptism with the Holy Spirit, and so my prayer is that you, the reader, will also know it being lifted as the Spirit enlightens God's Word for you.

Read your Bible in something like the way you would read a novel or watch a play. Take yourself into the life of its drama and let the feel of that life begin to flow through your life as you walk and talk with the ancient men of God and above all with Jesus. Lay hold of their vision and let it become yours as well. Let their longings be your longings and in the end let their joys be your joys, for therein lies the life God wants you to know in Christ.

All Biblical quotations are taken from the New International Version of the Bible. To avoid confusion, the conventions of the NIV translators have also been adhered to beyond the quotations, e.g., 'he' rather than 'He' for God, 'the Most Holy Place' rather than 'the Holy of Holies', 'Spirit' (of God) rather than 'spirit' in the Old Testament (contrast RSV).

PART ONE

INTRODUCTION

1

God's History of Redemption

Our intention is not simply to study history or to examine doctrines, but to learn the ways of faith, to discover the power of obedience, and above all to savour the grace of God. History and doctrine cannot be avoided, but without the divine, faith dynamic they are sterile. It is the Spirit that gives life! Our story is therefore not just about some men who turned their minds to heavenly things, but about God and the world he created and cares for. It is his history as much as it is man's.

God has a purpose for his world. At the dawn of time he invited man to participate in it, but man messed it up. In due course he invited one particular man to co-operate with him. This man caught the vision and served it faithfully throughout his life. His children continued to treasure it and though they fell upon hard times, they became the nucleus of a nation at whose heart it remained burning, if but dimly.

God rescued this beleaguered people, took them to himself and renewed the invitation he had given to their forefather, promising blessings if they co-operated in his plan. They eagerly committed themselves at first, but their enthusiasm quickly evaporated. Though they repeatedly suffered the consequences of rebellion, God continued to uphold them. He led them to the land he had promised to give them and there they became established as a national state. He did many things to help them keep the vision alive: he gave them a system of worship, priests to instruct them, judges and kings to govern them, prophets to speak his word to them.

But all that was only further preparation for what was to be the next major step in the outworking of the vision he had shown their first forefather, and so in due time he sent his

Son ... and through him his Spirit for all who believe ... to strengthen them for continuing participation in his purposes as the work of redemption spreads to all mankind.

1. WHEN THE TIME HAD FULLY COME ...

When the time had fully come, God sent his Son, born of a woman, born under law, to redeem those under law, that we might receive the full rights of sons.

(Gal. 4.4-5)

Before tracing the early stages of God's dealings with his world in detail, it will be helpful to have a simplified, introductory overview of the whole Bible-story, so that we can read our Pentateuchal stories and New Testament books in historical perspective and in the context of God's total purpose.

To do that we shall use the pattern of a twelve-hour clock. The scheme is helpful only in as much as it gives a bird's eye survey, but it is no more than a structural simplification and has little regard for chronological exactitude. For example, the time lapse between hours one and two is immensely far greater than that between hours three and four. But at this preliminary stage all we need is the general overview.

12.00 (Midnight): CREATION (Genesis 1–2)
Note how it is repeated several times: 'God saw that it was good'. The Garden of Eden is exactly how God intended his world to be, a place of total peace and harmony—between man and woman, man and the animals, man and plant life.

1.00 a.m.: THE FALL (Genesis 3–11)
As a result of sin, 'God saw how corrupt the earth had become' (6.12). The Tower of Babel story shows the final end of sin's corruption on earth: man alienated from man and from God. The question now is what God can do to rescue his handiwork and restore Eden.

God's History of Redemption

2.00 a.m.: THE CALL OF ABRAHAM (Genesis 12–50; c. 2000–1500 or 2000–1300)
God chooses one man, Abraham, and promises to restore blessing to mankind through his descendants in a land of his own appointing. We are not told how, but as the story unfolds, we hear about some of the problems Abraham and his offspring had in living out the faith-implications of this promise. They end up as strangers in Egypt!

3.00 a.m.: MOSES AND THE LAW (Exodus – Deuteronomy; mid-fifteenth or mid-thirteenth century)
God again chooses one man, Moses, through whom he leads his people out of captivity. At Mount Sinai, on their way back to the Promised Land, he gives them his law, the pattern of holiness by which he wants his redeemed people to live. He also comes to dwell among them by his presence in a new sanctuary that he commissions as a place of sacrifice to deal in mercy with the sins that separate them from him. However, because of continuing rebellion, they have to spend forty years wandering in the wilderness.

4.00 a.m.: THE CONQUEST (Joshua; c. 1400 or 1230)
After the death of Moses, Joshua leads the people into Canaan and is able to conquer most of the land.

5.00 a.m.: THE SETTLEMENT (Judges; fourteenth or twelfth to eleventh centuries)
Because the people turned away from God in disobedience, they found themselves oppressed by invaders, etc., but on repentance the LORD sent them deliverers ('judges') who drove out the invaders and restored peace.

6.00 a.m.: THE KINGS (1 Samuel – 2 Kings; c. 1050–597)
Because of Philistine aggression the people asked for a king. Saul was chosen, but his rule turned sour through pride and disobedience, then the choice passed to David, who established a dynasty that ruled till 597 BC.

7.00 a.m.: THE PRIESTS (Chronicles, Ezra, Nehemiah; 950 BC – 70 AD)
Solomon built the temple in Jerusalem and it became the

focus of religious practice and belief in Israel. From it the priests exercised an authority second only to the kings, and after the Exile, virtually second to none.

8.00 a.m.: THE PROPHETS (Samuel, Kings, Isaiah–Malachi; 1050 – 400)
Starting with Samuel, Israel had a succession of prophets, whose activities peaked at crisis times. They were charismatic enthusiasts who spoke out God's word of judgment against unrighteousness and who called Israel back to the promises and faith of her forefathers, foretelling also the day of a New Covenant, a coming Anointed One (Messiah) and an outpouring of the Spirit of God.

9.00 a.m.: THE EXILE (2 Kings 24f, etc.; 597–538)
On the death of Solomon (931) the kingdom split into Judah (in the south) and Israel/Ephraim (in the north). Israel was destroyed in 722 by the Assyrians, and Judah was taken by the Babylonians in 597. The people of Judah and Jerusalem were taken as exiles into Babylonia, but were allowed to return in 538, after Cyrus the Persian took Babylon.

10.00 a.m.: THE JEWS AMONG THE NATIONS (597 – today)
The Exile left Israelites (now known as Jews) scattered all over the ancient map. Some returned and rebuilt Jerusalem; a few prophets (e.g. Haggai, Zechariah, Malachi) kept faith alive, but the Jews gradually settled down to live and let live and to wait for the day their Messiah would come. They were ruled first by the Persians and then the Greeks. They gained independence for a while in the second century BC, and then finally were brought under the rule of the Romans.

11.00 a.m.: THE ROMAN PEACE (63 BC – 70 AD)
The Roman Empire brought peace to the ancient world. Travel was safer than at any time before. There was religious toleration during the early first century AD. The Greeks had left the world with an international language and culture. There were Jews in every land and in every main city, men of faith waiting for their Messiah. By and large the lessons of Moses and the prophets had been learned by

God's people. The time was ripe as never before for Christ to come; all the preparation needed had been accomplished.

11.55 a.m.: THE BIRTH OF JESUS CHRIST (5 BC !)
'When the time had fully come, God sent his son.' (Gal. 4.4)

11.57 a.m.: THE SPREAD OF THE GOSPEL IN THE ROMAN EMPIRE
A glance at the list of those present in Jerusalem in Acts 2 shows how well prepared the international scene was for the gospel.

12.00 (Noon): THE END (70 AD)
The sacrifice of Christ had been offered and time had been allowed for the news of it to reach God's ancient people, the Jews, everywhere. The temple and its sacrifices were no longer needed; the Romans destroyed it in 70 AD. The morning of God's history of the world was fully past, but the afternoon time of Christian history is another story to be told somewhere else.

It is an amazing story, how God raised up from one man, Abraham, a whole nation of people on the soil of Palestine, and then scattered them through the ancient world so that there were men prepared for Christ's coming strategically positioned everywhere. The course of spiritual preparation is also amazingly precise: first the teaching about the oneness of God and the need to relate to him in faith, then about his righteousness (in the Law) and the need for obedience, both essential themes for salvation and life in Christ as presented in the New Testament. Thirdly, he taught them about Messianic hope through the Davidic kings, fourth about sacrifice for sin through the priestly system, and fifth about the power of the Spirit through the prophets, all of which prepared the way for the coming of Christ, his sacrificial death on Calvary and the gift of the Holy Spirit at Pentecost.

2. THE BEGINNING OF THE STORY

In the Old Testament section of this book we shall be looking in detail only at the first stages of the story, and the theological emphasis will be mainly on faith, obedience and sacrifice. We shall discover how men laid hold of the vision of God's purpose and learned to respond to it in faith, how they were invited to participate in its outworking and sought to live in obedience to what that call required of them. We shall also discover how they found it difficult to maintain themselves in this vision and call, how their faith lagged and their obedience failed. But equally we see they were men who chose to sacrifice everything for the call and through them the work does increase and expand. It will be like watching a spring burst forth from dry ground, become first a trickle, then a stream, then a river, which is eventually, beyond the story we trace here, to widen into a vast estuary flowing out towards the mighty ocean of global humanity. What started with one man 4,000 years ago has today become that vast estuary, as the vision God showed Abraham draws nearer to its ultimate fulfilment.

We shall also see that the secret of its progress is not man's tenacity in the vision, but God's faithfulness in encouraging and upholding him in it. We shall watch men flounder again and again, indeed sometimes so much so that we wonder whether the vision can ever attain fulfilment. But then we shall see God pick them up and restore them to faith and obedience once more. His purposes are never thwarted, neither then nor today.

Reading these ancient tales does nothing but encourage us now to stand firm in our own faith and obedience as we see the day of fulfilment approaching. God still looks for men of vision, men who will commit themselves to serve the vision he gave first to Abraham, then to Israel, then through Christ, and finally to his Church. He looks for a people who will unite in that vision, serving it as one, with undivided loyalty to himself and his call. The vision is, after all, of an earth restored to the Paradise he first envisaged it would be, and to serve such a vision cannot but be good.

Strangely, however, we do find such faithfulness difficult

to maintain. But the secret of success is found in the story. It lies in recognising that the vision is God's, not ours, that we are invited to co-operate in it, not create it, and that the strength to do so comes from God, not from us. He communicates the vision and instructs us in its ways by his Word, but he supplies us with strength to be faithful by his Spirit. The Pentateuch is mainly a story about preparatory teaching, about how God first taught men the vision and its ways, and is therefore more an account of God's communication by his Word than by his Spirit, but even so, we shall certainly see clear evidences of the Spirit's workings in many of its stories, and beyond that we shall catch occasional glimpses of a promise of a fuller outpouring of the Spirit that he was preparing to make available to all men.

From beginning to end the Bible is full of stories about men on whom the Spirit rested, who saw visions and dreamed dreams, who lived and moved in a world of miraculous signs and wonders, who prophesied in words given to them by God, who knew the authority of God's Word and the power of his Spirit. We do find them in the Pentateuch, but there first and foremost we are reading about the laying of foundations of revelation. Without that the development of the prophetic/charismatic vision has little meaning, for the Spirit is given to impart both revelation and the power to fulfil it.

3. STUDYING THE PENTATEUCH

What is the Pentateuch?
The word 'Pentateuch' simply means 'five books' (Greek: *penta* = five, *teuchos* = book) and is used to refer to the first five books in the Bible: Genesis, Exodus, Leviticus, Numbers and Deuteronomy. The Jews call them 'The Torah' (Hebrew: *torah* = law or teaching), because they contain most of the Bible's legal teaching.

Since the Jews do not recognise our New Testament as sacred Scripture, they do not refer to the Hebrew Bible as 'The Old Testament'. Their name for it is 'The Law, The Prophets and The Writings' (*Torah, Nebi'im uKethubim*).

'The Law' refers to the Pentateuch.
'The Prophets' refers to
   (i) the history books Joshua, Judges, Samuel and Kings ('the former prophets');
   (ii) the prophetic books Isaiah, Jeremiah, Ezekiel and the twelve Minor Prophets from Hosea to Malachi ('the latter prophets').
'The Writings' refers to everything else.

The books in the Hebrew Bible are arranged in that order, which is different from the English order, and the Law is its first main section.

The names of the five books mostly relate to their content:

Genesis means 'origin' (of the world and Israel's history).
Exodus means 'departure' (from Egypt).
Leviticus means 'Levitical book' (that is, concerning the Levites and their priestly regulations and practices).
Numbers is so called because of the census at the beginning and end of the book.
Deuteronomy means 'Second Law' (or the re-presentation of the law by Moses at the end of his life).

Who wrote the Pentateuch and when?

The Pentateuch is sometimes called 'The Five Books of Moses', and each book separately referred to as 'The First Book of Moses', 'The Second ...', etc. These titles reflect ancient Jewish and Christian tradition that Moses was their author, but since the Reformation that tradition has often been questioned and in this century virtually abandoned by Biblical scholars who prefer to think of the Pentateuch as having been put together from different sources. We shall not be discussing their hypotheses here since they do not greatly impinge on our approach, which is concerned with matters of faith rather than literary analysis.

How we date the Pentateuchal writings depends entirely on our view of authorship. The scholarly views place most of the sources they identify at various points between the tenth and fourth centuries. The traditional view, of course, relates the whole to the time of Moses himself.

Outline of Contents.

Gen. 1–11 contains stories about beginnings, relating to what we today would call prehistorical times.

Gen. 12–50 is mostly made up of stories we call 'the Patriarchal Narratives', because they recount the exploits of the patriarchs or forefathers of Israel, that is, before Israel became a nation.

Exod. 1–19 tells of the departure from Egypt and arrival at Mount Sinai.

Exod. 20–40 gives the stories of what happened at Mount Sinai and details of various laws.

Leviticus is almost entirely made up of religious laws.

Numbers is a mixture of laws and stories relating to the last stages of the wilderness wandering.

Deuteronomy presents Moses addressing the Israelites on the east bank of the Jordan, on the eve of his death and of their entry into the land, reminding them of the laws and exhorting them to obedience.

This brief summary shows fairly clearly that while the Pentateuch tells a continuous story from creation to the time of Moses, it contains quite a variety of material. We find:

- Stories of a historical and biographical nature, particularly in Genesis, Exodus and Numbers.
- The stories of Creation, the Garden of Eden, the Flood and the Tower of Babel which belong to the world of prehistory.
- Genealogical lists summarising long stretches of history;
- Poems and Songs, some outlining historical episodes, but others not.
- Law-codes of various shapes and sizes.
- Sermons on the law or on history (especially in Deuteronomy).
- Some scholars would like to add sagas, legends and other literary categories to this list.

The main thing to note at this stage is that the style can change from page to page and sometimes it is important to recognise what kind of literature any particular passage contains in order to understand properly what it teaches. We shall see, for example, how our understanding of Deuteronomy changes when we read it as mostly sermon rather than just law, or how our understanding of Gen. 1–11 is affected by reading it as an account of pre-history rather than history.

Historical Background.

The stories of the Pentateuch concentrate almost exclusively on the people who became Israel without too much reference to other nations. But Israel was a relative late-comer on the historical scene. The map of the ancient world (see p. 29) was dominated by two large culture-blocks, Egypt and Mesopotamia. In both the birth of civilisation dates back to around 3,000 BC. Abraham probably lived soon after 2,000 BC and David around 1,000 BC. Geographically Israel was placed between these two major civilisations and her history was always governed by their relative strengths and weaknesses.

However, the Bible's attitude to the surrounding nations is largely to ignore them, except where their doings impinge on Israel's own life. More than that, our story for the first 500 years or so after Abraham's call is only about a family, not even a nation, and as such is hardly what we normally call history. We may call it family history or saga, but not national, international or political history.

Archaeologists have unearthed a great deal of material illustrating the life and culture of the ancient world, and we shall occasionally refer to their findings, but only when we find it helpful for our purposes, which are not primarily to write a history of Israel and the ancient Near East. Our intention is to trace the story of faith, which is also the Bible's main purpose.

The Religion of the Patriarchs.

Every ancient, pagan religion was *polytheistic*, i.e. had many gods.

Some of these drew little distinction between good and evil, but simply associated gods with rivers, trees, mountains and all geophysical phenomena. Such religion we call *animism.*

Some distinguished two groupings of gods, good and evil, and viewed the world as a kind of battle-field for the two groups. Neither group was classified as finally victorious;

life continued to depend on which group had the upper hand at any particular season. We call such religion *dualism*.

Some distinguished a single supreme god among all the others, one that could be regarded as a worshipper's sole god, but in no way denying either the existence of other gods or their power. Such religion we term *henotheism*.

Israel's religion, which recognised the existence of only one God was unique in ancient times. We call it *monotheism*.

Though Abraham's background was polytheism, his call must have made him a monotheist overnight (Josh. 24.2f). At least we never find him offering allegiance to any other god, though equally we never find him trying to convert anyone to his beliefs. Most of the peoples he mixed with in Canaan would have had dualistic views, for their religion was very much linked with seasonal conflict. To them Baal was the god of winter's rains bringing life to the earth, and his adversary was Mot, the god of summer's heat bringing drought and death. The Canaanite cults attracted some Israelites in later days, but apart from warnings about them in the law, the Pentateuchal stories contain hardly any references to them.

The pressing issues for Abraham and his descendants were not doctrines and debates about monotheism and polytheism, so much as the challenges of faith and obedience required in response to God's promises to them and his call upon their lives. Their questions were not about which god, but about how to walk in faithfulness with *this* God, the LORD, who had so dramatically put his hand upon them.

Just as our story is not about nations, so it is not about gods. It is the story about the One God and the people he chose to co-operate with him in his work of redemption.

2
Paradise Lost

GENESIS 1–11

Gen. 1–11 is pre-history rather than history. Israel's history only begins properly in Gen. 12 when God calls the first forefather, Abraham. Gen. 1–11 is like a prologue to that history, setting the scene for the action, so to speak. Unlike the later chapters that lead us carefully through the years with fairly detailed stories about the lives of men, Gen. 1–11 sweeps over vast reaches of time from the very dawn of creation, painting only a handful of brief artistic sketches to explain how things are as they are.

There are only six sketches altogether:
- Creation (ch. 1)
- the Garden of Eden (ch. 2)
- the Fall of Man (ch. 3)
- Cain and his descendants (ch. 4)
- Noah and the Flood (chs. 6–9)
- the Tower of Babel (ch. 11)

These sketches hardly cover the full story of mankind before Abraham's day, and though some of the gaps are filled out with genealogical lists that transport us rapidly down the centuries (chs. 5 & 10), we cannot help feeling that the purpose behind Gen. 1–11 is not simply to relate history.

What we have here is rather a portrait in words painted by a master artist, showing us the goodness of God's creation and the mess man has made of it. His stories are told to depict broad truths on a large canvas so that we can see, before we start looking at history itself, exactly what the challenges facing God and man are. And as we shall discover, they raise dramatic questions that set the scene for a play that promises to be exciting and yet relevant to the real issues of daily living.

Our purpose is to examine that portrait and highlight its significance for our lives rather than discuss issues of science or ancient history, though some of these will inevitably be touched on in passing. Other books can be found that deal with such matters; they are not central to our present aim.

1.1 – 2.3: In the beginning ...

The whole universe is paraded before our eyes in a series of vast panoramic views corresponding in arrangement with the days of a week. It is a matter of debate whether the author intended us to think of creation actually happening within the course of one week of seven 24-hour days, or whether his arrangement is purely schematic, like the arrangement of the visions of the end-times into series of sevens in Rev. 6–11; 15–16. (Incidentally, we shall discover that the picture of the end-time corresponds in many ways with the picture of the beginning. That is because the Bible's ultimate vision is of the curse of sin reversed and all the goodness of the original creation restored.)

However we choose to believe it all started, what we do need to notice particularly is that God's purpose in creating was good. Six times it is said that God looked at what he had created 'and saw that it was good' (1.4,10,12,18,21,25), and then at the end 'God saw all that he had made, and it was very good' (1.31). The picture is one of total satisfaction, of something complete and thoroughly wholesome. God is able to rest on the seventh day, because his handiwork does not need to be added to or touched up at places where it is unsatisfactory. God's work is always complete; he never has to reassess it, as we often do ours, with regret that it was not done this way or that. Similarly Jesus, at the end of his life, was able to say 'It is finished.' (John 19.30)

A second point that calls for comment is the place of man in God's scheme of things. The account of creation is arranged in eight acts spread over six days:

Day One   – light (day) and darkness (night)
Day Two   – the expanse of the sky
Day Three – dry ground (land) and waters (seas)
             – vegetation (plants and trees)

Day Four – sun, moon and stars (to mark seasons, days and years)
Day Five – sea creatures and birds
Day Six   – land animals, both domesticated and wild
          – man

The survey before we reach man is rapid, factual and without very much detail. God simply says 'Let there be ...', and each created thing appears. But when we come to man, we are given some insight into the reasons why he was created—we are told something about God's thoughts beforehand and about his communication with man afterwards. The heart of the matter is that man is made by God to rule over the earth as his viceroy. For that purpose he is made in God's own image and is given authority over all animal and plant life (cp. Ps. 8.5-8). God has created a good earth and in his goodness has given it to man to care for and enjoy. It is a precious and very happy picture.

Thirdly, note the method of God's operation. Before Day One his Spirit hovers over pre-creation formlessness, and then it is by his Word that everything is brought into being. Compare Ps. 33.6:

By the word of the LORD *were the heavens made,*
their starry host by the breath of his mouth (= his Spirit).

It is as though the Spirit and the Word are God's two hands. He uses them to create, and later, as we shall see, they continue to be the means by which he communicates with his creation, especially with man.

Fourthly, just as the last act of creation has particular significance, so also has the first. When God created the light on Day One, the sun had not yet appeared, nor even the sky. All that was there was a watery darkness (1.2), a kind of pre-creation cosmic soup! When God bade the light appear, he was doing what any workman would, switching on a light in his workshop to enable him to work. Christians through the ages have believed the source of this primordial light is the same as the source of light in the end-time, when there will no longer be any sun or moon, namely God himself (Rev. 21.23; 22.5)—that the light of Day One is light from God himself. And as at the beginning, it continues to be God's way that when he is about to create or recreate he will first cause his light to shine in our darkness. So it was when he sent Jesus into the world (John 1.5), and also when he entered our individual lives to recreate us (2 Cor. 4.6). After all, God is light (1 John 1.5), and the only way the chaotic mess of our lives will ever be sorted out is by his light shining into it. The principle of conversion is the same as that of creation.

Gen. 1 clearly does not tell us everything about earth's earliest stages. The chaos of something 'formless and empty' with 'darkness over the surface of the deep' existing before Day One is an unexplained mystery.

There is also a spiritual world that is never mentioned. When we reach ch. 3 we discover that Satan is already active in the serpent, but we are not told whether his fall occurred before, during or after earth's creation. If, as many Christians believe, the comparison in Isa. 14.12-15 between the king of Babylon and the 'morning star (literally 'bright one'—Latin: *lucifer*), son of the dawn' contains revelation about Satan's downfall, then it presupposes the existence of the earth, stars, mountains and clouds, but of course the language could be poetic, symbolising spiritual activity in the heavenly places, in which case it tells us nothing about the timing of the fall. On the other hand, Ezek. 28.12-19, which is also commonly assumed to refer to Satan's downfall, places it firmly in Eden, which is what the wording of Gen. 3.14 actually implies, for there God's curse is put on the serpent precisely 'because you have done this', that is, because he deceived Eve and so caused Adam's downfall.

There are many other questions left unresolved by Gen. 1, particularly in relation to issues raised by today's scientific hypotheses concerning earth's origins. But then it is not the purpose of Gen. 1 to deal with such questions. We have seen what it seeks to teach us—about the heart of God: that he created something good; filled darkness with light, formlessness with order, emptiness with life, and blessed it; that he made man in his own image to take charge of it; and in the end he was thoroughly satisfied with all he had made. Gen. 1 shows us God's heart, that he wills good, light, order, life and blessing to all he has made.

2.4-25: *The Garden of Eden.*

The sense of satisfaction and goodness is now enhanced as the story-teller invites us to take a closer look at man and the life God purposed for him. He paints for us a picture of a beautiful garden in a region called Eden (or 'Delight'), planted with 'trees that were pleasing to the eye and good for food' (v. 9), a place where a river flows to water the garden (v. 10). Here man lives at peace with the animals (vv. 18-20) and enjoys a uniquely happy and innocent relationship with his wife (v. 25). The picture is every man's Utopia: a life of peace removed from strife, a happy marriage, the company of friendly birds and animals, food in plenty free for the gathering, and the gentle occupation of caring for the world's most luxuriant garden. God's will for man is to live in such conditions, in Paradise itself!

There is a requirement, however. Man is different from the animals, made in God's image and therefore with ability to choose and be creative. God gives him large freedom of choice, but warns him of one danger, of trying to work it out himself without God, which is what the tree of the knowledge of good and evil in the garden symbolises. As long as he obeys God he will live and enjoy all his blessings, but the instant he disobeys he must lose it all. Here God establishes the principle of two ways that is to govern all subsequent history, the way of obedience that leads to life and blessing, and the way of disobedience that ends in curse and death. (See further, p. 96.)

Ch. 3: *The Fall of Man.*

Sadly man chooses the wrong way and his rebellion, sin, disobedience (call it what you will) results in the loss of this Paradise with all its benefits. Immediately we find ourselves face to face with man as we know him today, full of shame, guilt and fear (vv. 7-10), seeking excuses and blaming everyone but himself: Adam blames Eve and God, then she blames the serpent (vv. 11-13). But God is not interested in excuses. Suddenly we hear him cry, 'Cursed ... Cursed ...' (vv. 14,17), and the idyll is shattered. The beautiful canvas painted by our dramatic artist is ruined and man is banished from the Garden of Eden for ever, now to face a life of hardship, suffering and pain.

In Eden there were two special trees, representing the two ways, of death and life: 'the tree of the knowledge of good and evil' and 'the tree of life'. Driven from the garden man now has access to neither. He tasted of one, but that has left him in a condition of sin with some pretty warped notions. Deprived of the other, his only future is death. These two trees also represent the twin poles or foci of all God's dealings with men (his two hands in creation), corresponding to his Word (tree of knowledge) and his Spirit (tree of life). They symbolise the knowledge and the life of God himself, and as the drama of the Bible unfolds, we shall watch him gradually restoring men to a proper relationship with them, first through patriarchs and prophets, then more fully through Jesus, and finally in all fullness in the New Jerusalem of the end-time (Rev. 22).

4.1-24: Cain and his descendants.
Sin now tightens its hold, spreading through the human race and down the generations. Cain's jealousy leads to the murder of his brother, Abel, resulting in further curse and expulsion. Nevertheless, he establishes a city and by the fifth generation it has become a centre of culture and industry, but the heritage of his sin is not thereby expunged or even diminished, for presently we hear Lamech boast of a murder he considers much more spectacular than Cain's ever was.

Note how in v. 7 sin is likened to someone crouching at the door ready to pounce. Sin is no mere impersonal force, but something very personal, almost indistinguishable from Satan, 'and it desires to have you' (cp. Rom. 7.7-25).

4.25 – 5.32: Seth and his descendants.
God had had a purpose for Abel. Cain saw that and in his jealousy killed him, but God's purpose was not to be thwarted, so Seth was born 'in place of Abel' and soon afterwards 'men began to call on the LORD.' The atmosphere in this family is very different from that in Cain's. At one level there are similarities in their heritage: both had descendants called Enoch and Lamech and others with similar sounding names, like Irad and Jared, or Methushael and Methuselah. But such comparison only highlights the

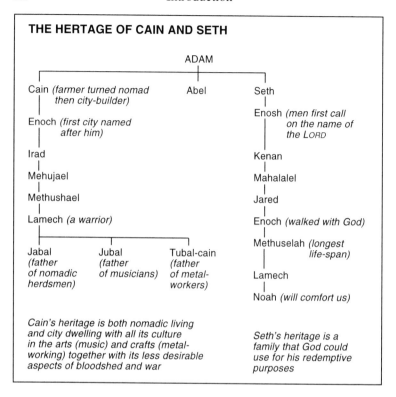

contrast. Cain's Enoch gave his name to a city, Seth's Enoch 'walked with God; then he was no more, because God took him away.' Seth's Methuselah was blessed with a longer life-span than any other man in history. Cain's Lamech boasted about his murderous revenge, Seth's Lamech became the father of Noah, whom he raised to be a righteous man, walking with God (6.9). Seth's family founded no memorable centre of cultured civilisation like Cain's, but God had his hand on them. They were like a people in the world, but not of it. Noah's father, Lamech, realised something of this truth and saw that behind it lay some redemptive purpose; he foresaw that his son would 'comfort us in the labour and painful toil of our hands caused by the ground the LORD has cursed.' (5.29).

Certainly sin is multiplying, but God has not forsaken his world.

Chs. 6–9: Noah and the Flood.

Seth's descendants apart, mankind is now totally lost in sin, and perversions, some of which we can no longer fully understand (6.1-7), have multiplied on earth. God, who so recently looked on his creation and 'saw that it was good', now looked down and saw 'how corrupt the earth had become' (6.12), 'was grieved that he had made man on the earth, and his heart was filled with pain' (6.6). The contrast between what God intended the world to be and what man has made of it is shattering. The earth is now fit only for destruction (6.13).

The story of the Flood and Noah's Ark is so familiar that it seems needless to retell it here. The tradition of this great primeval flood is so embedded in folk-memory that its story is found in the writings of other ancient civilisations. The 'earth' particularly affected by it must have been around Mesopotamia where Biblical man is generally located at this time and where the clearest extra-biblical records of it are preserved. Some of the details in the Babylonian account are strikingly parallel to those of the Genesis story.

The intention of the biblical account is very different from these others. It is told to show God's righteous anger against sin, that he cannot allow it to take over his earth. But equally it is to show that God's ultimate purpose is not destruction. While the flood checked the progress of sin, it did not resolve the problem. Shortly after it, we read about Noah becoming drunk and the unsavoury mess that resulted, issuing finally in the cursing of one of his sons. Some other answer will be needed ultimately.

After the Flood God promises that destruction will never be his purpose (8.21f), but the fallen condition of the earth is now an established fact and so he modifies some of his original instructions to Adam in recognition of the changed circumstances. Though he blesses again and still commands man to fruitfulness, he no longer commissions him to rule the earth. His relationship with its creatures is now governed by fear and God permits him to have the animals for food, just like the plants, though the blood (which is the life, cp. Lev. 17.11) is not to be eaten.

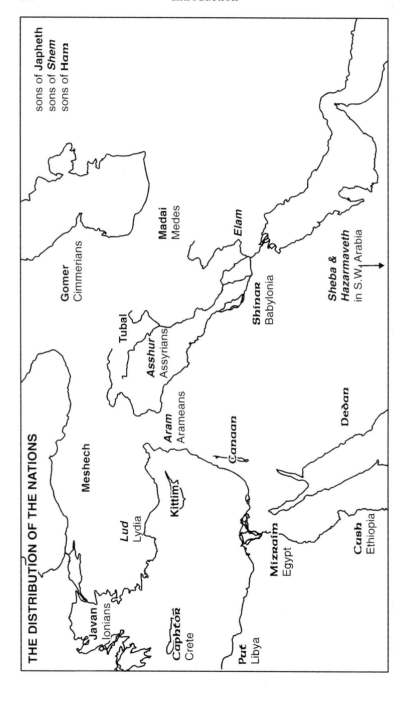

Ch. 10: The Distribution of the Nations.
Our prologue's portrait is now almost complete. The storyteller briefly surveys the peoples of antiquity, dividing mankind into three broad ethnic groups, corresponding to the three sons of Noah: Shem, Ham and Japheth.

Japheth represents the Indo-European races spread out across the north of the ancient map between the Aegean and the Caspian Seas.

Ham represents the southern peoples of North Africa, Ethiopia, Egypt, Arabia, Canaan and Southern Mesopotamia.

Shem represents those we today call Semites, then mainly located across the middle of the map, stretching from southern Turkey (Lud) through Syria (Aram) and Mesopotamia (Asshur) to Iran (Elam). It is from this branch of Noah's family that Abraham comes.

Ch. 11: The Tower of Babel.
We are now transported to Shinar (= Sumer, later Babylonia), a flat alluvial plain with no mountains, and so no rocks for building. Here men set themselves to build a city with clay bricks and in it a tower, an artificial mountain, reaching up into the heavens. That in itself was a pretty harmless pursuit, but the motive was not. Their intention was to 'make a name for ourselves' as a strong, integrated political unit, and so, presumably, to lord it over the rest of mankind. While God gave man authority to rule over animal and plant life in the beginning, he never gave him authority to raise himself above his fellow men. That prerogative belongs to God alone. In effect their tower would usurp the authority of God himself. Similar ambitions had led to Satan's downfall (Isa. 14.12-15), and now they are to lead to the further collapse of man. The outcome is total confusion—scattering of the peoples and division of earth's languages.

The final effect is complete alienation. In the Garden of Eden man and God had lived in perfect harmony. Adam's sin led to the breaking of that harmony between man and God; the sin of Babel now leads to the final shattering of any possible harmony between man and man. What we are left with is political and cultural division, which through history is to result in war and bloodshed.

The Challenge of Genesis 1–11.
These chapters have confronted us with some simple truths about God and man:
1. *God* is good and his purposes for his creation and for man in it are good (chs. 1 & 2).
2. *Sin* is no mere neutral principle, but something active in opposition to God (ch. 3).
3. *Man* is caught in a spiritual battle in which sin tries to lay hold of him and turn him from God (cp. 4.7).
4. Fallen man is weak, unable to resist temptation and conquer sin, even after God offers him a fresh start (ch. 9).
5. Though God has the power to create and destroy and has no intention of letting corruption control his earth, he clearly does not propose to restore his Eden by violent means (chs. 6–9).

Consequently, we are left asking:
- Is Paradise lost for ever? Or can it be regained?
- Has sin thwarted God's good purposes?
- Can man's headlong plunge into corruption be halted?— or perhaps even reversed?
- And if God can do anything about it, what can he do and how can he do it?

The questions are much the same as those people tussle with today, such as, 'If God is good, all-powerful, just, loving, etc., how can he allow such terrible things as we see around us to happen?' That is essentially the challenge of Gen. 1–11.

However, we have already been granted a few little glimpses of his way of working. We saw how he selected Abel, and then Seth and his descendants to bring 'comfort' to man in his 'labour and painful toil'. Will he not perhaps do something similar again? Strikingly Gen. 11 ends with a new hint of such things, for here our eyes are suddenly focused on a small family that sets out from Ur in Southern Mesopotamia to go to Canaan. They stop and settle in Haran in Northern Mesopotamia where the aged father of the family, Terah, dies. No explanations are given, but our attention is alerted. Why have we been introduced to this family? Is God perhaps about to do something through them as he did through Seth's children?

PART TWO

THE CALL OF FAITH

Faith is the most basic ingredient in a man's relationship with God and so it is only right that our Bible study should start with it as the main theme. So basic and essential is it that 'without faith it is impossible to please God' (Heb. 11.6); so necessary is it for every conceivable aspect of Christian living that the gospel is about 'faith from first to last' (Rom. 1.17).

This faith is not simply a set of beliefs or doctrines, but a response to God's word, his call, his promise, etc. Faith calls for action, not just consent, as we shall see when we examine Abraham's story. Basically it is trust that God will do what he says he will do, trust that enables us to respond to him in obedience when action is required, in patience when waiting is called for, in expectancy when something is promised, and in gratitude when something is offered.

'Faith is being sure of what we hope for and certain of what we do not see. This is what the ancients were commended for.' (Heb. 11.1f) In the pages that follow we shall begin to see how and why.

3

The Promise and the Patriarchs

GENESIS 12–50

It is a wonderful privilege to read the Old Testament as a Christian enlightened by the Holy Spirit. St. Paul says it is like reading with a veil lifted (2 Cor. 3.14-18). Before Christ it is not always very clear what God's plan of salvation is, but after receiving the illumination of his Spirit everything fits into place and it all makes new sense. We begin to see how God has been dealing with the challenges of Gen. 1–11 and we discover how to live beyond the dramatic tensions we have just outlined. For example, the greatest challenge of Gen. 1–11 is alienation and the need for reconciliation, but now we know through our experience in Christ the truth of the fact that that problem is being radically dealt with 'because God has poured out his love into our hearts by the Holy Spirit, whom he has given us' (Rom. 5.5).

We see the effectiveness of this in many ways. Of course, there is the obvious blessing of the reversal of the curse of Babel enjoyed in charismatic circles through the gift of tongues which enables people of different nationalities to worship together in harmony, and sometimes to cross the language barriers in communication. But more radical is the Spirit's work of breaking down barriers of suspicion, envy, hostility, etc., in the heart and replacing them with his love. In the power of that it is possible today to recapture something of the flavour of Eden.

But such blessings still belong to the future as we begin to read Gen. 12, and to get the true flavour of Abraham's and his descendants' hope we need to remember 'they did not receive the things promised; they only saw them and welcomed them from a distance' (Heb. 11.13). God revealed to them only as much as they needed for their time, but the lessons of faith they learned are the same in quality as those we need to learn for today. There is, of course, one significant difference in perspective in that their faith looked forward to a focal point, to which ours now looks back. Abraham believed God would do what he had promised; we believe he has done it. (Faith, of course, still has a future aspect as well.) The focus of the promise is the same for both, resting in the life, death and resurrection of Jesus Christ, and either way, whether viewed from before or after, the faith has to be the same, and that is why the words spoken of Abraham's faith, 'it was credited to him as righteousness', can apply equally to our faith today (Rom. 4.20-25). Although we live today at the other side of the cross, there is still much we can learn from Abraham, Isaac and Jacob, particularly about faith and obedience (cp. Heb. 11).

1. THE WORLD IN PATRIARCHAL TIMES

The patriarchs lived and moved along that part of the ancient world we call 'the Fertile Crescent', stretching up through Mesopotamia and down through Syria (Aram) and Canaan to Egypt. The civilisations of Egypt and Mesopotamia were already old when Abraham's father left Ur. His departure was probably associated with the sack of Ur, round about 1950 BC, when the city, a major centre of Sumerian society, was destroyed by Elamites from the east. Apparently Terah, his father, had had it in mind to migrate to Canaan, but he only got as far as Haran in Northern Mesopotamia, a city that was in many respects a twin of Ur, for both were centres of commerce and both well known for their patronage of the Moon-god.

Mesopotamia had enjoyed a period of considerable culture and imperial power under its Sumerian and Akkadian rulers at the end of the third millennium, but it became divided into smaller city-state units in the early second. Assyria and Babylonia first emerged as important political entities at this time, though it was mainly Assyria

The Promise and the Patriarchs

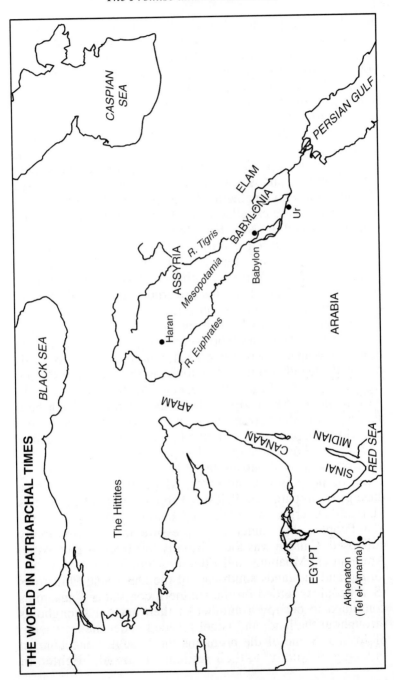

that showed expansionist tendencies. From 1500 to 1100 it was one of the leading states in the ancient world, but then it entered a period of weakness and only revived again about 900 BC. Apart from being the birthplace of Abraham and a source of wives for Isaac and Jacob, Mesopotamia plays no major part in the Biblical account of the history of God's people during the second millennium.

Egypt was the main external influence on Israel in its earliest history. About 1720 foreign kings known as the Hyksos came to power. Like Joseph and his brothers, they were Semites, and so would probably have received the Hebrews more sympathetically than native Egyptian rulers might. They were expelled in 1570 by Amosis, an Egyptian, who established the New Kingdom and turned Egypt into an empire that exercised control over Canaan for most of the following 350 years. Letters from the royal archives of Akhen-aten (Tutenkamen's father-in-law) found at Tel el-Amarna, tell of problems his governors had in Palestine in the fourteenth century controlling rebel elements called *Aperu*, who seem to have been of the same ethnic background as the Hebrews who were in Egypt at the time. The last great emperor was Rameses II, who ruled for two-thirds of the thirteenth century, but towards the end of his reign Egyptian power began to weaken. At this time a folk-movement of 'Sea Peoples' from the islands and northern shores of the Mediterranean down the coast of Palestine and into North Africa was beginning to erode Egypt's strength.

The Israelites came out of Egypt in Rameses' time. They are first mentioned outside the Bible in an inscription giving a list of peoples his successor, Merniptah, fought against during a campaign in Palestine about 1220. Most of this Pharaoh's energies were taken up stemming the influx of the Sea Peoples, but under their pressure the empire finally collapsed. Canaan was then virtually left free for the taking. Ammonites, Moabites and Edomites took control of Trans-jordan and the lands south-east of the Dead Sea; Philistines (Sea Peoples) settled on the southern coastland; Canaanites continued to occupy a number of their ancient strongholds throughout the land; and Israel invaded under the leadership of Joshua. Some of the problems the Israelites encountered in trying to hold on to their settlements are highlighted in

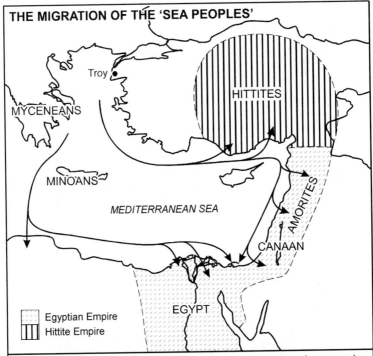

The migration of the Sea Peoples, as well as draining Egyptian strength, hastened the collapse of the Hittite Empire. Their movement was caused by an influx of new peoples into Greece from the north bringing an end to the Mycenean power that had controlled most of the Mediterranean sea-trade routes up to the thirteenth century. The upheavals of this time are also related to the fall of Troy which ended a long war between the Myceneans and the Trojans, about which the Greek poet Homer wrote in his *Iliad*.

the Book of Judges; Israel was only established in strength under David, who built up his own little empire, but that takes us beyond the history of the period we are studying here.

Although knowledge of the ancient Near Eastern background helps us to place the Bible stories in context, it is important to recognise that the stories themselves make little reference to international affairs. They are not written to give an account of ancient history. They are family tales, or sagas, tracing the private life-story of a man and his offspring, and they only cross-refer to world events and person-

The Call of Faith

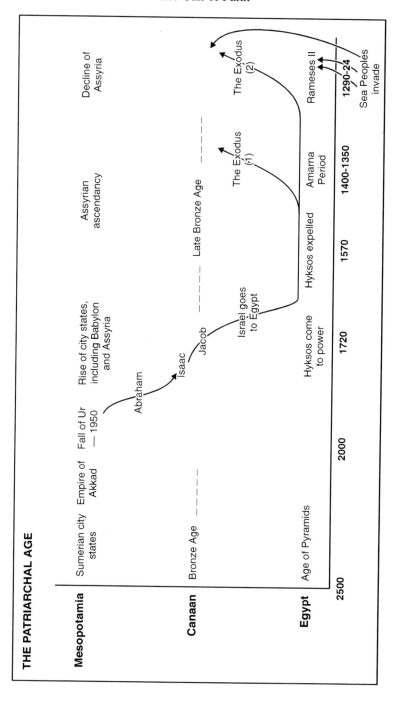

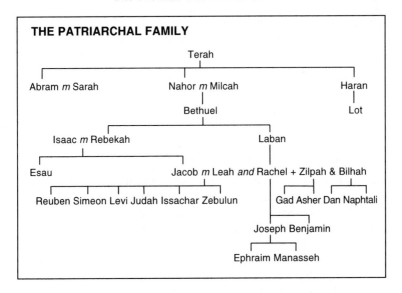

alities where necessary. Our story is about a chosen people and their God, about how they learned to respond to his ways, and about his purposes to use them for the salvation of mankind.

2. ABRAHAM (GEN. 12–25)

Abraham's story is of a man pulled out of paganism (Josh. 24.2,14), granted a vision of God's purpose for his world, invited to play a part in it, then learning what it means to respond in faith. It is a tale of groping faith on Abraham's part, and of unfailing faithfulness on God's. All the dramatic tensions of Gen. 1–11 come fully into play once more as we begin to trace Abraham's adventures. The date is sometime in the early second millennium BC.

12.1-3: God's call and promise.
Whatever reason Terah had had for going to Canaan, Abraham continues with the journey at God's command, leaving most of his relatives in Haran, where later he will send for a wife for his son, Isaac (ch. 24). At this early stage

Abraham is known as Abram, though for simplicity's sake we shall use only the longer name. (See ch. 17 for the change.)

God's word is very clear and very simple. He promises Abraham will:

1. receive a new homeland,
2. become father of a great nation,
3. receive personal blessing from God,
4. become a source of blessing for all peoples on earth.

The last component in this promise contains within itself the seed of a much wider vision that is to clarify itself more fully in later years, of Eden finally restored on earth (e.g. Isa. 11.6-9; Ezek. 47.6-12). For the present, however, that vision is but dimly perceived. The Garden of Eden is irretrievably lost, and practical realism offers no more than a knowledge that God will restore something of its flavour to men in this fallen world. The vision relates to future developments that lie far beyond Abraham's day, and so, apart from providing an over-arching focus of hope, it plays no immediate and active part in the story of Abraham's trials that follows.

The third component mainly operates of its own accord—there is not much Abraham can do about it anyway. We shall simply watch him become 'wealthy in livestock and in silver and gold' more or less automatically (cp. 13.2).

The first two components, by contrast, are the testing ground of his relationship with God. The drama centres mainly on his response to them, and several times we shall watch him try to work out God's purposes his own way, generally with dismal results.

God speaks with Abraham many times in the chapters that follow, but that is generally just to reaffirm these promises he gave right at the start. His later words add more details and more colour to the bald summary we have here, but they add no new promises. God has said it all at the start, and that is generally how it is when God calls a man, even today.

The Promise and the Patriarchs

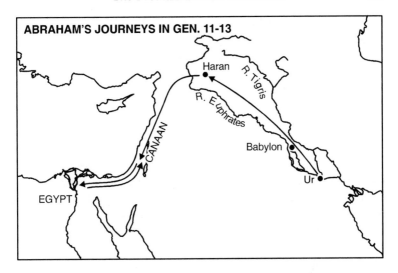

12.4 – 13.18: Abraham arrives in Canaan.

Initially our hearts thrill as we see Abraham go straight away in response to God's call, accompanied by his wife, Sarah, his nephew, Lot, and some servants. Without any delay he arrives in Canaan, and at Shechem God shows him that this is the land he has promised him. Delightedly we watch Abraham establish a base near Bethel and wander south exploring his new homeland (12.4-9).

Then everything seems to go wrong. Famine strikes, and Abraham goes to Egypt, where he gets himself in a mess. Fear, rather than faith, now dominates as he hides the truth about Sarah. Certainly he prospers financially, but Sarah is taken into Pharaoh's harem, and in the end God has to intervene and rescue the situation (12.10-20).

A calmer, more trustful mood prevails as he returns to Canaan, to his base near Bethel, back for a fresh start. We see faith surface again as he allows Lot to separate from him and choose the richest portion of the land for his home. Then comes God's reassurance: Abraham, this is the land I want you to live in; I will give it all to you; go and explore it; but stay in it, for this is the land! (ch. 13)

In this little story we see clearly God's faithfulness to his promises as he rescues Abraham, gives him a fresh start, and continues to enrich him despite himself, but we also recognise continuing drama as Abraham's action appears to put God's purposes in jeopardy. The challenge to Abraham, and so to us as we read about him, is about standing firm in faith in the vision God gives. Thankfully we shall watch him grow in that faith as the story progresses.

Ch. 14: God, not any man, will make me rich.

Abraham's encounter with Kedorlaomer and his allies, in which he rescued Lot and the prisoners and plunder taken from Sodom, resulted in the King of Sodom offering to reward him with the goods he had recovered. Abraham refused; he did not want anyone to be able to say, 'I made Abram rich' (v. 23). God had promised to do that for him, and this time Abraham stands firmly in the promise. (On Melchizedek, see pp. 174-7.)

Ch. 15: A moment of revelation and faith.

The tensions of faith we see in Abraham's response to God's promise of land are virtually duplicated in his response to the promise of offspring. Abraham is thinking his servant, Eliezer of Damascus, will have to be his heir (vv. 2-3), but God assures him he will have proper descendants of his own, so many he will not be able to count them. At that moment Abraham 'believed the LORD and he credited it to him as righteousness' (v. 6), whereupon God sealed his word, both about descendants and the land, in a dramatic and solemn covenant ceremony that Abraham must have vividly remembered ever after.

Ch. 16: Will Ishmael be my heir?

Strangely, despite the profundity of his experience in ch. 15, Abraham, in an amazing moment of rationalisation, agrees to get himself an heir by Sarah's maid, Hagar. Just as his flight to Egypt had caused havoc, this act also results in nothing but trouble. Sarah and Hagar are soon at loggerheads and Hagar runs away. Again God has to intervene to sort things out. Abraham is now 86.

Ch. 17: I shall have a true son and heir.

Thirteen years later God reassures him about his promise.

Abraham still hesitates and asks God to receive Ishmael as his heir, but finally he accepts that he will have a true son of his marriage to Sarah and seals his faith with circumcision.

18.1-15: Fulfilment is now at hand.

Now that Abraham is firmly established in God's promises, God announces, in an angelic visitation, that the time has come. Sarah thinks the whole affair ridiculous, just as Abraham had done a few months earlier (v. 12; cp. 17.17), but we are reminded that we are dealing with matters of faith and with a God whose purpose will be fulfilled, One for whom nothing is too hard (v. 14). He may have had to wait a long time for Abraham's full assurance of faith, but then the faith is about as important as the baby, and God was prepared to wait for both.

Before completing the story about Abraham's offspring, we are taken back for a moment to see how he is faring in the meantime with his faith in the promise about the land.

18.16 – 19.38: Vindication of an earlier faith decision.

Lot had chosen to live beside Sodom because, in contrast with the land God was offering Abraham, it seemed 'like the garden of the LORD' (13.10). But God knew what he was doing and Abraham had chosen well to trust him. Outward appearance can be thoroughly deceptive. Sodom was rotten to the core, fit only for destruction.

Ch. 20: A final crisis of faith.

About twenty-five years have passed (cp. 12.4 & 21.5) since Abraham arrived in Canaan and almost messed things up in Egypt. Here he nearly does it again. He goes to Gerar, which is on the road to Egypt. There he suddenly gives way to fear (v. 11) and we find ourselves watching an almost exact replay of his earlier Egyptian fiasco. But God rescues him as before. The message is clear: the man who has learned faith over many years may still falter, but if his sin is not deliberate rebellion, God will not let him fall. After all, God's desire is to encourage and build up faith, not destroy it, to have our co-operation, not to wash his hands of us.

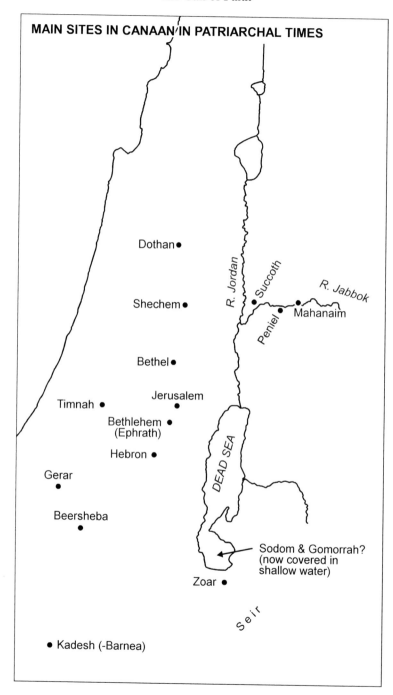

The Promise and the Patriarchs

21.1-21: Isaac is born.
We now reach Abraham's moment of fulfilment. Isaac is born, and in due course Ishmael is sent away to fulfil a different calling.

Ch. 22: Abraham is asked to sacrifice Isaac.
Then, when there is no other possible heir left, God asks Abraham to sacrifice Isaac as a final test of his faith. But Abraham has now learned to trust God and to walk in total obedience to his word.

In the 'sacrifice' of Isaac we can see a foreshadowing of the whole Israelite sacrificial system and of the final sacrifice of Christ, for Mount Moriah is, according to 2 Chron. 3.1, the site on which the temple was later to stand. But the time was not yet either for temple sacrifices or the sacrifice of the 'only Son'. In this episode, which has the same moving quality as the crucifixion story, God was only granting a foretaste of what it was all going to cost him himself.

21.22-34 & 23.1-20: Abraham finally settles.
After the birth of Isaac Abraham establishes a home at Beersheba, and then when Sarah dies he buys a burial plot at Hebron. In both actions we see tokens of his faith that God will one day fulfil his promise to give this land to his descendants.

Ch. 24: He arranges Isaac's marriage to Rebekah.
All that is left now is for Abraham to arrange for his son to be married and so ensure continuity for this second part of the promise.

25.1-11: The Death of Abraham.
Abraham is laid to rest beside Sarah in the plot of land he had bought, the faith-token of fuller possession yet to be.

Some of the stories we have skipped so lightly over in these last few chapters are among the most beautiful and moving in the Old Testament, but more detailed analysis of them would add very little to the theme we have traced. Basically we have been watching Abraham learn to live with the vision and call God gave him at the beginning. The verdict of both Testaments is that he was a giant of faith: in 2 Chron. 20.7 and Isa. 41.8 he is called God's 'friend' and Paul in Rom. 4.20 rightly says that 'he did not waver through unbelief regarding the promise of God'. The fact is that Abraham never lost his basic belief in the vision and the promises that God gave him. We never see him reject his call, or rebel against God, or turn away to any other god. Certainly he faltered from time to time, but his problem was not so much loss of belief as difficulty in seeing how God's purposes could be attained without him working out solutions himself. But that was not what God wanted; the co-operation he required was simple belief, trust or faith. He was not asking Abraham to do impossible things, but to trust him to do them, and all Abraham's own efforts ever achieved was to leave a trail of havoc behind him.

Abraham was just like us. We too have to learn the ways of faith, and so it is immensely encouraging for us to note that, as Abraham went on, he 'was strengthened in his faith and gave glory to God' (Rom. 4.20). Something of that glory shows through in the closing stories in chs. 22–25. There we see the fruits of God's encouragement. He never condemned Abraham for floundering, but rather restored him to faith and encouraged him in it with repeated reminders of the vision he was called to serve. God knows our frailties when he calls us, and he wants to encourage us in our co-operation with him, not condemn us for the very weaknesses from which he wants to rescue us. (However, it is otherwise when it comes to deliberate rebellion, as we shall see later when we come to look at the wilderness stories.)

3. ISAAC (GEN. 21–35)

Though born as a child of promise (ch. 21) and dramatically protected by an angel of God on Mount Moriah (ch. 22), Isaac's story is fairly colourless. He appears as little more than a bridge between Abraham, Israel's great forefather, and Jacob, the nation's immediate father.

Ch. 24: He marries Rebekah.
Abraham sends to his own kinsfolk in Northern Mesopotamia for a wife for Isaac, thus preserving the promise in the family. God's approval is evident. Here is one of the most smoothly flowing faith-stories in Genesis. Rebekah's brother and father sum it all up very neatly: 'This thing is from the LORD; we can say nothing to you one way or the other. Here is Rebekah; take her and go.' (v. 50)

Ch. 25: Jacob and Esau are born.
When Abraham died, he left everything to Isaac, as God had said he would (v. 5). In a most matter of fact sort of way we are informed that Rebekah was barren, but Isaac prayed, the LORD heard and Rebekah became pregnant (v. 21). And so the twins, Esau and Jacob, were born.

Ch. 26: Stay in this land!
Here we have the only story telling of anything Isaac did during his life, apart from fathering his boys and passing on his blessing to Jacob, and it is a very pointed story, for it is virtually a replay of chs. 12 and 20. 'Now there was a famine in the land—besides the earlier famine of Abraham's time'—and Isaac headed off down towards Egypt, doing exactly as his father had done before him. Significantly it is at Gerar (cp. 20.1) that God stops him—'Do not go down to Egypt; live in the land ...'—and he only narrowly escapes falling foul of the same sin as Abraham. However, like Abraham, God continues to bless him, too much for the liking of some of his neighbours!

It seems that the main point of this story is to impress that the lessons of faith and obedience need to be learned afresh in each successive generation and that the Garden of Eden is not going to be regained simply by evolution, or education, or with the passage of time. Man's tendency will always be to escape to an 'Egypt' where conditions seem less harsh, rather than stay firm in faith. The challenge will arise again in the next generation, and sadly the book of Genesis is to end with God's people firmly removed to Egypt, again because of famine.

We hear little more about Isaac after this, save that he distributed his blessing to his children (ch. 27) and was eventually buried by them (35.27-29).

Isaac's is hardly a story full of great excitement, but it still plays an important part in our great drama of salvation. God asked no major new decisions of him, only to hand on the call and blessing to his son. His faith is therefore seen in that he accepted and believed the promises God had made to his own father and that he executed this simple task faithfully, thus preserving continuity for the next generation and for a time when God might act dramatically again. Not all the Biblical characters are great adventurers like Abraham. The majority are fairly ordinary men leading fairly ordinary lives. That, of course, is as it should be, for life is mostly lived by every-day people, not super-heroes, and it is good to know they too perform a thoroughly purposeful role by their simple faithfulness.

4. JACOB (GEN. 25–50)

The story of Jacob shows us how strong is God's determination to see his purpose fulfilled, for Jacob is a most unlikely candidate to become the bearer of the promise. It is a story of God patiently, over many years, refining and remoulding a man to make him a suitable channel for his will.

25.19-34: Jacob deprives Esau of his birthright.
Any optimistic illusions we might have cherished about human potential for moral and spiritual progress down the generations are ruthlessly undermined by our first few glimpses of Jacob's early life. The second-born of twins, he is of quieter temperament than his brother. Esau strikes a manly figure, 'a skilful hunter, a man of the open country,' and his father's favourite, but Jacob is a stay-at-home, spoiled, mother's boy. Our first introduction to him reveals a rather despicable personality, for it tells how he ruthlessly extorted Esau's birthright (his share of his father's estate) from him at a moment when he was too weak and exhausted to think of anything other than simply staying alive.

The Promise and the Patriarchs

27.1-40: He steals Esau's blessing.
The second story is equally off-putting. With his mother's help he cunningly deceives his aged and now blind father into giving him the blessing that should rightfully have been Esau's, even using God's name to back up his lie (v. 20).

27.41 – 28.9: Then he has to flee from Esau.
Esau becomes murderous and Rebekah, fearing for Jacob's life, sends him to her brother, Laban, in Haran. She obtains Isaac's approval with a plea that Jacob should not marry a local girl since the two Esau had married had caused so much trouble (cp. 26.34f). So Isaac sends Jacob off with his blessing and with a prayer that his son's offspring will see the fulfilment of the promises God made to Abraham. In a fit of rage Esau then goes and marries another local girl to spite his father!

28.10-22: As he flees he meets with God.
As we watch Jacob go, we cannot help asking how this lost soul, this haunted fugitive, can possibly become the new custodian of God's promise. But fortunately God does not judge by our standards. Jacob's vision at Bethel is impressive, not least for its majesty, but also for the fact that it expresses no condemnation. It speaks only of God's ultimate purpose, assuring Jacob that Isaac's last prayer was entirely in accord with his will, and that everything he had promised Abraham he was now promising Jacob. The encounter itself is sufficient to bring Jacob under conviction and cause him to pledge himself to God's service. The Jacob who continues on his way is a different person, now walking in awe of the God whose name he had used so lightly before.

Chs. 29–30: Twenty-one years an exile in Laban's household.
Jacob meets his match in Laban and finds himself on the receiving end of the sort of treatment he had given his brother. However, they prove to be happy years for him. He marries first Leah and then Rachel, and by them and their maids has eleven children. Meanwhile his flocks increase and, despite an attempt by Laban to cheat him of his rightful reward, he 'grew exceedingly prosperous and came to own

large flocks, and maidservants and menservants, and camels and donkeys' (30.43).

We begin to see that God is indeed fulfilling his promises in this man's life, and now the desire is stirring in him to return home (30.25).

Ch. 31: Jacob's unseemly departure.

Relationships at Laban's farm are strained. His sons are jealous of Jacob's increasing wealth and Jacob is uncomfortably conscious of the changed atmosphere. The LORD now prompts him to leave with a reminder of his calling, but governed by fear rather than confidence (v. 31), he flees stealthily with his family. Laban is, of course, furious, and particularly since his household idols have disappeared. Eventually Laban and Jacob part on good terms, but the story in its details is not very edifying. Jacob has changed a lot since he left Canaan, but he has not yet become a man whose conduct inspires great confidence.

Ch. 32: On his way back to Canaan Jacob meets with God again.

The nearer he gets to home, the more his fear grows. He knows God's angels are with him (v. 1), but the prospect of meeting Esau terrifies him and he resorts to tactics of desperation. But he also prays (v. 9). Then sending his possessions, his flocks and servants, and finally his wives and children on ahead, he is left alone, and there at the Jabbok he 'wrestles' with God. He emerges from this struggle crippled, but a new man, and with a new name—Israel.

Ch. 33: He is reconciled with Esau and settles at Shechem.

As Esau approaches, Jacob no longer hides in the rear, but boldly goes ahead alone to meet his brother (v. 3). The tension is over as the two are reconciled. Jacob then goes on to Shechem, where Abraham had first stopped when he came from Haran (cp. 12.6f), and there, like his great forebear, builds an altar, but now he can dedicate it to 'the God of Israel' (v. 20). Israel, or at least the nucleus of the nation, has now arrived in the promised land!

The Promise and the Patriarchs 45

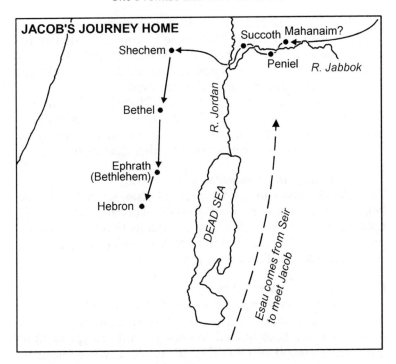

Ch. 34: Two of his sons massacre the Shechemites.
Strangely, much as he has changed, Jacob is still prepared to lie. He has no intention of going to Seir (Edom), where Esau now lives, but he is unable to say so openly (33.14). We are not dealing with unreal people who attained sinless perfection, but folk just like ourselves who still need God's grace, even after he has done so much in their lives. That truth is nowhere better illustrated than in this chapter where we watch the wonderful sense of promise in Jacob's arrival at Shechem being spoiled by the conduct of some of his children. To be sure, Jacob is furious, but the outcome is that he has to move elsewhere.

Ch. 35: So he moves to Bethel and settles there.
After rededicating himself and his family, he returns to Bethel, where he first encountered the LORD, and there he settles. He erects a new altar and there God reaffirms the promises he had first given to Abraham. He then sets out to

visit his aged father. On the way two tragic events take place: Rachel dies giving birth to her second son, Benjamin, and his oldest son, Reuben, sleeps with Bilhah, Rachel's servant who has already fathered two of Jacob's children. Then soon after Jacob's arrival, Isaac dies.

Much as we rejoice at the arrival of Israel in Canaan, the story continues to have threads of tragedy and sin running through it. We are dramatically reminded that what progress has been achieved is thanks to God rather than men.

Ch. 36: Esau's descendants.
This chapter gives us an overview of Esau's line before we begin to follow the story of Jacob's. Theologically it adds nothing to our story, other than remind us that God's saving purposes lie with the children of his choice, not with all Abraham's descendants.

Ch. 46: Jacob's descent to Egypt.
Towards the end of his life we discover Jacob has learned important lessons of faith, so much so that, whereas Abraham and Isaac both tended to drift towards Egypt in their later years, Jacob is unwilling to go there when the time comes, and has to be assured by God himself that this time it must happen: 'Do not be afraid to go down to Egypt, for ... I will go down to Egypt with you.' (vv. 3f)

Chs. 48–49: Jacob's last days.
Our final scenes are therefore of a great man of faith in his old age blessing his children and grand-children, reviewing the fulfilment of promises God had given him in his renegade youth (48.3f), and prophetically looking down the years to a day when God would fulfil them completely by restoring Israel to its land (48.21f).

5. THE SONS OF JACOB/ISRAEL (GEN. 37–50)

Since there are now twelve descendants of Abraham, the drama no longer focuses on one man. However, the problems remain essentially the same: man's tendency and

God's will continue to conflict with each other. The main difference now is that that conflict is multiplied many times over, because the tensions are no longer simply between one man and God's purposes for him, but now also between the various individuals in the group. And as we watch, we see the group riven asunder by jealousy and strife. If we wondered before how God could achieve his purposes through men like Abraham and Jacob, how much more must we wonder now? How can a strife-torn people ever be a source of hope, not just for themselves, but for the rest of mankind?

The date is probably some time after 1720, when the Hyksos came to power in Egypt (see p. 30).

Ch. 37: Joseph is sold into slavery.

The story of this generation, like that of the last, opens with our attention focused on a spoiled child: 'Israel loved Joseph more than any of his other sons' (v. 3). Like father like son, it seems, and sure enough, though the details are of course different, the progression of the story is similar: Esau wanted to murder Jacob, the brothers want to kill Joseph (v. 20); Jacob fled into exile, Joseph is sold into exile (v. 28).

But there are also striking differences. For example, before his flight Jacob seemed quite unconcerned about the seriousness of his calling, whereas Joseph is highly conscious of his. In fact it is that sense of his vocation that is to sustain Joseph through his dark times and later protect him from vengeful reaction in the day of his power (see 45.5-8; 50.15-21). From his childhood dreams he knew God had a plan for his life. It must have been hard at times to see how that could ever be fulfilled, but he apparently lived in trust that it would, and therein lies much of the attractiveness today of this ancient of faith.

Again unlike Jacob, Joseph is not the sole bearer of the promise. Jacob was chosen in preference to Esau, as Abel and Seth were chosen rather than Cain, but Joseph was not to be separated from his brothers in the same way. All twelve make up the infant people of Israel together. And yet within the group Joseph is specially chosen, if only as the one through whom its corporate calling is to be secured. Throughout the Bible it is normally God's way to work through a man. That vocation is regularly a source of terrible jealousy among those around the man chosen. Such jealousy caused Abel's death and repeatedly endangered the work of Moses. Here it almost destroyed God's infant nation, and similar jealousies continue to endanger the LORD's work in churches all over the world today.

Ch. 38: Judah and his family sin.
Our hearts sink even further as we read how Judah, one of the brothers who came out reasonably well in the last chapter and so might have been a source of hope for better things, becomes involved in a sordid chain of events that by no stretch of the imagination can be said to glorify God.

Chs. 39–41: But the LORD is with Joseph.
In Egypt Joseph becomes slave to an army officer, but is thrown into prison, even though innocent of any offence. After he interprets Pharaoh's dream, he is elevated to the court and given charge of the nation's economy. Thanks to his careful preparations, Egypt has plenty and to spare when famine comes.

The story of Joseph's rise is a masterpiece of literature, but its primary significance for us here is found in the way it gives God the credit for all that happened: 'The LORD was with Joseph and he prospered', 'the LORD gave him success in everything he did' (39.2,3; cp. 39.5,21,23; 41.16,51f). Even Pharaoh acknowledges that God's hand is on this man, that he is 'one in whom is the spirit of God,' and it is for that reason alone, not just because he manages to interpret a dream, that he raises him to his high position of authority (41.38f). We are thus vividly reminded that the final outcome of our story does not depend only on Jacob's twelve sons—and therein lies our real ground of hope.

Chs. 42–45: Joseph is reunited with his brothers.
Meanwhile in Canaan men go hungry. In a profoundly moving narrative we read how Jacob's sons go down to Egypt for corn, and end up being invited to settle in the land by the brother they had tried to kill.

The moment Joseph makes himself known to his brothers he also unfolds to them the divine mystery behind all that has happened. It was God! 'God sent me ahead of you,' he says, 'to preserve for you a remnant on earth and to save your lives ... it was not you who sent me here, but God.' (45.7f)

46.1 – 47.12: Jacob, his sons and their families settle in Egypt.

Whilst we can see God's hand behind all that has happened, we have not heard his voice for a long time. He spoke frequently to Abraham, expounding and re-asserting his promise (chs. 12–22); he spoke twice to Isaac, reminding him of the promise to Abraham and transferring it to him (26.2-5,24); he spoke to Jacob as he fled and as he returned home, again mainly about his role as inheritor of the promise (28.13-15; 31.3,13; 32.22-32; 35.1,9-12). But since Jacob's return to Bethel his voice has been silent. Now he speaks once more, for the last time in Genesis, and what he says takes us by surprise (46.2-4).

Abraham and Isaac had both drifted towards Egypt in time of famine and had had to be brought back by God, and now here is Jacob being taken to Egypt in similar circumstances. Understandably he is hesitant, and we cannot help but ask along with him whether the move is going to endanger God's work again. Strangely God says it will not: 'Do not be afraid to go down to Egypt.' The advice is the opposite to that given to his fathers, but God assures him he will continue to work out his purpose in Egypt and eventually bring his people back to Canaan again. If we did not know the sequel, it would be difficult to comprehend the intention of God, but it is at points like these that faith is tested, just as Abraham's had been tested when he was asked, in contradiction to all he had hitherto understood, to sacrifice Isaac. It took a miracle to tidy up the mess made by one man who went to Egypt, but here we have an embryonic nation and the problems potentially involved are unthinkable. God's words, 'Do not be afraid', therefore, invite us as well as Jacob to lay aside our apprehensions and to face this enigma and the future in trust.

47.13 – 50.14: Jacob blesses his children before his death.

The famine runs its course, but thanks to Joseph's careful management his family are well cared for.

Jacob is now old. He has Joseph promise to bury him in Canaan; he blesses Joseph's two sons, Ephraim and Manasseh; and then he utters a kind of prophetic blessing over each of his own twelve sons. In due course he is laid to rest in the family burial plot, beside Abraham and Sarah, Isaac and Rebekah, and his own wife Leah. The story speaks hope rather than sadness. It directs our thoughts out of Egypt back to Canaan—the return with Jacob's body is like a foretaste of some greater return. But then, such was Jacob's faith: 'I am about to die, but God will be with you and will take you back to the land of your fathers.' (48.21)

50.15–26: *Joseph also speaks hope and vision before he dies.*

After Jacob's death, Joseph reassures his still apprehensive brothers that God's hand has been in everything that has happened (v. 20), and with his dying breath he seeks to arouse their faith once more in God's vision for their future: 'God will surely come to your aid and take you up out of this land to the land he promised on oath to Abraham, Isaac and Jacob.' (v. 24)

And the promise of blessing to all the families of the earth?

The dramatic question raised by the Genesis story is about continuing tension between God's purposes as expressed in his promises and man's apparent inability to co-operate fully with unflinching faith in the vision they inspire. Jacob goes back to Haran, the very land his grandfather had been told to leave in the first instance. Abraham and Isaac head towards Egypt in their times of trial, and the twelve sons of Jacob end up there. The human tendency is always away from the land of God's promise, the place where his purposes are to be worked out, and the question we are left with is whether God can possibly ever win through with folk like these, who are essentially no different from us today.

The problem, which showed itself also in relation to the promise of offspring, is a perennial one, but we can see something of the answer to it as we hear God reassert his promise time and again, as we watch him rescue his people and restore them to the place of promise time and again, and as even in the final moments of this first act of our historical drama we hear Joseph remind them of God's continuing promise to visit them once more. In other words, left to man all would be lost, but thankfully man is not left to his own devices for ever, and so we can look forward with a sense of anticipation as we wonder what God will do next to rescue his purposes and bring them to fruition.

The Genesis story:
1. reminds us that we shall never bring back Paradise by ourselves,
2. tells us God has said he is going to do it,
3. calls us to have faith that God can do what he says he will do.

In essence faith is very simple. It does not ask us to do what God says he will do, but only to trust him to do it. Theoretically that should take the strain out of much of life and even make it enjoyable, yet strangely we do find faith difficult, particularly when moments of crisis arise. However, we see God appreciates that too as we watch him repeatedly give encouragement and assurance to sustain the patriarchs in their faith. And as he does so, they do mature and grow in it. So it is still today.

Nevertheless, it is becoming clear that some solution more radical than that given in Genesis is going to be necessary as the number of those to be taught faith increases. Genesis is only first stirrings; there is much yet to come.

God's Word and his Spirit were both active at creation and were both represented by trees in the Garden of Eden. Re-creation will also require the activity of both. We have seen God's Word begin to become active in communicating vision and faith to Abraham and his children. We shall watch it become more active still, and alongside it we shall see his Spirit stir until finally both are in full flood in the life of Jesus Christ.

4
God's Grace in Salvation

EXODUS 1–18

The story of the Exodus and the wilderness wanderings, like the stories of Genesis, is essentially the story of a man of faith and his God. Moses was surrounded by other men and women, many of them people of stature: his brother, Aaron, who became a priest, as did his sons; his sister, Miriam, who was a prophetess; Joshua, Hur and Caleb, who were leaders of men; Jethro, his father-in-law, who taught him many things; Hobab, his Midianite brother-in-law, who stayed faithfully by him throughout the forty years' discipline in the wilderness; Bezalel and Oholiab, the skilled craftsmen who fashioned the tabernacle and its equipment; and many others, mostly unnamed, like the seventy elders who helped him govern the people, who faithfully supported him as he led God's people on their impossible journey. But like Abraham, Isaac, Jacob and Joseph, Moses has in the end to bear the burden of faith largely by himself, and so the Exodus story is Moses' story, for the two are inextricably intertwined.

That personal quality, however, clothes the bare facts of history with warm flesh and blood, transforming them from dry information into that which lives and imparts life. Just as our study of Genesis was an invitation to enter into the vitality of the drama and tap the heartbeat of its main actors, so here the invitation remains the same. We may not remember the names of the Pharaohs and the dates of their reigns, we may not fully understand who the Midianites, Amalakites, Edomites, Moabites and Ammonites were, let alone the Amorites, Hittites, Perizzites, Canaanites, Hivites

God's Grace in Salvation

and Jebusites, but if we can learn some of the lessons of faith Moses learned, if we can catch something of the vision he caught, if we can feel some measure of the vibrancy of God's power he felt, these things will live with us for ever and become for us an eternal source of encouragement and strength.

1. THE WORLD OF THE EXODUS

There are two main theories about the date of the Exodus, one that it happened in the fifteenth century BC, the other in the thirteenth.

Biblical tradition places it 430 years after Joseph and his brothers arrived in Egypt (Exod. 12.40f). If the descent to Egypt occurred some time after the Hyksos came to power about 1720 (see p. 30), then the Exodus should be dated some time after 1290, during the reign of Rameses II. According to Merniptah's inscription there were Israelites in Canaan by 1220, so the entry to the land must have taken place some years earlier. If we date the Conquest shortly before 1230 and the Exodus before 1270, then Moses must have fled from Egypt at the end of the fourteenth century.

In Exod. 1.11 we are told that Israelite slaves helped to build Pithom and Rameses. Rameses is though to have been the old Hyksos capital, Avaris, in the Nile Delta (the same as Zoan in Num. 13.22), and we know that it was rebuilt by Pharaoh Sethos I as his capital using forced labour. He was Rameses II's immediate predecessor, reigned about 1305–1290, and, on this dating of the Exodus, would have been 'the new king, who did not know about Joseph' (Exod. 1.8).

We have a very slight problem accommodating the date of Moses' flight from Egypt, forty years before the Exodus according to Acts 7.30, to an oppression in Sethos' time. To do that we must assume the figure forty is an approximation rather than an exact number. Anyhow, Exod. 1.11 seems to help us to pin-point the time of the oppression to this general period at the end of the fourteenth and the beginning of the thirteenth centuries, suggesting that the Exodus may have occurred sometime in the reign of Rameses II.

On this view we have also to assume that the date in 1 Kings 6.1, 480 (or 440 according to the Greek text) years between the Exodus and the building of Solomon's temple, is also a round number indicating something like twelve generations (twelve times forty), or just a very long time.

If we do regard it as a precise date, that would place the Exodus around 1440, some 200 years earlier. Until recently it has been difficult to fit this date with what we have known about the ancient world at that time, but recent archaeological discoveries have suggested that this earlier date may possibly be the right one after all. If so, that would push the dates for Abraham and his descendants further back than those we have used in this book. The debate is a very complex one and need not delay us unduly here. Whenever the Exodus actually happened, the story of faith remains the same. The alternative historical outlines are as follows:

DATE	EGYPT	ISRAEL
c. 1870		Israel goes down to Egypt (1)
1720	The Hyksos come to power	
c. 1700		Israel goes down to Egypt (2)
1570	Amosis expels the Hyksos	
	A pharaoh who did not know Moses	Israelites work as slaves and Moses flees from Egypt (1)
c. 1440		The Exodus (1)
c. 1400		The Conquest (1)
1305-1290	Sethos I rebuilds Avaris/ Rameses with forced labour	Israelites work as slaves and Moses flees from Egypt (2)
1290-1224	Rameses II	
c. 1270		The Exodus (2)
c. 1230		The Conquest (2)
1224-1211	Merniptah	
1220	Merniptah invades Canaan	& encounters Israel in Canaan

2. THE EXODUS, A TRIUMPH OF FAITH (EXOD. 1–18)

The story we are about to trace in Exodus to Deuteronomy is in many ways a tale of triumph, but in others one full of the same kind of dramatic tensions we encountered in Genesis.

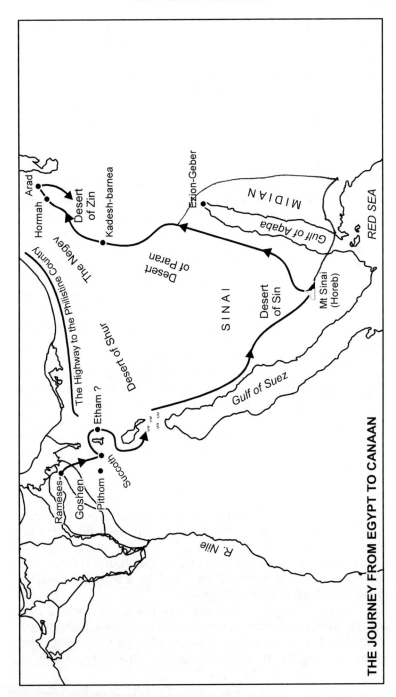

THE JOURNEY FROM EGYPT TO CANAAN

We shall watch Moses successfully lead the people out from Egypt and down to Mount Sinai to meet with God. But we shall also hear them grumble and complain as they go and at every stage thereafter, until finally we shall watch them lose God's opportunity for entering the land and wander for a generation in the wilderness before finally reaching the borders of Canaan again. But at least we start with a story of triumphant faith.

Ch. 1: Slaves in Egypt.

We know virtually nothing about the Israelites during their time in Egypt, except that they grew in numbers. But they always saw the hand of God in that quiet period of hidden growth, that is, those who had the faith-eyes to see it. Jacob knew from the start that it would be happening (Gen. 46.3), and the Israelites remembered it ever after as a purposeful part of their history every time they went to the sanctuary to offer the firstfruits of their harvest (Deut. 26.5). It is strange, therefore, that the 300 or so years between the death of Joseph and the birth of Moses are so completely undocumented (vv. 1-7).

When at last we emerge from the mists of this forgotten history, we find ourselves in an Egypt anxious about the Hebrew population-explosion, taking repressive measures to restrict their growth and freedom. But it is all to no avail. The numbers keep on growing, for it was God's will that they should increase. Oppression from outside seldom hinders God's purposes as much as lack of faith within the community.

Ch. 2. Moses to the rescue!

Moses, born of a Levite family, was raised as an Egyptian courtier. One day a sense of calling to help his Israelite brothers rose within him, but the gallant action he took resulted only in his flight from Egypt. He found refuge with Jethro, here called Reuel (2.18, cp. 3.1), a Midianite priest, and married his daughter, Zipporah.

During his long exile tending Jethro's sheep, Moses, like Joseph in prison, must often have asked himself about the meaning of his life. But God knew what he was doing—he was preparing his man for the action ahead. According to

Acts 7.23 & 30 (cp. Exod. 7.7), Moses spent forty years in Pharaoh's household and forty years roaming the wilderness in search of pasture. By the end of that time he must have known both the corridors of power in Egypt and the ways of the desert as well as any man could. God was preparing his man well.

Meanwhile, back in Egypt the Israelites were crying out for God to send them help. The Pharaoh who had sought to arrest Moses (perhaps Sethos I) died and the way was now clear for him to return.

3.1 – 4.17: God sends Moses to take Israel out of Egypt.

The scene is set and the chief actor has been trained for his part; all he needs now is his script and the prompting to step on stage. But when that comes, impressive as the appearance of God in the burning bush at Horeb (= Sinai, where later Moses will receive the law) may seem, Moses shows considerable unwillingness to play the part. Five times he objects, and five times God refuses his objection:

Who am I? I'm not fit for a job like that!
– I will be with you (3.11f).

How am I to explain to the Israelites who you are?
– Tell them that I AM, the God of their fathers (3.13-22).

What if they will not believe me?
– Here are three miracles you can use to convince them (4.1-9).

Lord, I am no speaker!
– Who made your tongue? I will help you (4.10-12).

Lord, please send someone else!
– Your brother, Aaron, will stand by you and speak for you, if you need that, but you are the one I have chosen. *You* must go (4.13-17).

In the course of this conversation God gives Moses careful instructions about what he is to do and what he is to ask from Pharaoh:

1. He is to bring the Israelites out of Egypt (3.10).
2. He is to bring them to worship at this mountain (Sinai, 3.12).
3. He is then to lead them to Canaan (3.17).

4. But he is only to ask Pharaoh to let them take a three-day journey into the desert to offer sacrifices to the Lord (3.18).
5. And he is not to leave Egypt furtively, but openly, laden with gifts from the Egyptians (3.21).

In the story that unfolds we shall watch Moses stand firm in his faith before Pharaoh, refusing to leave Egypt until he can go freely and in accordance with this blue-print God has given him. If at first Moses showed himself unwilling, he is soon to prove the depth and tenacity of his commitment, and in so doing also to prove the power of God available to the man who is obedient to and has faith in God's word. In the end he did not have to rely on Aaron to speak to Pharaoh for him.

4.19-31: Moses returns to Egypt.

On the journey, we read, 'the LORD met Moses and was about to kill him', but Zipporah circumcised their son and so saved Moses' life. The story is very strange and we cannot pretend to understand every detail of it, but it does show us how seriously God wanted Moses' total obedience, how unwilling he was to overlook his smallest disobedience, and doubtless Moses himself did not readily forget the lesson.

On his return, the elders of Israel are thrilled at all he has to tell them, but, as we shall see, their enthusiasm soon dissipates when testing comes. Before long Moses and Aaron will be standing alone.

5.1 – 7.5: First encounter with Pharaoh.

Just as God has instructed, Moses asks that the people be released to take a three-day journey into the desert to offer sacrifices to the LORD. The outcome is disastrous: increased oppression for the slave-people and hostility towards Moses from their leaders (5.1-21).

So 'Moses returned to the LORD' who assured him he would do every thing he promised (5.22 – 6.8).

Thus reassured, he returned enthusiastically to the Israelites, but this time 'they did not listen to him because of their discouragement and cruel bondage.' This is just what we might have expected, as also is the doubt that begins to nibble at Moses' soul: 'If the Israelites will not listen to me, why should Pharaoh listen to me, since I speak with faltering lips?' (6.9-12) There is nothing like a bit of crisis to challenge our stance in faith; most of the patriarchs in Genesis learned that, and now Moses has to learn it. But it is at such points we discover the faithfulness of God. Just as Moses is tempted to return to his original doubts, God reminds him of his original answer to these doubts, that Aaron can speak for him. And so God sets Moses back on his faith-feet with a strong reminder of his promise and commission (6.28 – 7.5).

Chs. 7–12: Pharaoh's hardness versus Moses' faith.

To Pharaoh the first two plagues seemed no more than tricks his magicians could copy, but by the third even they were advising him that 'This is the finger of God' (8.19). The rest of the plagues have in common that mysteriously no Israelites were affected by them. In the case of the tenth that was because they were forewarned and so could take suitable precautions, but otherwise it was because the effects of the plagues were supernaturally limited to Egyptian quarters. The evidence of God's hand is manifest and so it is surprising that Pharaoh resisted so long.

The impression we get is that the plagues followed each other in fairly rapid succession over one season between springtime and harvest.

1. First the Nile, the source of Egypt's water and so of its life, turns to blood causing fish to die and rot.
2. A week later hoards of frogs leave the stinking water, only to die among the Egyptians' houses, thus increasing the stench.
3. Then comes the plague of gnats
4. and flies—perhaps the putrid fish- and frog-carcasses had provided a breeding ground for them.
5. Presently disease breaks out among cattle,
6. and then among the Egyptians themselves.
7. A freak hail- and thunder-storm ruins the harvest,
8. a wind blows in locust-swarms that ravage what the storms have left,
9. and then the land is cloaked in darkness for three days.
10. Finally Egypt's first-born die, while the Israelites shelter under the protection of the blood of the Passover lambs.

The hardening of Pharaoh's heart.
Pharaoh proved hard to impress. The reason at first was partly because his magicians were able to copy the miracles (7.22; 8.7), but thereafter the only explanation given is progressive hardening of his heart. At his first encounter with Moses he simply asked in some surprise and annoyance, 'Who is the LORD, that I should obey him? I do not know the LORD' (5.2), but at his second encounter he positively refused to listen and his 'heart became hard' (7.13). As we read through the account of the plagues, we learn that after each of them that hardness continued to increase as he dug his heels in and refused to let Israel go:

> 'Pharaoh's heart became hard; he would not listen' (7.22).
> 'he hardened his heart and would not listen' (8.15).
> 'Pharaoh's heart was hard and he would not listen' (8.19).
> 'this time also Pharaoh hardened his heart' (8.32).
> 'his heart was unyielding and he would not …' (9.7).
> 'the LORD hardened Pharaoh's heart and he would not listen' (9.12).
> 'he and his officials hardened their hearts' (9.34).
> 'the LORD hardened Pharaoh's heart, and he would not …' (10.20).
> 'the LORD hardened Pharaoh's heart, and …' (10.27).
> 'the LORD hardened Pharaoh's heart, and he would not …' (11.10).

This progression from chs. 5 to 11 is very telling. At first there is no mention of hardness, but as he opposes God's will a hardness begins to appear, then in ch. 8 he positively and deliberately hardens himself against God, until finally God enters the process himself and makes use of it to attain his purposes.

It is noteworthy that God, while he made full use of this progression, did not actually initiate it. And yet, long before Moses ever appeared before Pharaoh, God told him he would harden his heart, and even that the plagues would have to run their full course through to the death of Egypt's firstborn (4.21-23; cp. 7.3f). God knew what kind of a person he had to deal with in Pharaoh and so knew full well beforehand what would happen, but he is not a heartless tyrant and has never hardened the heart of any man who has not first hardened his own heart. Presumably God would have welcomed a change of heart in Pharaoh, and at first he allowed room for that to happen, but he knew it would never be so in reality, told Moses as much, and used Pharaoh's hardness to achieve his end anyhow. Israel had to come out of Egypt, with or without Pharaoh's willing co-operation.

There is always an easy and a hard way of co-operating with God! The lesson of Pharaoh's heart is a lasting memorial to that truth, and still today too many choose the hard way of resistance when God asks them to do something. Israel was also slow to learn. In the wilderness we shall see them again and again fail to co-operate willingly with God—and they seldom got as many chances as Pharaoh did!

The persistence of Moses' faith.

At several points in the story we watch Pharaoh bend a little, but never enough to satisfy Moses. After the first four plagues he summons Moses and gives him permission to hold his sacrificial festival somewhere in Egypt. Moses is not impressed; God told him to ask for much more than that (8.25-32). After the next three plagues Pharaoh gives his permission for the Israelite men to go alone and offer their sacrifices in the desert. Again Moses is not impressed (10.8-11). After the eighth and ninth Pharaoh allows the men, women and children to go, on condition that they leave their flocks and herds behind, but Moses refuses again as before (10.24-27).

Then finally, after the tenth plague Pharaoh gives in completely to Moses' demand: 'Go, worship the LORD as you have requested. Take your flocks and herds, as you have said, and go' (12.31). Now Moses accepts, and as he goes, the Egyptians shower the Israelites with presents, glad to see them depart. This was at last the fulfilment of the promise God had given him at the burning bush.

A weaker man might have accepted some of Pharaoh's compromise offers, glad to have achieved as much as seemed reasonably possible. Moses was not such a man. He stood uncertain at the burning bush, but now he stands a man of amazingly courageous and persistent faith. He knew the vision, the promise and his own commission, and he stood firm until he saw God's word fulfilled. Pharaoh could harden his heart as much as he wanted, but here he was face to face with a man of iron will—and with God on his side. The encouragement in a story like this for our faith today is well nigh limitless.

12.1 – 13.16: The Exodus.

The Passover night, dreadful for the Egyptians, meant salvation and freedom for Israel. For ever after the Passover would be celebrated in a festival (see p. 128) that would keep its memory alive, when the story of God's great saving act would be taught to Israelite children down their generations. Centuries later a new and much more far-reaching act of salvation was to be wrought at Passover-time, when Jesus transformed the Passover meal into the Eucharist or Communion and offered himself as the ultimate Passover lamb (1 Cor. 5.7; see also p. 136), whose blood now procures eternally for all men the protection from judgment and death that the blood of the Exodus lamb once afforded the people of Israel.

The children were also to be taught about Israel's salvation when firstborn animals were being sacrificed and firstborn children were consecrated in memory of that fateful night (13.1-16).

We are told that about 600,000 men left Egypt (12.37). With women and children included the total company must have been nearer 2,000,000, a number quite impossible for the wilderness to support, but then the Old Testament does say the provision was miraculous and supernatural. Whether we find such numbers hard to cope with or not (some would retranslate the Hebrew so as to reduce the total estimate to about 500,000), it is important to realise that the Exodus-Wilderness story is essentially a tale of God's wonders, of things men could never have achieved by themselves.

13.17 – 15.21: Crossing the Sea.

The Israelites were first led south from Rameses to Succoth (12.37), because the coastal highway to Canaan was patrolled by Egyptian army units. If some of the Israelites wondered why they were heading in the wrong direction, they must have become even more perplexed when Moses

God's Grace in Salvation

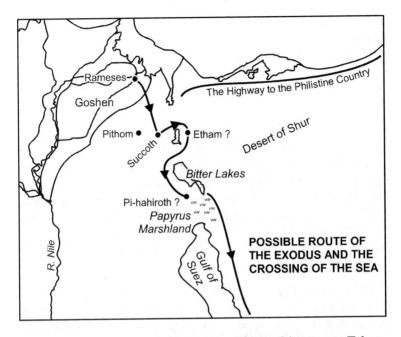

POSSIBLE ROUTE OF THE EXODUS AND THE CROSSING OF THE SEA

then led them back from the desert-fringe at Etham towards Egypt again. But God knew what he was doing (13.17; 14.3). When the reports of their strange movements reached Pharaoh, he concluded that the Israelites were lost, seized the opportunity, and set off in pursuit (13.20 – 14.9).

Suddenly the Israelites find themselves trapped. The next few verses are most illuminating—crises often reveal hidden depths of character. When the people panic and blame Moses, he preaches them an amazingly faith-inspiring sermon: 'Do not be afraid ... The LORD will fight for you; you need only to be still' (14.13f). Yet inwardly he is at a loss, for we immediately hear God say, 'Why are you crying out to me? Tell the Israelites to move on' (v. 15).

Here we see Moses' true frailty. Despite his gigantic faith in Pharaoh's presence and his powerful preaching to the Israelites, at heart he is no different from any one else. It was no special natural ability that enabled him to do all he did, but only his faith in God. And here is encouragement for our faith: when a time comes for the praying to stop and action to begin, as it must, and our hearts fail us, we do well to remember Moses.

The moment Moses steps forward, the miracles begin and suddenly the crisis is over. Presently we are listening to Moses and the Israelites singing their song of triumph. Where a few hours earlier it was cries of panic, now there is a surge of enthusiasm and faith as they rejoice in what God has done and boldly sing of the victories that lie ahead as they approach Canaan (15.1-21).

The site of the miraculous sea-crossing is unknown. The Hebrew *Yam Suf* actually means 'Sea of Reeds' rather than 'Red Sea', suggesting a location somewhere near the Bitter Lakes, north of the Gulf of Suez, where papyrus reeds grow. (*Yam Suf* is also used of the Gulf of Aqaba, the northern arm of the Red Sea itself; cp. Num. 14.25; Deut. 1.40; 2.1; 1 Kings 9.26; etc.)

15.22 – 17.7: The Israelites grumble, but God supplies.

The Israelites' euphoria was short-lived. From this point on we shall hear them repeatedly grumbling and complaining, against both God and Moses, because of hardships they have to endure in the wilderness, mainly over their food supply and shortage of water, as we should expect in a desert area. Repeatedly we shall see God provide, but the memory of his miracles soon fades and every new crisis calls forth fresh complaints. Moses handles each new situation by turning to God for the answer. He shows amazing patience most of the time, though occasionally a sense of frustration surfaces, until finally, in Num. 20, tested to the limit, he loses his temper and throws away his own opportunity of entering the promised land.

The provisions we read of here are water, manna and quails. Migrating quails do cross the Mediterranean to this region, and so we find the Israelites gathering them again on another occasion, when 'a wind from the LORD' carried them in from the sea (Num. 11.31-34). There have been various attempts to identify manna with natural substances in the region, but none of the suggestions explains the miracle of the abundant daily provision that lasted forty years and then suddenly stopped the day the Israelites crossed into Canaan (Josh. 5.12). The miracle of provision of water, as we should expect, is repeated more than once (15.22-27; 17.1-7; Num. 20.1-13; 21.16-18). Both Rephidim in Exod. 17 and Kadesh in Num. 20 are called Meribah, place of 'quarrelling', and perhaps both are called to mind in Ps. 95.

'There (in Egypt) we sat round pots of meat and ate all the food we wanted' (16.3). Later we even hear the Israelites cry, 'We remember the fish we ate in Egypt, at no cost—also the cucumbers, melons, leeks, onions and garlic' (Num. 11.5). It is amazing the tricks memory can play under stress.

17.8-15: Battle with the Amalakites.
No sooner is one crisis resolved than another arises. Israel is attacked by Amalekites, nomads who roamed the desert lands south of Canaan. Almost every time we meet them they are fighting with Israel (Num. 14.42-45; Judg. 3.13; 6.3; 7.12), but ultimately they were to pass from history (Deut. 25.17-19; 1 Sam. 15). In the meantime it seems everything would try to stop Israel reaching Sinai.

Moses takes Aaron and Hur up a nearby mountain to oversee the battle. Hur seems to have worked closely with Aaron in helping Moses to govern the Israelites during this time (cp. 24.14), that is, before Aaron was appointed priest at Sinai.

Every leader, religious or other, needs an overall, mountain-top perspective. But the man of God atop the mountain has to do battle on behalf of his people in a manner unknown to the secular leader. His is a battle in the spiritual places (cp. Eph. 6.10-12), a battle of prayer, but as he wins through, so do his people in the valley of life. Sometimes this struggle is so demanding that he needs the support of friends who understand these matters and will stand by him.

Ch. 18: Moses meets up with his father-in-law.
The sense of triumph in this chapter is almost as great as in ch. 15, as Moses and Jethro, two great men of God, rendezvous not far from the mountain where Moses had first met God, and rejoice together in all the LORD has done.

Israel does not yet have its own priestly system, and so Jethro, the priest of Midian, leads in the sacrificial worship. Then he gives Moses some fatherly advice about using the more capable Israelites to help him with the tasks of leadership before he wears himself out.

Jethro, the Kenites and the LORD.
When we first meet him, Jethro is introduced as a Midianite priest (Exod. 2.15 – 3.1). The Midianites were found on the desert-fringes in Transjordan, east of Moab, down southward past Edom and to the east of the Red Sea. Here we see them well-disposed to the Israelites, but forty years later they join forces, first with the Moabites (Num. 22–25) and then with the Amorites (Josh. 13.21), to halt their progress, and in the days of the Judges Gideon has to fight them when they invade Canaan (Judg. 6–8). Either their attitude changed after Jethro's death, or else he belonged to one of their clans that viewed the Israelites differently from the rest of his kinsmen.

In Judg. 1.16 Jethro is said to be a Kenite, as also in Judg. 4.11 is Hobab, who is introduced to us in Num. 10.29 as Jethro's son. Kenites are first mentioned in Gen. 15.19 in a list of peoples in Canaan in Abraham's time. Some of Jethro's Kenite descendants entered the land with Joshua and settled in the Negev, south of Judah (Judg. 1.16; 1 Sam. 27.10). Both Saul and David were kindly disposed to them (1 Sam. 15.6; 30.29). The descendants of Rechab (the Rechabites), who belonged to the Kenite clan, were excessively zealous for the LORD in Elisha's and Jeremiah's time, (1 Chron. 2 .55; 2 Kings 10.15f; Jer. 35). Whatever the general Midianite attitude to Israel, their Kenite section seems to have been very friendly, and surprisingly devoted to the LORD for non-Israelites. But then their name probably links them with Cain (the spelling is similar in Hebrew), and despite all his failings, the LORD had put his mark on him from earliest times (Gen. 4.15). If we are not misinterpreting, that could mean that Jethro already knew the LORD before Moses arrived, and hence we see another amazing instance of how carefully God's guiding hand was on Moses. Perhaps it was no accident that he found refuge with Jethro's family when he fled from Egypt. That would certainly explain why he was happy to let Jethro preside at the sacrifice in Exod. 18.

However, Jethro is not an Israelite and so has no continuing role in God's saving work. Hence, as the Exodus story draws to its close, as Israel prepares for the last lap of the journey to Sinai to meet with God, we watch him depart to his own people, not with sadness, but with satisfaction about all he has done to aid the LORD's work (v. 27).

PART THREE

THE CALL OF OBEDIENCE

If the Exodus-story taught faith, the challenge of the Sinai-story is primarily obedience. Of course the two are inter-related. Abraham and Moses both had to obey as well as have faith, and so in one sense our division at this point is artificial. Nevertheless it is helpful, for we do see a shift of emphasis. The vision given to Abraham does not change, and so faith is still needed, but new ingredients now enter the story speaking more strongly about need for obedience and we find ourselves reading more stories about rebellion and disobedience than before.

Obedience is the response required by God to his law. It is not the means of salvation for Israel, since salvation has already taken place in the Exodus. Salvation was not a reward; it was freely given by God when he took Israel out of Egypt. Hence the law was never intended to be a test by which Israelites could earn salvation through keeping it, though that was what the Jews had made of it by New Testament times (Rom. 10.1-5). Rather it is God's pattern of life for his people, those he has already saved and made his own, the pattern by which he asks his chosen ones to live so that he can finally fulfil his purpose through them.

True, certain rewards and punishments are attached to the laws, and these are relevant to continuing enjoyment of the fruits of salvation, but they are not in themselves that salvation. The law is for God's saved people; it is not a prescription for earning salvation.

5

God's Grace in Revelation and Discipline

EXODUS 19 – NUMBERS 36

As we sweep through the many chapters covered in this section our aim will mainly be to follow the story they tell. We shall take a closer look at some of the laws later.

God had chosen Abraham to be the forefather of a nation through which he would restore blessing to mankind and he had chosen Canaan as the place where he would work out that purpose. We have watched the nation come into being and are about to watch it being brought home to its promised land. But before it sets out for Canaan, God reveals the way of life by which it is to fulfil its destiny as a socio-political unit there.

However, even before they reach Canaan, we shall see the Israelites repeatedly grumble and rebel and each time we shall watch them experience the Lord's discipline as he teaches them the seriousness of their calling.

1. AT MOUNT SINAI: A NEW BEGINNING (EXOD. 19 – NUM. 10)

Exod. 19: Moses prepares the people to meet God.
The two words that best sum up the pattern of life the law requires are righteousness and holiness. We shall examine their meaning more fully at a later stage, but already, even before any law is given, we see a growing consciousness of the need for the latter.

OUTLINE OF THE SINAI STORY IN EXODUS 19–40	
Ch. 19	Israel arrives at Sinai, the people consecrate themselves and God descends on the mountain.
Ch. 20	God announces the Ten Commandments.
20.21 - 23.33	Moses ascends Sinai and God shows him the content of 'The Book of the Covenant' embodying many basic laws that are to govern the social, moral and religious life of Israel.
24.1-11	Moses and seventy elders pledge Israel to keep its laws.
24.12 - 31.18	Moses goes up on the mountain alone for forty days and is given detailed instruction for constructing the tabernacle and consecrating its priests.
Ch. 32	Meantime the people forsake their pledge and worship Aaron's golden calf. Moses smashes the Covenant Tablets in anger.
Ch. 33	Moses pleads with God and his anger is averted. Moses is then reassured of his continuing presence.
Ch. 34	New Covenant Tablets are made and Moses comes down from Sinai radiant.
35 - 40	The tabernacle is constructed according to the design given to Moses in chs. 25–31 and God's glory comes to reside in it.

Three months after the Exodus, Israel pitched camp at Mount Sinai and 'Moses went up to God', who spoke to this effect: I have brought you to myself and if you are prepared to obey me, you will be my treasured possession. But are you prepared to enter into covenant with me, to be my priests on earth, a holy nation? (vv. 1-6)

When Moses brought the people's response, God sent him to proclaim two days of consecration to prepare for his coming (vv. 7-15).

Then on the third day God descends on the mountain amid thunder, lightning, cloud, fire, smoke and the sound of a trumpet. Moses is summoned into his presence a third time and sent to warn the people not to come near onto the mountain (vv. 16-25).

20.1-21: God speaks from the mountain.
If the preparation was awesome and God's coming wondrous, his voice inspired terror as it spoke out the Ten Commandments. Trembling, the people plead with Moses to

God's Grace in Revelation and Discipline

mediate between them and God, and so he approaches God on their behalf to receive the rest of the laws himself.

The Ten Commandments are essentially a summary of the covenant between God and Israel and are thus unique among the laws. That is partly shown by the fact that they alone were spoken to the people directly by the voice of God from the mountain (cp. Deut. 5.22), while the rest were mediated through Moses, either alone on the mountain, or later at the tent-sanctuary.

20.22 – 23.33: Moses receives the Book of the Covenant.
This first selection of laws provides a summary outline of the kind of society God desires for his people. It contains a mixture of civil and religious laws which, by contrast with the laws of most other ancient societies, show a high respect for human life and a strong emphasis on fair justice.

It concludes with promises of blessing for the obedient and a reminder that it is God's purpose to give Israel the land of Canaan (23.20-33).

THE BOOK OF THE COVENANT

A. *Introduction*
20.22-23	A call for faithfulness to God
20.24-26	On building an altar for his service

B. *Various Civil Laws*
21.2-11	The treatment of slaves
21.12-17	Some offences meriting the death penalty
21.18-27	Compensation for bodily injury
21.28-36	Legal responsibility for animals
22.1-15	Laws concerning damage to property
22.16-17	The rights of a seduced virgin

C. *Mixed Social, Moral and Religious Laws*
22.18-20	Loyalty to God
22.21-27	Caring for the weak in society
22.28-31	Offerings made to God and personal holiness
23.1-9	Principles of truth, justice and mercy
23.10-13	Sabbaths for the land, the people and working animals
23.14-19	Festivals and offerings

D. *Conclusion*
23.20-33	God promises to guide, protect and bless the people if they continue to obey him.

24.1-11: *The covenant is sealed.*

God has asked if the people are prepared to enter into covenant with him (ch. 19), has outlined his requirements (ch. 20), and has given Moses a survey of the nature of the society he envisages (chs. 20–23). Now he invites them to pledge themselves to the patterns he has described. Moses therefore reads the Book of the Covenant to the people, and when they agree to obey it, he seals the agreement with sacrifice. As he sprinkles the blood, we hear him say, 'This is the blood of the covenant that the LORD has made with you,' words that are to be re-echoed centuries later as Jesus, at the Last Supper, inaugurates the New Covenant in his own blood (Mark 14.24).

The ceremony ends in an astounding moment of intimacy when Moses and other leaders are granted a vision of God and permitted to dine in his presence (vv. 9-11). Again we see foreshadowings of the Last Supper when, in a similar context of intimacy at a meal, Jesus is to announce the New Covenant.

24.12 – 31.18: *Moses is shown the patterns for Israel's worship.*

Moses now leaves Aaron and Hur in charge of the people (cp. 17.10), and goes up to spend the next forty days on the mountain alone with God.

There he learns about God's desire to 'dwell among' his people and is given precise instructions for constructing a sanctuary for him, the tabernacle with all its furnishings (chs. 25–27; 30–31), for making the priests' garments and consecrating the priests to the service of the tabernacle (ch. 28–9), for the provision of materials and money for the tabernacle, and for the composition of the oil and incense to be used (chs. 25 & 30). For fuller discussion, see pp. 119-22.

After final instruction about the importance of keeping Sabbath (31.12-17), the LORD gives Moses 'the two tables of the Testimony, the tablets of stone inscribed by the finger of God' (v. 18). And at that point Moses' time on the mountain should have been finished!

32.1-6: *Sin—The people break covenant.*

About five weeks pass and Israel forsakes its pledge; so

soon does commitment wane. Aaron, the very man God has in mind to be high priest, fashions a golden calf-idol and identifies God who brought Israel out of Egypt with it.

32.7 – 33.3: Judgment—God's anger.

Naturally God is angry, but Moses pleads for mercy. However, when he sees for himself what has happened he momentarily forgets his pleadings and his own anger burns. He smashes the Covenant Tablets, calls to himself all who are for the LORD and sends them to execute the very punishment he had pleaded with God to revoke. (The fact that the Levites were the ones who responded may have been one of the reasons why it was they who were later appointed to the service of the sanctuary; cp. Deut. 33.9).

Amid all his anger, we still hear Moses pleading for his people (32.31-2). Emotions and reactions in such circumstances are bound to be exceedingly complex, and clearly Moses was torn apart by his. Transgressing God's covenant has serious personal repercussions for both people and leaders. Sadly Israel would soon forget the lesson—too many similar stories are found scattered through the Old Testament. In each of them we find Moses pleading for his people in the same way, time and again, even when they turn against him personally with threats of violence.

Perhaps the most unbearable consequence of rebellion is awareness of the withdrawal of God's presence and blessing. However, God never revokes his promise. He said he would take Israel to Canaan and so it will be, but now he is unwilling to go himself lest his anger burn against them again, and so he proposes that an angel lead them.

33.4-23: Repentance—Moses pleads for assurance of God's Presence.

The people are distressed, but Moses is determined not to give in: If your Presence does not go with us, what's the point of your having taken us this far or of our going any further? The Moses that stood firm in faith before Pharaoh in his palace now stands firm in prayer before God at his temporary 'tent of meeting', and God rewards him with visible proof of his restored presence in a vision of his glory.

Moses' relationship with God is beautifully summarised

here: 'The LORD would speak to Moses face to face, as a man speaks with his friend' (v. 11).

Ch. 34: Restoration—the covenant is renewed.
Now that personal relationship with God has been restored, Moses is summoned up the mountain to have the Covenant Tablets remade. He is first reminded of some of the lessons to be learned from his experience at Sinai thus far: that God is faithful to his word, that he is compassionate and merciful, but that he also demands justice, loyalty and obedience. A number of new commands are given, mostly relating to worship, and then the Tablets are remade.

Moses' face as he descends the mountain this time is aglow. So it could have been the first time. We have finally arrived at the place God originally intended we should be at. Rebellion has added nothing but a great deal of unnecessary delay, suffering and heartache.

Chs. 35–40: Making and setting up the tabernacle.
Moses now gets on with the job he was instructed to do during his original forty days atop the mountain and has the tabernacle and its furnishings constructed according to the plans outlined in chs. 24–31.

40.34-38: The Glory of the LORD.
Ever since the Israelites left Egypt they had been led by the LORD in a pillar of cloud by day and of fire by night (13.21f; 14.19f). Also, until the tabernacle was constructed, Moses had erected an interim 'tent of meeting' outside the camp where the LORD would meet with him in the pillar of cloud (33.9f). Now the cloud moved to the new Tent of Meeting and God's glory filled the tabernacle. It was the symbol of God's Presence with the Israelites on their journey and they only moved camp when the cloud lifted from the tent. Christians have often found their example a useful guide to following the Spirit today.

Though Israel stayed at Sinai for almost a year (Num. 10.11), Moses never had to go up the mountain again. The tabernacle was now to be the regular meeting place—hence the name 'Tent of Meeting'. The laws in Leviticus and Numbers were given there, at the foot of the mountain. The mountain top was the place of God's initial appearing and of his covenant-making, but it was never God's intention that men should have to climb mountains every time they needed to speak with him. By his own ordaining he could now be met in his Presence indwelling the tabernacle ('There ... I will meet with you,' Exod. 26.22), then later the temple, and ultimately in his Spirit indwelling the Christian tabernacle, which is our body (1 Cor. 3.16f; 6.19).

LEVITICUS
(The details of the laws are discussed more fully on pages 109–131. For the present our concern is to trace the story.)

Chs. 1–7: The laws of sacrifice.
At the Tent of Meeting God outlines to Moses the forms of regular sacrificial worship to be used there.

Chs. 8–10: Consecration of the priests.
Now that the tabernacle is ready and the forms of worship are given, Moses consecrates Aaron and his four sons to be priests according to the instructions in Exod. 29 and the sacrifices start. As the first draws to its conclusion, while the people are being blessed, the LORD puts his seal of approval on all that has been done by sending supernatural fire to consume the remaining sacrificial offerings on the altar.

Sadly the rejoicing is spoiled when two of Aaron's sons, Nadab and Abihu, decide to do things their own way and have to pay with their lives. The message is clear, and is as sharply imparted as it was to Moses himself when he first set out to serve the LORD (Exod. 4.19-26), that God requires complete obedience to his instructions in every detail from those he calls to serve him.

Chs. 11–15: Laws of purity and impurity.
An important part of the priest's duty, besides the sacrificial, is to 'distinguish between the holy and the profane, between the unclean and the clean' and to teach the people the decrees of God that encapsulate that distinction (10.10f). That is, of course, partly a religious function relating to sacrifices, offerings and ceremonially holy living, but it also

governs what we would regard as secular, though Israel did not draw the distinction. Hence the laws in this section mainly relate to daily living, to what we today would refer to as diet, health and hygiene. Some of the regulations may seem rather quaint, but they were to the ancients what our modern techniques of refrigeration, food and health control and preventative medicine are to us today.

Ch. 16: The Day of Atonement.
A third main function of the priest is to stand between his people and God pleading for their forgiveness and offering sacrifices for their atonement (their *at-one-ment* with God).

Chs. 17–26: The Holiness Code.
These chapters contain a mixture of social, moral and religious laws, demonstrating what we have already observed, how little the LORD distinguishes between secular and religious matters. God's call is to be holy, and that applies to every aspect of life, not just religious affairs. The teaching is summed up in the commandment: 'Be holy because I, the LORD your God, am holy' (19.2), and it is because this demand for holiness is so strong throughout that these chapters are commonly referred to as 'The Holiness Code'.

THE HOLINESS CODE	
Ch. 17	forbids eating blood, for the life is in the blood.
Chs. 18–20	prohibit certain social and ethical practices found among Israel's neighbours (cp. 18.3). Holiness is complete separation from all that is unholy (20.1-8).
Chs. 21–22	lay down further, even more stringent rules for priests.
Ch. 23	outlines the regulations for holy days and festivals.
Ch. 24	gives instruction about the oil and bread regularly in use in the tabernacle, and concludes with a ruling about blasphemy.
Ch. 25	prescribes that land should lie fallow every seventh year and that debts should be cancelled and property restored every fiftieth year (Jubilee).
Ch. 26	details various blessings and curses relating to obedience.
Ch. 27	discusses the purpose of vows and tithes.

God's Grace in Revelation and Discipline

Ch. 26 aptly rounds off this collection of laws with its promise of blessings for obedience and warning of the disasters that will result from disobedience. Its picture of blessing is truly a description of Eden: flourishing vegetation (vv. 3-5), peace in nature and society (vv. 6-8), people being fruitful and multiplying (v. 9), plenty to eat (v. 10), and God walking among his people once more (vv. 11f). It thus reminds us that the laws of Sinai are all part of God's plan to fulfil his promise to Abraham and restore his world to what it was originally intended to be. History may have moved on, but God's purpose remains unchanged.

The theme of ch. 27 is that everything belongs to God, and as a token of that fact firstborn of men and beasts, firstfruits of harvest, and tithes of grain and cattle are his by right. Some of these may be redeemed, as may persons or possessions dedicated to God in a vow. This reminder that everyone and everything belongs to God makes a most fitting conclusion to a book that demands obedience and dedication. His law asks no more than we owe him.

NUMBERS

Chs. 1-2: Moses takes census of the people and organises the camp.
Having imparted the basic patterns for worship and social life, the LORD now bids Moses get the community properly organised. First he has to discover who exactly he has with him, and then he has to arrange their camp emplacements in an orderly fashion to avoid confusion once they set out on their journeys again. Their time at Sinai is drawing to a close.

Chs. 3-4: He then organises the Levites.
God accepts the Levites in place of Israel's firstborn who by right belong to him (Lev. 27). They are set apart for special service, and so are numbered and organised separately from the other tribes.

Chs. 7-8: Final arrangements at the tabernacle.
Moses now receives gifts and offerings from the tribal

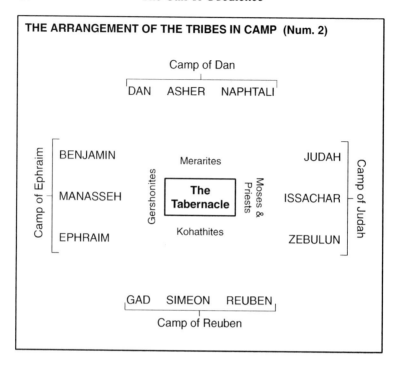

leaders at the dedication of the tabernacle, has the lamps lit, and consecrates the Levites to their work.

9.1 – 10.10: Final celebrations and preparations for the journey.

A year after the Exodus, as their time at Sinai draws to an end, the Israelites keep Passover once more, and Moses has trumpets made for summoning the people.

On the cloud and the Tent (9.15-23), see pp. 76 & 82.

Additional Laws in Numbers.

Moses continued to receive laws and instructions from God at different stopping places in the wilderness. Many of them expand on laws already given, others are additional to them.

Ch. 5   deals with impurity in the camp and lays down tests for adultery.

Ch. 6   describes the Nazirite vow, a vow of special consecration that any Israelite could take.

God's Grace in Revelation and Discipline 81

Ch. 9	permits Passover to be celebrated a month late if circumstances prevent it being held in the first month.
Ch. 10	gives instruction about the use of trumpets to assemble the people and at festivals.
Ch. 15	prescribes additional offerings to be brought after entry to the land, distinguishes how to deal with unintentional and deliberate sins, gives a ruling about Sabbath-breaking, and requires that tassels be worn to remind the wearer of God and his law.
Ch. 18	lists some of the duties of the Levites and details the tithes and offerings that are to be their means of upkeep.
Ch. 19	details a ritual for removing defilement after contact with a dead body.
Chs. 28–29	outline in greater detail the offerings and rituals for holy days and festivals (cp. Lev. 23).
Ch. 30	explains conditions under which a woman's vows may be revoked (a man's vow is unconditionally binding).

We shall look more closely at the purpose of the laws and the priestly rituals in our next chapter. In the meantime let us press on with the story.

2. FROM SINAI TO KADESH (NUM. 10–20)

This next stage of our story is dominated by accounts of grumbling, complaining and rebellion. If we were surprised to hear the Israelites complain after experiencing the miracle of the Exodus and after the appearance of God in the fire of Sinai, then it is perhaps even more surprising to hear them complain at this stage, on what should have been the last leg of their journey to Canaan. At another level, it is not at all surprising, for it is a common experience with Christians that the spiritual struggle intensifies the nearer God's objective approaches. Jesus knew that struggle too in Gethsemane.

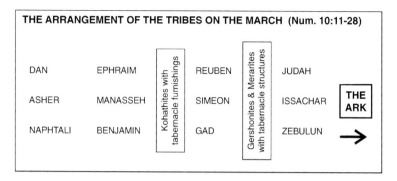

Num. 10.11-26: The Israelites leave Sinai.
After just over a year the Israelites strike camp and move north by stages. Within a few months they are to reach the southern borders of Canaan and should have entered the land then, their journeying ended. God's plans were not at all wasteful:

- three months from Egypt to Sinai—a very short time for the journey considering the numbers involved;
- just under a year at Sinai—a necessary length of time to get the community and its life-style organised;
- then the last lap to Canaan.

However, because of their disobedience this last lap was to take thirty-eight years. In many ways this is the most distressing section of the Pentateuch, but it does have its beautiful highlights, the first of which is the account of their departure from Sinai.

In Num. 9.15-23 we were reminded that the Israelites only moved when the cloud at the Tent of Meeting moved (cp. Exod. 40.34-38). Now at last the cloud lifts and the people set out in orderly formation, tribe by tribe, as the LORD had commanded (cp. Num. 2).

Moses invites Hobab, his brother-in-law, Jethro's son, to accompany them, knowing that his intimate knowledge of the desert will be particularly useful on the journey. Here we have a most interesting example of God's power and man's skill working together: we have just read that God had given a cloud to lead Israel, and yet here is Moses welcoming human expertise as well. There is no contradiction in that, as long as man works in harmony with God; problems only

God's Grace in Revelation and Discipline

arise when he goes his own way, depending solely on his own abilities, as Nadab and Abihu did (Lev. 10). After all, when God wanted the tabernacle constructed, he used two craftsmen with considerable expertise, Bezalel and Oholiab (Exod. 35f); and he also made sure that Moses was very thoroughly equipped with the necessary human skills before calling him to confront Pharaoh. Hobab's family stayed with Israel throughout their wanderings and eventually settled in southern Judah (Judg. 1.16).

And so the tribes set out, full of enthusiasm and determination, crying triumphantly:

> Rise up, O LORD!
> > May your enemies be scattered;
> > may your foes flee before you.

11.1-3: The grumbling begins.
It seems the tribes had not gone very far before the complaining started. We are not told much about this first incident, but in it we find the ingredients of similar incidents that went before and that are to follow:

1. the people complain,
2. the LORD is angry,
3. judgment overtakes the people,
4. Moses prays for them and
5. the judgment abates.

The sequence is not always the same, but the basic story is.

11.4-35: Manna and quails!
The first time the Israelites craved the food of Egypt, the LORD gave them quails and manna (Exod. 16). Now they are tired of the manna, so the LORD gives them quails again, this time in such surfeit that it makes them sick. Sometimes the LORD's way of dealing with our selfishness is to grant us our desires so that we can learn by experience the effects of our greed.

11.10-30: The elders and the Spirit.
Interwoven with this story of grumbling is an account of an episode that is of primary importance for understanding

the message of the Old Testament, and indeed of the whole Bible. Moses pleads that he finds it impossible to carry the burden of this complaining people all by himself, whereupon God asks him to summon seventy of the best elders to the Tent of Meeting. There he endues them with the Spirit that is already on Moses himself and they begin to prophesy, presumably rejoicing in seeing something of the revelation God gave Moses on the mountain, thus equipping them to share leadership with him. The nature of their prophesying is not actually explained to us, but when Joshua is offended by it and wants to have it stopped, Moses turns to him and says, 'I wish that all the LORD's people were prophets and that the LORD would put his Spirit on them!' (v. 29)

Clearly Moses recognises that something very precious has happened, so much so he longs for it to be shared by all his people. Much later in Israel's history other men on whom God's Spirit rested were to experience the same longing, but more than that were to realise it was going to be fulfilled one day. For example, Isaiah 44.3 speaks of God pouring out his Spirit on Israel's offspring, Ezek. 36.26f tells that the Spirit will be put within them, and Joel 2.28 declares that then they will all prophesy. The fulfilment of these prophecies, of course, begins on the day of Pentecost described in Acts 2, when the disciples of Jesus are filled with the Holy Spirit and speak in other tongues. There Peter explains that this is the prophesying foretold by Joel, but clearly Moses, more than twelve to fourteen centuries earlier glimpsed the potential of it. Num. 11 is therefore in some way like an early foretaste of Pentecost.

Here we have a first hint of a stream that is to surface from time to time in Israel and finally to burst forth in full flood in and through the ministry of Jesus and his disciples. It is this stream of the Spirit that will give our story coherence as it develops, linking the men of faith of the Old Testament with the Christians of the New. Moses glimpsed and longed for it, others later saw it coming, it arrived with Jesus, and the disciples lived and ministered in the fullness of it. It was to bring blessing to all who received it, in line with God's promise to Abraham, and was to impart new life to them, thus restoring a measure of what man had lost when deprived of access to the tree of life in the Garden of Eden.

Ch. 12: Does the LORD only speak through Moses?
Jealousy of the LORD's call and anointing led to Cain's downfall, it caused disruption among Jacob's children, and now Moses suffers from it. But as in the earlier stories, it rebounds on the heads of those opposing him, in this case his own brother and sister. Like Joseph before him, Moses harbours no ill will. Sadly we see the scene re-enacted in the life of many congregations today. However, it still remains true that, while God will grant many in a church the gift of prophecy, he will normally speak more directly and clearly to the one he has appointed as leader and shepherd of the flock (cp. vv. 6-8).

Chs. 13–14: Tragedy at Kadesh.
When Israel arrives at Kadesh (13.26) on the southern borders of Canaan, presumably only a few months have passed since leaving Sinai. Faith, obedience, patience and every virtue have been sorely tested at every stage, then at the last crucial moment, when Israel should have gone forward in faith to win the land, fear grips the people as they listen to the spies' reports about the apparent strength of the Canaanites.

The grumbling this time is so virulent that it cannot be quelled. Moses, overwhelmed by the tragedy of the situation, pleads with God for his people, but while the LORD agrees to withhold his anger, he refuses to permit any of the adults (over twenty) who had seen his wonders in the Exodus and at Sinai to enter the promised land. They are to wander homeless for forty years until their generation has completely died off. Their sons will then enter, along with Joshua and Caleb who alone remained faithful.

The knowledge that they have lost their opportunity, of course, turns their rebellion to remorse, but when they try to enter the land now, they find the way firmly closed to them. While God was backing them, what seemed impossible would have been straightforward, just as the apparently impossible journey from Egypt to Kadesh had been; but now that he is not, all they feared proved true.

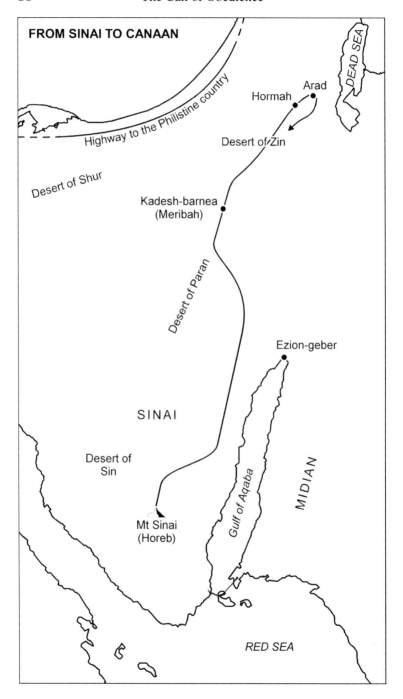

God's Grace in Revelation and Discipline

Faith demands that we move forward in obedience to God's command, leading or prompting when he speaks; fear will cause us to shrink back in disobedience. The way of faith and obedience leads to fulfilment, the way of fear and retreat leads only to anguish. The same is true still today; and the cost of disobedience can be just as high as it was in Israel's day. (The best Christian commentary on these events is in Hebrews 3.7 – 4.13 and 10.19-39; see below, pp. 174, 177.)

Chs. 15–19: The years of wandering.

We know hardly anything about the long years of Israel's wanderings in the desert, but these chapters tell us two important things. Firstly, despite the harshness of God's judgment, Israel was still his people and it remained his purpose to bring them to Canaan. So he continued to prepare them, speaking to them through Moses and giving them further laws. (See pp. 80f.)

But secondly, the grumbling continued. The rebellion of Korah and 250 Israelites was apparently motivated partly by continuing jealousy of Moses' leadership (16.3) and partly by disgruntlement that he had not succeeded in taking them into the land (16.14)—such is the perversion of man! God's judgment is sudden and sharp, but after it the whole Israelite community starts to complain again (16.41). Plague breaks out and Moses once more pleads for the people. God then performs a miracle with Aaron's staff which is thenceforth to stand as a sign that Moses and Aaron do indeed exercise their leadership by God's appointing, the intention being to put an end to the jealousy and complaining once and for all.

20.1-13: Back at Kadesh.

'In the first month', presumably of the fortieth year, they arrive back at Kadesh, the place from which they originally should have set out for the land, years and years, a whole lifetime, lost through rebellion and disobedience. And the tune has hardly changed. Still they grumble and quarrel, this time because of shortage of water. Of course God has his supply and he tells Moses how to get it—'Speak to that rock.' But this time Moses, who had been so long-suffering and had faithfully pleaded for the people all these years, finally snaps and in a fit of rage hits out at the rock with his staff as he shouts roughly at the people. That momentary lapse was to cost him the privilege of entering Canaan himself: 'Because you did not trust me enough to honour me as holy in the sight of the Israelites ...' (v. 12). Later we are to hear him justly blame the people for this judgment (Deut. 1.37), but in the end the sin was his, not theirs.

And so, on this sad note, this unhappy period of our history draws to its close. It stands eternally as an object lesson on the cost of failure to walk in faith and obedience, and neither Israel nor the Church have been allowed to forget it (Ps. 95; 106; Heb. 3–4).

Moses' sister, Miriam, died at Kadesh (v. 1), his brother, Aaron, died soon after the tribes left Kadesh, and Moses was to die himself before the year was out. Despite all their failings, this family had served the LORD well. Though it is sad that none of them ever entered the land, their role in history was actually over and we sense a rightness as we see first Aaron and then Moses hand over their leadership to younger men.

3. FROM KADESH TO THE PLAINS OF MOAB (NUM. 20–36)

The thirteenth century saw considerable upheaval in the Middle East. Egyptian power was severely eroded by the influx of Sea Peoples from across the Mediterranean, amongst whom were the Philistines who settled on the southern coast of Canaan. About the same time, as Egypt's hold on Canaan weakened, the small kingdoms of Edom, Moab and Ammon began to emerge as strong political units along its southern and eastern borders. And, of course, in the land itself some Canaanite cities were taking advantage of their new-found freedom to strengthen their fortifications. If the Israelites had gone forward in faith forty years earlier they would have encountered less well organised opposition. Ch. 13 suggests that their original plan was to go straight up from Kadesh into the southern hill-country, but now they have to weave their way around the borders of the new kingdoms until at length they arrive in the Plains of Moab,

God's Grace in Revelation and Discipline 89

across the Jordan from Jericho, where Joshua will eventually lead them into the land. (The story is told again in Deut. 1–3.)

20.14 – 21.20: The journey round Edom and Moab.
Though the Edomites did not allow the Israelites to pass through their territory, they did not harass them as they made their way round. But the journey was far from uneventful. Shortly after they left Kadesh Aaron died, then they were attacked by the people of Arad, they suffered from a plague of serpents, and at least twice they experienced water-shortage. But we can see the LORD's hand at work in each of these crises.

Aaron's death was no sudden, unexpected calamity, but was coupled with the orderly and peaceful handing on of his priestly authority to his son, Eleazer (20.22-29).

Arad is in the hill-country the Israelites had dismally failed to take in their own strength thirty-eight years earlier; now that the LORD is with them, they have no problem in winning it (21.1-3; cp. 14.40-45).

The plague of serpents was God's response to a final bout of grumbling and was dealt with when Moses prayed and held aloft a bronze serpent (21.4-9). This bronze image was later put in the temple in Jerusalem, though it was eventually thrown out when the Israelites started worshipping it (2 Kings 18.4).

The provision of water is also again the LORD's, just as it had been at Rephidim and Kadesh (21.10-18; cp. Exod. 17; Num. 20).

21.21-35: The conquest of Transjordan.
From their base camp in the Plains of Moab the Israelites defeated Sihon, King of the Amorites, who held southern Transjordan, and Og, King of Bashan, further north beside the Sea of Galilee (cp. Deut. 2.26 – 3.11).

Chs. 22–24: The Moabites seek to destroy Israel.
Balak, King of Moab, pays Balaam, a famous pagan prophet, to come and curse Israel, but in a unique demonstration of his sovereignty, God intervenes and virtually turns Balaam into a prophet of his own. First he impresses

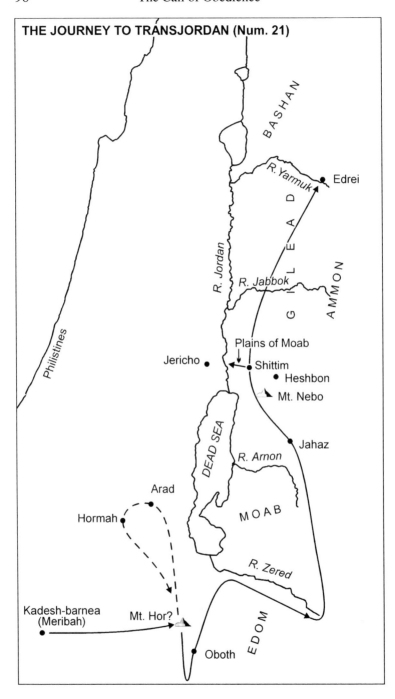

his will on him by night visions, by an angelic visitation and by giving his donkey voice (ch. 22). Three times Balak tries to obtain his curse, but each time he has to listen to Balaam bless Israel. Finally Balaam is granted an amazing vision in which he sees a king arise in Israel and establish imperial rule over Edom and Moab (the star of Jacob in 24.17 is David)—then even beyond that to the Assyrian conquest in the eighth century.

Ch. 25: Israel sins at Baal-Peor.
Despite his amazing visions, Balaam was a pagan. After he left Balak he must have had some corrupting influence on Israel through the Moabites and Midianites around them, and as a result their women were enticing Israelites to worship the local Baal of Peor (cp. 31.16). This is the episode referred to in Rev. 2.14.

Chs. 26–27: Moses starts preparations for entry into Canaan.
Firstly, Moses assesses his fighting strength by counting the men of military age. This census, the second since leaving Egypt, reveals that after forty years Israel has not grown in numbers, but has even decreased slightly (26.51; cp. 1.46). The desert must have taken its toll, but even so God's promise was multiplication (Lev. 26.9). That, of course, was dependent on obedience—the lesson is clear. The Levite count shows a slight increase, but only slight (26.62; cp. 3.39).

Secondly, he seeks the LORD's guidance about a particular problem of inheritance that could have led to squabbles in apportioning the land. The right granted here is for brotherless women to inherit, and that was unusual in the ancient Near East. However, a proviso is later added that such women must marry within their own tribe (see ch. 36).

Thirdly, he has Joshua publicly commissioned to take command after his death. We do not hear a great deal about Joshua before this. He had led Israel's fighting men against the Amalekites at Rephidim (Exod. 17.8-13), he accompanied Moses as his personal assistant when he went up Mount Sinai (Exod. 24.13), and later he stood guard over the tent of meeting (Exod. 33.11). He was puzzled by what was happening when the Spirit came on the seventy elders (Num. 11.28), but he and Caleb were the only ones among the spies to maintain the faith perspective about entering the land (Num. 14.6-9). Now he is himself recognised as one who has the Spirit and he is to exercise an authority beyond that of any elder.

Chs. 28–30: see pp. 81 and 128.

Chs. 31–32: The Transjordanian settlement.
A final battle in which the Midianites are thoroughly routed brings Israel's conflicts in Transjordan to an end. (Balaam is killed in this battle; 31.8, cp. v. 16.) Reuben and Gad appeal to Moses for possession of the Transjordanian territories and, along with Makir, a section of the tribe of Manasseh, are granted their request, on condition they also help the other tribes to conquer Canaan.

Chs. 33–36: Territorial arrangements for Israel in Canaan.
After reviewing the stages of the wilderness journey, Moses preaches to the Israelites about the importance of eradicating paganism from Canaan, otherwise the Canaanites 'will become barbs in your eyes and thorns in your sides' (33.55).

Then he outlines the limits of the territory they plan to take and appoints tribal leaders to be responsible for the division and apportionment of the land (ch. 34).

He allocates towns for the Levites to live in since they are to have no territory of their own, and he nominates certain cities of refuge to which men accused of murder can flee for protection until brought to trial (ch. 35).

Then finally he gives a ruling to ensure that tribal lands remain within the tribe if one of its families has no sons (ch. 36).

The story we have followed thus far is consistent and coherent. Moses demonstrated tremendous faith as he brought Israel out of Egypt, and then amazing patience as he bore with their grumblings, pleading for them time and again to avert God's anger, even on one occasion when they were preparing to stone him (Num. 14.10). We see in him a

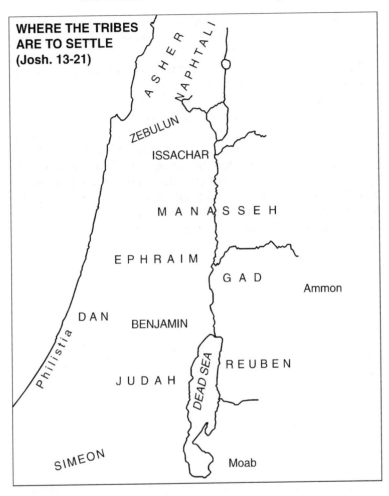

man of faith and vision, one who knew what he had to do and where he had to lead his people, whether they were willing or not, and at whatever cost. One or two men stood by him, some with greater constancy than others, but for the most part he had to stand alone with God.

At Sinai a new dimension enters the story as God outlines his plans for his people's future, his purpose to dwell among them in mercy, and the blessing that he promises to give them when they follow his commands. Sadly we watch them lose credit time after time until finally they are turned back at the borders. For forty long years they drift aimlessly in the wilderness, until finally God leads them forward into the Plains of Moab, winning victory after victory.

Repeatedly we see God's faithfulness to his promises and purposes. He punishes, but he also forgives and restores. Despite persistent disobedience he continues not only to feed and support his people, but also to prepare them for entering the land at last. As they sit on the Plains of Moab he gives final instructions about apportioning the land and as Moses numbers his men and makes his last preparations, we sense that we are about to enter into the vindication of that faith that had inspired not only Moses, but also men like Joseph long before him, who had foreseen this day when Israel would finally return home.

6

Now Choose Life

DEUTERONOMY

The Book of Deuteronomy does not so much give us an additional set of new laws (although its name does mean 'second law': Greek *deuteros* = second, *nomos* = law); rather it is a re-presentation of the laws already given. As we have seen, the Israelites are thoroughly taught and prepared for crossing into Canaan by this time. God is not suddenly throwing a whole lot of last minute teaching at them as if he were suddenly remembering all the things he should have said but never got round to saying. That is how we commonly operate, but God's work is always well-planned and thorough. We saw that when we looked at the story of creation, and we shall see it again when Jesus dies with the words 'It is finished' on his lips (cp. pp. 15, 176).

In fact Deuteronomy, unlike the legal portions of the rest of the Pentateuch, is not, for the most part, a record of words spoken by God to Moses. It is almost entirely a long speech made by Moses, a farewell sermon in which he pleads with the Israelites as they prepare to cross into Canaan to pay heed to the things God has already taught them, both in the laws and through their wilderness experience. His theme is basically this:

Chs. 1–11:
See that you do not forget what you have learned over these past forty years about God's love and faithfulness and about the cost of rebellion. You know his will is to bless you.

Chs. 12–26:
When you apply the laws, do so with gratitude to God, and love and humanity toward each other. You are called to be God's holy people, so live as such, in faithfulness to him, in unity together and in obedience to his laws, so that it may go well with you.

Chs. 27–31:
The LORD is giving you a choice, whether to obey him and live, or to disobey and die, to have blessing or curse.

Chs. 32–34:
These chapters conclude Moses' life-story.

Deuteronomy's challenge is summed up in its description of 'The Two Ways' in 11.26-28 and 30.15-20: the way of obedience leading to blessing and life, and the way of disobedience leading to curse and death. God had already established the principle in Eden (see p. 18) and we encountered earlier teaching about it in Lev. 26. Now it becomes the overarching theme as Moses makes his last impassioned plea to his people.

It should, however, be noted that this doctrine is not a recipe for obtaining salvation. The Israelites were already granted that when God rescued them from slavery in Egypt. Deuteronomy, like all the law of Moses, is rather an account of how to continue living in salvation: it describes the kind of life God wants his saved people to live. Salvation in the Bible story is not something man earns, but something God does for him. Paul emphasises the truth of this again in Romans.

The quality of life among God's people required by Deuteronomy may be summed up in two words: grateful love—love shown to God himself by serving him in total faithfulness (chs. 1–11, cp. 10.12f), and love for fellow Israelites shown in humanitarian behaviour and in care for the poor and needy (chs. 12–26, cp. 15.7-15)—love arising from hearts that are thankful for all God has done for Israel. What God longs for is a people that will love him and serve him out of gratitude, not just out of a sense of duty. Such service will, of course, lead only to greater blessing, which in turn should lead to an increase of love and gratitude.

With that sort of teaching Deuteronomy brings us very close to the New Testament. It takes us into the heart of God that undergirds the law and is in many ways like an intermediate stepping stone between the law of Sinai and Christ's law 'written not with ink but with the Spirit of the living God, not on tablets of stone but on tablets of human hearts' (2 Cor. 3.3).

Thus Deuteronomy, while it looks back to Sinai and the wilderness experience, is also a prophetic book. Immediately it looks forward to life in Canaan, but it also speaks of a more ultimate vision. Moses had had revelations of God's purposes granted to no other in his day—he knew God's heart, for he spoke with him 'face to face, as a man speaks with his friend' (Exod. 33.11). When the seventy elders glimpsed something of what he saw it overwhelmed them and lifted them forward into a foretaste of things that lay hundreds of years ahead of them (Num. 11). It is therefore little wonder that his speech has such a strong flavour of things to come. But then, he was a man of the Spirit and part of the activity of the Spirit is to do precisely that, to reveal 'what is yet to come' (John 16.13).

In Deuteronomy, as well as tapping the heart and mind of God, we begin to uncover the heart and mind of man filled with God's Spirit. It is, after all, Moses, not God, who speaks and those who know the reality of God's love poured into their hearts by the Holy Spirit will find themselves very much at home with his thought-patterns and heart-feelings as he expresses his own appreciation of God's love and challenges us to respond accordingly.

1. THE MESSAGE OF HISTORY (CHS. 1–11)

Chs. 1–4: Learn the lessons of your desert journeyings and obey God.
We are now right at the end of the wilderness period (1.3f). Moses begins his address by reviewing the main incidents since leaving Horeb (the name used for Mount Sinai in Deuteronomy, cp. Exod. 3.1).

Ch. 1: When God told us to leave Horeb, he bade us go straight to the land he promised our forefathers he would give us (vv. 6-8, cp. Num. 10). On the way I had to appoint elders to help me carry the burden of all your complaints (vv. 9-18, cp. Num. 11). At the border I knew we had to go in boldly and take possession, and our spies told us it was a good land (vv. 19-25, cp. Num. 13). But, despite all my pleadings, you would not trust God and so he condemned us to wander in the wilderness (vv. 26-46, cp. Num. 14).

2.1 – 3.20: Throughout those forty years God looked after us well, and then he led us round the territories of Edom, Moab and Ammon, which were not promised to us anyway (vv. 1-23, cp. Num. 20-21). But now we have taken Transjordan, the lands of Sihon and Og (see map on p. 90). That has been straight-forward enough because God gave it to us—it was promised territory—and I have apportioned it to Reuben, Gad and part of Manasseh (2.24 – 3.20, cp. Num. 21 & 32).

3.21-29: Joshua will lead you into Canaan; I cannot go with you. You have seen how easy it is to conquer when God is with you, so go forward this time and do not be afraid. I have to pay the cost of my disobedience. It is not easy and I have pleaded with God about it, so whatever you do, remember the lessons of these forty years.

Ch. 4: Be sure to listen to what God is commanding you now (4.1f). Remember what happened just a few weeks ago to those who turned to follow the Baal of Peor (vv. 3f, cp. Num. 25).

You have been given commandments that will make you wise among the nations (vv. 5-8). Make sure you do not forget them; teach them to your children. Remember them, they are God's pattern for your life in Canaan (vv. 9-14).

The God you met at Horeb is not like the pagan gods; do not be led astray to worship them; he is a consuming fire, a jealous God; I know that because I have felt his hand of judgment myself (vv. 15-24).

If a time comes that you do turn to other gods, you will again be removed from the land and you will only be restored to it after whole-hearted repentance—but you *will* be restored, for God will not forget the promise he made to

Abraham (vv. 25-31).

Just think of it, you have met the God of heaven and earth in an experience unique to man, and it is all because he loved your fathers. Now he is taking you home. Please keep his decrees (vv. 32-40).

Throughout these chapters Moses has repeatedly underlined God's love and goodness towards Israel, as well as the seriousness of his call. As we have seen, his love is as much our motive for obedience as the awesomeness of his majesty.

Chs. 5–11: Learn what the LORD asked of you at Horeb —to love and serve him.

Ch. 5: When God spoke out of the fire to your fathers, it was also to you that he spoke (vv. 1-4), and when you heard you stood in awe and pledged your obedience (vv. 23-27), but what the LORD really wants is the allegiance of your heart (v. 29).

The wording of the Ten Commandments here is slightly different from that in Exod. 20, but then Moses is freely rehearsing them as part of his sermon and is probably taking the liberty most preachers take when they want to get their point across. We see that particularly in the Sabbath commandment where he stresses again that obedience should rise out of a grateful remembering of all the LORD has done.

The same emphasis on love and gratitude, on remembering and not forgetting, as well as on faithfulness and obedience is found throughout the chapters that follow.

Ch. 6: When you enter the land with all its provision and luxuries, be careful not to forget the LORD. Love him with all your heart, soul and strength; teach the laws and the story of your salvation to your children; and obey the LORD so that it may go well with you.

Ch. 7: Do not form relationships with the pagans in Canaan; you are called to be a people holy to the LORD. You are his treasured possession, and that is not because you are particularly special people—on the contrary, you are a fairly insignificant race—but it is because the LORD loves you. Obey him and be faithful, for he will look after you and will gradually drive out the Canaanites, so long as you do not get involved in their detestable paganism.

Ch. 8: Beware! When you are enjoying the blessings of the land, you will be tempted to forget that it was the LORD who gave it to you, and then you will be in danger of losing it all.

Ch. 9: But you have not earned it. It was promised to your forefather, Abraham. Watch that you do not provoke God to anger as you did at Horeb when you made the golden calf—and at other places where you disobeyed him.

Ch. 10: That caused a lot of hassle, but God in his faithfulness and mercy renewed his covenant and promise. So fear, obey, love and serve him, because all he wants is to do you good. He chose you, he loves you, he is your praise, he is your God!

Ch. 11: Love him, obey him, remember all he has done for you. He is about to give you good things. Do not be led astray to other gods. You have a choice of two ways before you, one leading to blessing and life, the other to curse and death—be sure to obey him.

Moses must have been a powerful preacher! He had rallied his people many times before, but in Exodus to Numbers we only have snatches of his sermons. Here we see his heart.

2. APPLYING THE MESSAGE AT THE HEART OF THE LAW (CHS. 12–26)

As we are taken through different aspects of the law, Moses hammers home the same lessons. He is not concerned to give new laws so much as to draw out the heart of those already given, to teach the Israelites about the essential principles by which they are called to live in the land, and to remind them that obedience based on grateful love will lead to infinite blessing—as well as the converse, of course. We should continue to read these chapters as a sermon. A quick comparison of ch. 12 with Lev. 1–7, both on the sanctuary and its sacrifices, shows clearly that we are still reading a sermon, not just learning laws. Whereas Leviticus outlines all the practical instructions needed to perform the sacrifices at the altar, Deuteronomy speaks of the right attitudes with which to bring them to the sanctuary.

12.1 – 14.21: *You are the LORD's people; you must serve him alone.*

Ch. 12: Offer your sacrifices at the LORD's chosen sanctuary, not at a local Canaanite shrine. In Israel all slaughter was sacrifice, because the life is in the blood and that belongs to God. Slaughter should therefore normally be at an altar, but if the LORD's house be too far away, then either the animal should just be slaughtered at home and the blood allowed to run out on the ground, or it should be sold so that another animal can be bought to offer at the sanctuary, but on no account should it be offered at one of the local shrines with its pagan ways. The meat should be shared with the whole household, even the slaves—and all should be done with rejoicing and thanksgiving, because the LORD has blessed you (vv. 7,12,18).

Ch. 13: Whatever you do, do not worship other gods, not if the most convincing prophet, nor someone from your own family or friends, nor even a whole town-full of people should try to persuade you. Get rid of such influences from your life altogether.

14.1-21: You are the children of God, a holy people, the LORD's treasured possession. That truth must be reflected in every aspect of your living, even the food you eat.

14.22 – 15.18: *Be generous to your fellow Israelites.*
Do not neglect your tithes so that aliens, orphans, widows and Levites may eat. And be faithful in obeying the LORD's command to release your fellow Israelite from his debts and your Hebrew slaves from their bondage every seventh year. 'There should be no poor among you ... do not be hardhearted or tight-fisted towards your poor brother. Rather be open-handed and freely lend ... Give generously to him and do so without a grudging heart.' (vv. 4,7f,10) These sentiments were already expressed in Leviticus (cp. 25.6f), but Moses, the preacher, here exhorts the people to apply them and live by them.

15.19 – 16.17: Let festivals be times of joyful thanksgiving for all.
A glance at Lev. 23 and Num. 28f again reveals the striking contrast between preaching and legal instruction. Though Deuteronomy does refer to some of the regulations governing the sacrificial offerings, it would be well nigh impossible to celebrate Weeks and Tabernacles on the basis of the teaching given here, because it is almost entirely about the right attitudes with which to celebrate them: they should be times of remembering (16.3,12), and therefore of rejoicing (16.11,14f) and gratitude for all the blessings granted by God (16.1,10,17). And no-one, however poor or humble, whether children, slaves, Levites, aliens, orphans, widows, or whoever, should be left out of the celebrations. You need to remember you too were once poor and oppressed until the LORD rescued you (16.12).

16.18 – 21.23: Maintain holiness and humanity in your social structures.
Various aspects of the affairs of state are discussed: judges, law-courts, priests, prophets, the king, the army, the rights of sons, etc. No sharp distinction is drawn between secular and sacred institutions. After all Israel is the LORD's people and the distinctions we draw today between Church and State cannot always be applied in the same way. A brief review of these chapters shows that Moses is still preaching the same sermon, but now applying his basic teaching about fidelity to God, justice and humanity to Israel's religious, social and political institutions.

16.18-20: Judges and officials must maintain fair justice to secure life in the LORD's land.

16.21 – 17.7: Religious cases may be judged in secular courts—certain religious offences are so abominable that the secular courts have the right to execute offenders, provided the accusation can be properly sustained on the evidence of two or three witnesses.

17.8-13: Secular cases may be referred to religious courts and they are the final court of appeal for all cases, religious or secular.

17.14-20: If the nation is to prosper, the king, when you appoint one, must get himself a copy of the Law, read it every day, and live according to its teaching.

18.1-8: Every Levite must be allowed his fair share in both the duties and the benefits apportioned to him by law; he has, after all, no other way of earning a living since he has no tribal territory.

18.9-22: Pagan diviners are not to be sought after or heeded. The LORD has promised to provide a prophet like me, through whom he will speak. You will recognise him, because he will speak in the LORD's name and his words will come to pass.

19.1-13: Cities of refuge are to be places of protection for those charged with, but not guilty of murder.

19.14: Respect ancestral boundaries.

19.15-21: The evidence of witnesses must be verified so that justice is not perverted.

Ch. 20: War is to be fought fearlessly, but without wanton cruelty; principles of humanity and religious devotion need to be balanced with each other.

21.1-9: Unsolved murders can be dealt with by sacrifice so that no person or place needs feel a burden of blood-guilt.

21.10-14: Any woman taken for wife from prisoners of war must be treated with the respect due to a wife.

21.15-17: The inheritance of firstborn sons must be respected above all else.

21.18-21: If all discipline fails the courts may have to put a stubbornly rebellious son to death for failing to honour his parents.

21.22f: Do not sully the land by exposing a criminal's body beyond the day of execution.

Chs. 22–25: Miscellaneous laws.
Clearly it is impossible to comment here on all the individual laws in these chapters, but even a cursory glance through them shows that the same principles underlie their presentation.

(a) Humanitarian care: put a parapet round the flat roof of

your house so that no-one will fall off and get hurt (22.8); if a runaway slave takes refuge with you, protect him (23.15f); do not charge a brother Israelite interest (23.19); exempt a newly-wed man from military service for a year (24.5); do not take advantage of a poor man who works for you (24.14f); let the poor glean in your harvest-field (24.19-22); etc.

(b) Similar care for animals: if you see your neighbour's ox or sheep or donkey in trouble, help it for him (22.1-4); do not harm a mother bird when you take her eggs or young (22.6f); allow your ox to have some grain when it is working for you (25.4).

(c) Holiness: purity is demanded in marriage and sexual relationships (22.13-30); membership of the Israelite assembly must be carefully controlled to keep it pure (23.1-8); the army camp must also be kept clean and holy (23.9-14).

(d) Justice and honesty: be true to your vows (23.21-3); do not mete out excessive punishment (25.1-3); do not cheat with two sets of weights, an accurate set and a false set (25.13-16).

A number of the laws here have no exact counterpart in the other law-codes, but they are mostly further applications of the central principals we have outlined and so add nothing essentially new.

Ch. 26: Remember God's graciousness and be faithful to him.

The legal section closes here, not so much with further laws about firstfruits and tithes, as with a preacher's suggestion about using their offering as occasions for remembering God's saving acts, returning thanks for his gift of the land, and renewing our pledge to faithful service.

Aptly this part of the sermon ends with a reminder that Israel is God's treasured possession that he has promised in his love to bless—that in the end should be Israel's real motive for obedience (vv. 16-19).

3. BLESSING, CURSE AND REPENTANCE (CHS. 27–30)

Moses now follows up his sermon with further preaching of a different nature and with some practical suggestions aimed at securing the people's commitment to the covenant and ensuring that it is maintained once they are in the land.

Ch. 27: First he instructs them to set up large public monuments with the law inscribed on them for all to read. Then he outlines a ceremony in which they are to bind themselves anew in the covenant both with sacrifices and with public reminders of the blessings and curses attached to the laws.

It is significant that he should choose Mount Ebal and Mount Gerizim as the site where these things are to happen, because the town of Shechem lies at the foot of them and it holds a special place in the history of God's promise of the land. It was the first place where Abraham stopped when he arrived in Canaan (Gen. 12.6f), and it was there that Jacob first encamped when he returned from exile (Gen. 33.18-20). Both of these men built altars there, and now, as a first token of arrival back home, Israel is to build another altar at Shechem and pledge itself again in allegiance to the LORD. In later times the Samaritans built a temple on Mount Gerizim. It was destroyed about 128 BC, but they preserved the tradition of the sacredness of the site into New Testament times (John 4.20), and still do so even today.

Ch. 28: Moses spells out in great detail the kind of blessings and curses Israel can expect, depending on obedience or disobedience. The curse-list is considerably longer, but then Moses was a realist—he had already seen Israel's natural propensity to rebellion.

The blessings and curses relate to the tangible realities of life, not just to spiritualities. That is what we should expect if we recall that God's purpose is to restore his creation to what he first intended it to be. When he called first the patriarchs and now Israel, he offered them the potential to enter into a preliminary foretaste of that restoration, the full realisation of which, of course, still lies in man's future. He promised Abraham blessing and he became rich in livestock, silver and gold (Gen. 12.2; 13.2). Similarly his promise to Israel is 'abundant prosperity' (Deut. 28.11), indeed virtually to walk again in Eden (vv. 1-14). But the way is the way of obedience.

Ch. 29: Moses then reviews Israel's history, past, present and future, reminding the people again of God's graciousness to them since he took them out of Egypt (vv. 2-8), impressing upon them the seriousness of what they now do in pledging themselves again in covenant with God (vv. 9-21), and warning them once more of the disastrous consequences of rebellion (vv. 22-29).

Ch. 30: However, God's will is not to destroy, but to restore, and so the purpose of the curse is not vindictive, but to bring to repentance. Then 'The LORD will again delight in you and make you prosperous' (v. 9).

What the LORD is offering is something good and it should not be beyond your reach, but in the end of the day the choice is yours—so choose life. (See also above, pp. 96, 100.)

4. MOSES' LAST DAYS (CHS. 31–34)

Moses now commissions Joshua to succeed him, encouraging him to be strong in the vision (31.1-8). He also commissions the Levites to teach the law regularly to the people (31.9-13).

Then, for the first time in Deuteronomy, God speaks. He reveals to Moses how the Israelites will soon forsake the covenant and turn to other gods, and tells him to compose a song they can learn in order to make the message unforgettable. However, he still encourages Joshua to lead them into the land, since he promised on oath he would give it to them (31.14-23).

Moses relays this message to the Levites as he hands over the Book of the Law into their keeping (31.24-29), and then teaches the people his song (31.30 – 32.47).

His work now almost completed, God summons Moses to ascend Mount Nebo and view the land he himself will not be allowed to enter (32.48-52).

But first Moses blesses the people, prophetically visualising them settled in their tribal territories, most of them surprisingly secure and strong considering their predicted rebellion, but some needing his prayers for strength and protection (ch. 33).

Then finally, Moses climbs Mount Nebo and sees the land he has longed to enter all these years, the land promised to his fathers. The story of his death, like that of many great saints, is cloaked in wonder. Though an old man, he is in good health and strength. But his work for God is ended, and so he dies and is mysteriously laid to rest, no-one knows where (34.1-8).

A new day in Israel's history now begins as Joshua takes up his leadership. The people accepted him, not because he pushed himself forward as leader, but because he was already selected by God and commissioned by Moses (34.9). Joshua's story belongs to our next volume, but we may note in passing that Christian leadership is still recognised (in theory, at any rate) by the same double principle of anointing with God's Spirit and public appointing from the Church.

No prophet was known like Moses in Israel (34.10-12), at least not till Elijah's day. Both men lived at times when God had to perform mighty acts of salvation, Moses when Israel was in danger of extinction through slavery in Egypt, Elijah when Israel's faith was being eradicated from the land by the pagan Queen Jezebel (1 Kings 17 – 2 Kings 2). Both men were channels through whom God performed many miraculous signs and wonders, and both were in their own ways channels of revival. Both met with God on Mount Sinai, both were mighty prophets, both were taken from the earth in mysterious circumstances, both bequeathed their charismatic/prophetic anointing to younger men who carried their work to completion. In both we can see foreshadowings of Jesus Christ and his ministry. That is probably the main reason why it was with them that Jesus communed on the Mount of Transfiguration (Mark 9.4).

While we have not yet arrived at the stage in Israel's history where any prophetic movement has emerged, we at least see in the personal life and ministry of Moses many traits of the faith of later charismatics and so begin to get some feel of its potential. Moses is like a middle-man, standing half-way between a vision and its realisation. Adam's sin brought death, Abraham saw a vision of life restored; Moses caught that vision, longed for others to experience its reality and tried to share it with his people; later prophets were to see that it would be widely appreciated one day; and finally it came to fruition with Jesus. We must leave the middle part of the story for our other volumes, and now turn directly to the New Testament fulfilment, but at least we already have enough of the vision to understand its fulfilment.

7

The Heart of the Law

Before we leap forward over the centuries to study the New Testament sequel to these early stories that we have been following through the Pentateuch, we need to take a closer look at the laws God gave to Moses, partly to help us understand better what the New Testament has to say about them, but also to help us appreciate that spiritual dimension in the law itself which the Holy Spirit can bring so vibrantly to life in the personal experience of the Christian.

1. WHAT THE LAW CONTAINS

Categories and Collections of Law.
The laws can be divided into several broad categories:
- Cultic/sacral/priestly law, concerning sacrifice and priesthood.
- Criminal law, prescribing punishment by the state.
- Civil law, mainly concerned with property and recompense for damage.
- Moral law, concerning inter-personal relations.
- Religious law, governing man's attitude to God.

We shall discuss the first category (cultic law) in the next chapter; the last four are mainly found in:
- The Decalogue (Exod. 20 & Deut. 5), mostly religious and moral law, but also the basis of Israel's criminal law.
- The Book of the Covenant (Exod. 21–23), mostly civil law, but plenty of examples of the other three categories.
- The Holiness Code (Lev. 17-26), largely cultic in orientation, but containing a fair amount of religious and moral law (note the demand for holiness, Lev. 19.2).

- Deuteronomy (Deut. 12–26), mixed laws, with exhortations to obedience, humanity, holiness, etc., attached.

Forms of Expression of Law.
The individual laws are written down using different forms:
- Command, e.g. 'Honour your father and your mother.' (Exod. 20.12)
- Prohibition, e.g. 'You shall not steal.' (Exod. 20.15)
- Curse, e.g. 'Cursed is the man who carves an image or casts an idol.' (Deut. 27.15)
- Statute, e.g. 'If a man steals an ox or a sheep and slaughters it or sells it, he must pay back five head of cattle for the ox and four sheep for the sheep.' (Exod. 22.1)

Statute is the form normally used to express laws in other societies, but in the Old Testament the rest of the forms, particularly the prohibition, are also freely used. In that respect the Old Testament is unique in its codification of law, but then its law is God's law, and God does not simply legislate—he commands. His will is absolute.

That is the reason why we sometimes find these simple forms expanded with brief sermon-like, hortatory clauses or sentences, such as, 'for the Lord your God is holy', or 'so that it may go well with you in the land the Lord your God is giving you', or something much longer, like some of the preaching we have seen in Deuteronomy. Civil authorities do not normally preach sermons about their laws; God's ministers must preach his laws, for they are not simply good ideas thought up by men about how best to control society, but God's word to his people to direct them on the way that leads to life.

The Decalogue
The Ten Commandments are unique among the laws of the Pentateuch. They are the very words God spoke from the mountain to express the heart of his covenant with Israel. Hence they were the laws carved on the stone tablets and deposited in the ark.

They are all concerned with man's relationship with God (the first 4) and with his fellow men (the last 6), and, taken together, they represent the very essence of what God's call on ancient Israel was: total devotion to himself and total respect for other men. They are so important that they also formed the basis of Israel's criminal law, which is why many of the laws in the Pentateuch that are directly derived from them carry the death penalty (e.g. in Lev. 20). In a sense the rest of the laws could be said to be a commentary on the Ten Commandments, or instructions about their application in particular circumstances.

2. WHAT THE LAW REQUIRES

Justice and Righteousness

The principles on which criminal and civil law operate are really quite simple: the death penalty for the most serious offences; otherwise 'eye for eye, tooth for tooth' (Exod. 21.23-25; Lev. 24.17-22), with fair compensation permitted sometimes as a substitute. The standard is basically fair justice; and excessive or cruel punishment, frequently found in other societies, is not countenanced, sometimes even explicitly forbidden (Deut. 25.2f)

The words most commonly used to express these principles in the Old Testament are justice and righteousness. In the minds of many today they unfortunately suggest something very formal, legalistic and stuffy, but they are first and foremost a description of God's own character (cp. Deut. 32.4). They tell us that he is not uncaring about evil and all that men suffer through it, that he is active in limiting its effects and is in the process of having it finally eliminated from his world. He does, however, ask those he invites to share in his redeeming work to reflect the same qualities both in their private and their community living. The law sets out guide-lines to make that practicable and is therefore itself a reflection and expression of God's righteousness and justice. (The same words were later used to describe Messiah's mission in Isa. 11.4.)

Humanity and Love

God's righteousness and justice are thus at root expressions of his love and the laws his instructions how to respond to and mediate that love. We have noted how Moses drew out the law's emphasis on humanity in his preaching in Deuteronomy and we cannot fail to recall how Jesus was later to quote Deut. 6.4f and Lev. 19.18 when he summarised the law: 'Love the Lord your God with all your soul and with all your mind and with all your strength. Love your neighbour as yourself.' (Mark 12.30f) Paul says the same in Rom. 13.8-10: 'Love is the fulfilment of the law.' Righteousness and justice without love can be harsh and formal; love and humanity without justice can be sentimental and chaotic. The two sets of attributes are only different sides of the same coin, and both are required to make the coin complete. Our part in the relationship is beautifully summarised by the prophet Micah:

> *He has showed you, O man, what is good.*
>   *And what does the* LORD *require of you?*
> *To act justly and to love mercy*
>   *and to walk humbly with your God.* (6.8)

Holiness

This word completely encapsulates all we have said about righteousness, justice and love. Basically it means separation and is the one word that uniquely describes God. He is the One who is totally different: 'I am God, and not man—the Holy One among you.' (Hos. 11.9)

Places and objects can also be called holy if they are specially set apart for God. For example, Moses first met God on 'holy ground' (Exod. 3.5); the Sabbath was a holy day (Exod. 20.8); the main rooms in the tabernacle and the temple were known as 'the Holy Place' and 'the Most Holy Place' (Exod. 26.33).

But holiness was also what God required of his people, that they should mirror his own holiness: 'Be holy because I, the LORD your God, am holy' (Lev. 19.2). God's people were to be different from all others on earth, a people set apart with a different life-style that was to be the reflection of his own nature. They are therefore not to intermingle with the nations, 'for you are a people holy to the LORD your God. The LORD your God has chosen you out of all the peoples on the face of the earth to be his people, his treasured possession.' (Deut. 7.6) Their call, as Isaiah was to put it later, is to be 'a light for the Gentiles' (Isa. 42.6).

Moral Purity and Ceremonial Purity

Purity is as much part of holiness as justice, righteousness and love. In the Old Testament it is expressed primarily in the laws relating to sexual abuses, such as those in Lev. 18 & 20. As Paul rightly points out in the New Testament, sexual immorality is different from other sins, because it defiles one's body, and that is a temple of the Holy Spirit (1 Cor. 6.18-20).

However, the Mosaic law recognises that other things can contaminate the body, such as skin diseases, the wrong kind of food, contact with a corpse, and certain bodily discharges. There are various laws governing this kind of defilement in Lev. 11–15.

The difference in seriousness between the two kinds of impurity can be seen in the prescriptions for dealing with them. The second sort can normally be remedied by ceremonial means, by rites of cleansing and by sacrificial offerings. The first sort cannot be so easily removed. In relation to them the laws are absolute: 'Do not ... do not ... do not ...' (Lev. 18); 'If anyone does ... he must be put to death ... must be cut off ...' (Lev. 20). The law did actually distinguish degrees of intent and did not, for example, prescribe the same punishment for a girl who was raped as for one who wilfully committed adultery (cp. Deut. 22.13-30), but even so it does not prescribe for the removing of the consequent impurity through sacrifices. The sacrificial system was God's provision to deal with sins of ceremonial or outer impurity, not with impurity resulting from wilful violation of the basic requirements of the covenant. The covenant demanded obedience; sacrifice for sin was not an easy way round that demand.

3. WHAT THE LAW OFFERS

'The words of this law ... are your life.' (Deut. 32.46f)
We have tried in these pages to look beneath the skin of the law and lay bare its heart. What we have discovered is something that has life, a heart pulsating with righteousness and love. We have, in fact, touched the heart of God him-

self—which is what we should expect anyhow, since the law is his word.

For man's relationship with him in the law to be right, heart needs to meet heart. Hence we hear Moses, particularly in Deuteronomy, repeatedly call for a heart-response: 'These commandments are to be upon your hearts' (6.6), 'Fix these words of mine in your hearts and minds' (11.18), 'Take to heart all the words ...' (32.46). Particularly striking is the passage in Deut. 30.11-20, where Moses points out that the law is not a distant thing, difficult to lay hold of, but 'the word is very near you; it is in your mouth and in your heart so that you may obey it' (v. 14). And in the very next verses he adds that heart-response in obedience will mean life and prosperity.

The same truth underlies the long passages about blessing and curse resulting from obedience and disobedience respectively: 'You will be blessed in the city and blessed in the country ... You will be blessed when you come in and blessed when you go out ... The Lord will send a blessing on your barns and on everything you put your hand to ...' (Deut. 28.3-8). The atmosphere is not much different from that of Jesus' Sermon on the Mount in Matt. 5–7, where he too asks us to dig beneath the skin of the law and touch the heart that pulsates within: 'The words of this law are your life!'

'Observe them carefully, for this will show your wisdom.' (Deut. 4.6)

The Israelites were commanded to teach the laws to their children, not by sending them to some law-teacher or priest, but at home (Deut. 6.7; 11.19). Certainly priests and Levites were also told to teach the law (Deut. 31.9-13), but the law is first and foremost a matter of the heart and the place where the heart most intimately operates is in the family. It is there that children receive their education for life as distinct from their academic education or vocational training, and it is there that God's word must first be effective.

The same principle underlies the teaching in the Book of Proverbs, which in many ways is not unlike a lot of what we find in the Mosaic law. There we listen to the father of the family teach his children about matters relating to conduct in society and life in general. There too the father bids his son take the teaching into his heart and thus gain life. The one word that sums up the content of this family-teaching in Proverbs is 'wisdom' (cp. 4.1-9). Wisdom is that which gives a man status, enables him to rise in society, helps him avoid ways that lead to suffering and anxiety, and generally encourages him to get the best out of life. But at its root lies the wisdom God first revealed to Moses at Sinai—the law: 'for this will show your wisdom.'

'The precepts of the LORD are right, giving joy to the heart.' (Ps. 19.8)
Since the law is life and wisdom, we should expect to discover that living by its precepts imparts a sense of joy and well-being. Hence we occasionally find its praise being sung in the Psalms, as in Ps. 19, or the very long Ps. 119. Ps. 1.2 speaks about the man whose 'delight is in the law of the LORD' and about the solidity of such a man's life. The word used by Moses is 'blessed' (Deut. 28.1-14; cp. Ps. 1.1). The man who walks in its ways finds that at the heart of the law there is a song of praise that rings through creation, the song that Ps. 19 so vividly proclaims. But that is only as it should be, for after all, the law is the utterance of God himself: 'giving joy to the heart!'

'Your word is a lamp to my feet and a light to my path.' (Ps. 119.105)
However, the law was not given that men might sing its praises, but to be lived. The only positive requirement laid on the king of Israel is that he possess a copy of it, read it every day and live by it (Deut. 17.18-20). Joshua was instructed to meditate on it day and night (Josh. 1.8). The Levites were to read it regularly at festivals (Deut. 31.9-13), and we see something of what that instruction entailed as we watch Ezra reading the law to the people from his pulpit every day throughout the seven-day autumn festival and then reading from it to them again for quarter of a day a fortnight later (Neh. 8.1 – 9.3).

Coupled with each of these instructions to read the law is a promise that living by it will lead to good things. The law was to be like a map or a handbook from which the people and their leaders could learn how to run their lives and the lives of those in their care. Just as an instruction manual will tell how to get the best out of a new piece of apparatus, so the law was God's instruction manual telling how to get the best out of the new life he was about to give the Israelites in the land of Canaan: a lamp to their feet and a light to their path.

The Law and Legalism

By New Testament times attitudes to the law had changed a lot. Though there was some dispute about the authority of the rest of what became our Old Testament, all parties in Judaism accepted the Pentateuch as their basic Bible. Its strictest interpreters were the Pharisees. They were ardent believers in righteousness, but their approach to the law was petty and literalistic, judging by Jesus' repeated criticisms.

Paul was a Pharisee in regard to the law (Phil. 3.5), but when he became a Christian, a veil was lifted from his eyes and the Spirit showed him dimensions in his Bible that his fellow Jews did not even realise were there (2 Cor. 3.14-18). However his conversion never caused him to deny the value of the law. 'Rather,' he says, 'we uphold the law … the law is holy, and the commandment is holy, righteous and good.' (Rom. 3.31; 7.12) And yet several times we hear him argue vigorously for the freedom of the Spirit against the old life of bondage to the law (cp. Rom. 7–8; 2 Cor. 3; Gal. 5). Many have found his teaching at this point contradictory and confusing, but that need not be, for all he is saying is that the legalistic mentality of Judaism obscures the true heart of the law, yet when the Spirit opened his eyes he saw what Moses saw, what Jesus had taught, what God originally wanted to convey, that there is life in the heart of God's word which, when taken into a man's heart, gives life in a way that the letter never can. Indeed the letter obscures that life and even kills it. Literalism and legalism may be religious, but they spell death (2 Cor. 3.1-6).

PART FOUR

SACRIFICE AND THE CROSS

The further we go with God in faith and obedience, the more he unfolds his sacrificial heart to us. At every stage in our walk with him there is an element of sacrifice: Abraham had to sacrifice family relationships when he left his homeland; Moses recognised the sacrificial cost of his call from the start and pleaded to be released from it. But as they continued on their way, God began to unveil to them hidden depths of sacrifice that we can only describe as revelations of his own heart. Towards the end of his life Abraham was granted a glimpse of something of eternal significance on Mount Moriah, though he was probably quite unable to grasp its full meaning. The high point of Moses ministry was when he stood on Mount Sinai and received revelation of this sacrificial heart of heaven which he had then to translate into the systems of the earthly tabernacle. We shall see the same patterns in Jesus' life. At first he ministers faith accompanied by confirming signs and wonders, but soon he has to draw his disciples aside and speak to them of the sacrifice that is to be the culmination of his own ministry.

Faith and obedience draw us closer into the heart of God, and there we shall discover the Lamb that was slain from the foundation of the world. However, it is important to remember as we study this section that Christ's sacrifice was what released heaven to earth and opened the flood-gates for an outpouring of God's Spirit such as the world had never imagined possible. Our call to faith and obedience is in the end a call to share in his sacrificial work and so to further the release of his blessing, the blessing originally promised to Abraham who was first called to the walk of faith.

8

Sacrifice and Priesthood

After sealing the covenant on Mount Sinai (Exod. 24), the first thing God showed Moses, during his forty-day stay on the mountain, was the plan for the tabernacle, which would be the continuing place of their meeting and communing with each other thereafter (25–27 & 30–31; cp. 35–40), where, 'above the cover between the two cherubim that are over the ark of the Testimony, I will meet with you.' (Exod. 25.22)

The key to understanding the purpose of the priesthood and sacrificial system at the tabernacle lies in the opening instruction God gave Moses at that time: 'Have them make a sanctuary for me, and I will dwell among them.' (25.8)

A sanctuary is a holy place, set apart for God who is himself utterly holy. After the fall, he withdrew from among men, because, if his holiness and our sin were to mingle, the one would destroy the other. Either sin would taint his holiness and it would cease to be holy, or else he must destroy what is of sin in order to preserve his holiness. The relationship between the two is a bit like that between fire and water. They cannot mingle without the one destroying the other: either the water quenches the fire or the fire evaporates the water. They cannot co-exist unless there is a separation or barrier put between them. Water can only sit on fire if it is separated from it in a pot. So it is with sin and holiness.

In Eden God walked with Adam in an open relationship (Gen. 3.8), but from the fall to Moses he remained aloof in the heavens, communicating by his word, by angels, by visions and the like. Now he plans to come and live among sinful men in their tent-settlement in a tent of his own. For that to be possible, something must be done to ensure that their sin does not enter and contaminate the presence of his holiness. Hence the tent-sanctuary was to be constructed 'exactly like the pattern' God showed Moses, with clearly demarcated zones of holiness. The Israelites were mandated to present themselves before God at the tabernacle three times a year (Exod. 23.14,17), but no-one was permitted to pass the altar of sacrifice that stood there. That was the permanent barrier that no sin must pass. Beyond it lay the tent which was holy. Its first room was the Holy Place, which only the priests could enter, and that only after sacrifice to cleanse them from sin. The inner room was the Most Holy Place, to which the High Priest alone had access, and that only once a year at the feast of Atonement when the sin of the whole priesthood and community was dealt with very thoroughly.

Hence the priests were the go-between people, who stood at the altar-barrier and went before the Holy God to plead for the sinners who stood at the other side of the altar, until he returned bringing them knowledge of God's acceptance and blessing.

All of this was made possible by the blood of sacrifice. Because of Adam's sin, all men are under penalty of death: 'Dust you are and to dust you will return' (Gen. 3.19). Life is sustained by our blood pumping nutrients to the various parts of our bodies. When our blood is shed, or ceases to flow, we die. The life is in the blood (Lev. 17.11). God in his mercy agreed to receive substitute blood for ours, blood of an animal offered to him in sacrifice. The sinner brings his offering to the priest at the altar. He sheds its blood and presents it at the altar or in the tent. When God accepts it, the sin-penalty has been paid and the sinner can go free to live once more under blessing instead of curse.

The tabernacle was given by God as a place where he could have mercy on sinful men and restore them to live in his presence, freed from their sin and from his wrath. That is why the lid of the ark was known as the 'mercy seat' (KJV) or 'atonement cover' (NIV; Exod. 25.17). There God's glory resided in a special way 'between the two cherubim'. When Moses asked to see God's glory, he was shown his 'goodness' and heard him describe himself as 'the compassionate and gracious' (Exod. 33.19; 34.6). Here the sinner could come and find mercy and grace to help him in his need.

God's purpose is that we be freed to live again in his

presence and then to learn his ways of holiness. That is why it was also the priests' duty to teach the law, or the way of holiness, so that men could learn to live with the holy God as they were intended to do at the beginning. But to enable them to do so, their sin had first to be dealt with.

Ultimately the intention is that the relationship with God that was so beautiful in Eden be renewed, that the sin that spoils it be removed, and that the holiness that enables it be restored. The Old Testament sacrificial system provided for that to a degree, but never fully. The complete fulfilment of all that the priestly and sacrificial system foreshadowed had to wait until the coming of Christ, who was '*the* Lamb of God, who takes away the sin of the world' (John 1.29)

1. THE TABERNACLE

The basic lay-out of the tabernacle, and of the temple that later replaced it, was essentially quite simple. (See following page.)

In Heb. 8–10 we read that the tabernacle Moses made was 'a copy and shadow of what is in heaven' (8.5). It seems that as Moses stood on the mountain, God gave him a vision of his own 'dwelling-place' in heaven and instructed him to make an earthly copy, in miniature, as it were, where men could come to meet with him in the right context, one that would remind them of the spiritual reality it represented.

A glance at Isa. 6 shows something of what that could mean, for there we see Isaiah in the temple, but in his vision it has become for him God's heavenly throne-room and we are never sure as we read whether we are actually in the temple or in heaven. Somehow we are in both at once, for though he saw 'the LORD seated on a throne, high and exalted', 'the train of his robe filled the temple', and again, although he heard the seraphs worship around the throne, 'the doorposts and thresholds shook and the temple was filled with smoke', then one of the seraphs flew from God's throne and took a live coal from the altar (of incense). Isaiah must one day have 'seen' the curtain removed, the ark transformed into God's throne, the cherubim spring to life

122   The Sacrifice and the Cross

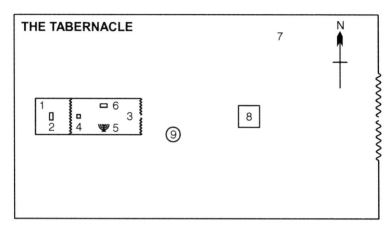

1. *The Most Holy Place*: sometimes called 'the Holy of Holies', entered only once a year by the high priest. It contained the Ark of the Covenant.
2. *The Ark of the Covenant*: a wooden box containing 'the Testimony', the two tablets with the Ten Commandments. The lid (the 'atonement cover' or 'mercy seat') was of solid gold and at both ends were the figures of guardian cherubim with their wings extended as a symbol of protection. The ark therefore symbolised God's throne (Isa. 6.1; Ezek. 43.7), where he could be approached 'above the cover between the cherubim' (Exod. 25.22).
3. *The Holy Place*: where the priests entered to minister before the Lord, separated from the Most Holy Place by a linen curtain.
4. *The Altar of Incense*: a small horned altar in front of the curtain where incense was burned morning and evening daily.
5. *The Lampstand*: a seven-branched, golden lampstand, the only source of light in the Holy Place.
6. *The Table*: also in the Holy Place. Twelve new loaves ('bread of the presence', sometimes called 'showbread') were placed on it as an offering each Sabbath.
7. *The Courtyard*: the tabernacle (and later the temple) stood at the west end of the courtyard.
8. *The Altar of Burnt Offering*: here the animal sacrifices were offered.
9. *The Basin*: a huge bronze basin used by the priests to wash their hands and feet before entering the Holy Place or before offering sacrifice.

as bright, shining beings (*seraphim* means 'burning ones') worshipping God in heaven, and yet he was still himself in the temple.

Clearly the tabernacle, then later the temple, was intended to be a God-given point where heaven and earth could meet and where God's presence could be known in a very special way.

2. THE PRIESTS AND LEVITES

The Priests
On the mountain God also gave Moses instructions about the appointment and consecration of priests to serve at the tabernacle (Exod. 28f; cp. Lev. 8–10, 21f). While the details of their dress and the many rituals they performed are interesting in themselves, they are not particularly important for our purposes here. The facts we do need to note are that:
- The priests came from the family of Moses' brother, Aaron, who was of the Kohathite division of the Levites.
- Their main function was to oversee and perform the sacrificial work at the tabernacle.
- Only the high priest had the privilege of entering the Most Holy Place, and that only on the Day of Atonement (Lev. 16).

The Levites
Because the tribe of Levi was faithful to God in the wilderness, it was set apart to serve him in a special way (Exod. 32.25-29; Deut. 33.8-11), but the nature of their service, unlike that of the priests, was not revealed until the tabernacle was already erected and functioning (Num. 1.47-53; 3.5-37; 8.5-26). The Levites were to be temple-servants, to assist the priests with the non-sacrificial duties of the tabernacle.

They are divided into three groups:
- The Kohathites, who cared for the tabernacle furniture.
- The Gershonites, who cared for the curtains and coverings.
- The Merarites, who cared for the tabernacle structures.

In later days men drawn from their ranks formed the temple choirs (1 Chron. 16,23,25) and some of them probably composed psalms like Pss. 85 and 87.

In Canaan the Levites were to have no tribal territory of their own but were to be supported by the people's tithes. 48 towns were designated for their use (Num. 18; 35; Deut. 18; Josh. 21).

Other Duties of Priests and Levites:

They formed a final court of appeal for deciding on questions no-one else was able to answer. Sometimes these would relate to legal matters, or sometimes to military or political decisions. To reach decisions the priest would sometimes consult the *Urim* and *Thummim* which were sacred stones kept in a pouch worn on the high priest's chest, the Urim answering 'no' and the Thummim 'yes' (Exod. 28.30; Deut. 17.8-13; 33.8-11).

Probably their most important duty was to teach the people the law of God, a task in which both priests and Levites shared (Deut. 31.9-13; 33.8-11; Neh. 8.1-12). According to the prophets it was a task they frequently failed to perform (Ezek. 44.10-14; Hos. 4.1-9; Mal. 2.7-9).

3. THE SACRIFICES

The first thing God showed Moses once the tabernacle was erected was the sacrificial system he wanted to operate in it (Lev. 1–7). Five different kinds of offering are distinguished:

1. *The (Whole) Burnt Offering*: This offering symbolised total dedication to God. After its blood had been sprinkled on the altar, the whole animal was burnt (Lev. 1 & 6.8-13).

2. *The Grain Offering*: An offering of flour, baked cakes, or raw grain, each with oil and incense. Part of it, a memorial portion, was burnt on the altar to ask God to remember the worshipper for good. The rest was given to the priests for food (Lev. 2 & 6.14-23).

3. *The Fellowship (or Peace) Offering*: Only the animal's fat, kidneys and liver were burnt; the blood was sprinkled on the altar and the meat was shared among the worshippers in a kind of communion meal (Lev. 3 & 7.11-34).

4. *The Sin Offering*: Offered 'when anyone sins unintentionally'. The sacrifices were similar to the fellowship offering, but the blood was sprinkled before the curtain and smeared on the horns of the altar of incense (for priest or community), or smeared on the horns of the altar of burnt offering (for a leader or a private individual), and poured out at the

base of the altar of burnt offering. The meat was given to the priests (Lev. 4 & 6.24-30).

5. *The Guilt Offering*: Basically the same as the sin offering. The distinction between the two is not entirely clear, though payment of compensation is also involved in the guilt offering (Lev. 5.14 – 6.7 & 7.1-10).

Sacrifice and Sin

These different sacrifices had different emphases. The burnt offering was an act of homage, dedication or thanksgiving, the fellowship offering was more an expression of harmony and restored relations with God and others, the sin offering was almost entirely an act of contrition. But every sacrifice of whatever kind was intended in some measure to atone for sin.

Now in the last chapter, when we looked at the distinction between moral and ceremonial purity, we noted that some sins were not readily covered by sacrifice. The regulations for the sin offering state clearly that its purpose is to atone for unintentional sins only (Lev. 4.2,13,22,27). Some examples of the sort of sin covered are given in Lev. 5— failure to testify in court, touching anything ceremonially unclean, touching human uncleanness, and thoughtlessly taking an oath. Similarly the guilt offering is to cover unintentional sins (Lev. 5.14,18), and the list of examples mentions lying, stealing, cheating, keeping lost property and swearing falsely; in these cases any restitution necessary had to be made in full and more before the sacrifice was offered (6.1-7).

The contrast between what can and cannot be covered by sacrifice is strongly reinforced again in Num. 15.22-31. Repeatedly it is unintentional sin that is spoken of, and the pointed statement is added: 'But anyone who sins defiantly blasphemes the LORD, and that person must be cut off from his people ... his guilt remains on him.' (vv. 30f) We shall need to bear this distinction in mind when we come to look at the Christian interpretation of sacrifice in Heb. 9–10.

If sacrifice only had such limited effectiveness in dealing with sin, we may well ask why God bothered to require it. The answer to that question lies partly in understanding the distinction between unintentional and wilful sin. Certain sins are fairly obviously unintentional, like the hurtful word that slips out almost unconsciously and is immediately regretted, or thoughtlessly touching things one ought not to touch, but it is difficult to conceive how some of the sins mentioned in Lev. 5 & 6 could be regarded as unintentional in that almost innocent sense.

The answer must therefore lie at a deeper level, in discerning what is an act of conscious *rebellion* against God. Any infringement of the first four of the Ten Commandments was such: worshipping other gods, idolatry, blaspheming God's name and Sabbath-breaking (for Sabbath was specially appointed for honouring God). With the next five differentiation was made between what was wilful and what was not. Thus a son who opposed his parents had to be disciplined, but if he proved unrepentantly stubborn and rebellious, drastic legal action was required (Deut. 21.18-21). The law also distinguished between murder and manslaughter (Deut. 19), being an adulteress and a victim of rape (Deut. 22.13-30), theft and retaining property that was lent, borrowed or found (Lev. 6.2f), consciously giving false testimony and failure to speak up in court (Lev. 5.1). Since the tenth commandment relates to inner attitudes of the heart, distinctions cannot be drawn in the same kind of way.

Any infringement of the law was sin, whether wilful or unintentional, and had to be dealt with somehow, but not all sin was an act of conscious rebellion against God. The sin that was not contaminated the believer himself and tarnished the holiness of God's covenant people, but that sin was covered through sacrifice which restored and purified the offerer and the community, thus delivering them from its consequences. The wilful sin, by contrast, was an act of rebellion, a declaration as it were of decision not to serve this God any more, or not to serve him in the way he desired. By such sin the sinner removed himself from the protecting cover of God's covenant promise and the benefits offered in it through the sacrificial system. The sacrifices were indeed intended to be comprehensive. They were given to cover all sin, but only for those who did not choose through rebellion to remove themselves from the covenant community.

It must also be remembered that the purpose of sacrifice

was not only to procure forgiveness. It could also express thanksgiving and worship (Ps. 96.8; 107.22; 116.17), or back up prayers for God's help (1 Sam. 13.8-12; Ps. 20.3), or demonstrate commitment to a pledge or covenant (Exod. 24.5-8), or celebrate particular festivals (Num. 28–29), or simply be a daily act of worship (Num. 28.1-8), etc. Basically a sacrifice is an offering made to God of something specially set apart for him, and so, in the ritual at the tabernacle, the worshipper would lay his hand on the animal's head thus formally identifying himself with his offering before God (cp. Lev. 1.4; 3.2; 4.4; etc.). In our every-day language the word 'sacrifice' is used to signify the costliness of giving something up, and it had the same significance in ancient Israel. Livestock was no less valuable then than today. Atonement was never cheap. In the end of the day, the only sacrifice for sin fully acceptable to God is, of course, that of true repentance, of a broken and a contrite heart (Ps. 51.16f).

A special Day of Atonement was held in the autumn, when sacrifices were offered to atone for the sins of priest and people (see below). The purpose of its rituals was to cleanse the sanctuary and the community thoroughly once a year, but the sins it covered were mainly of the same unintentional sort as those covered by the regular sin and guilt offerings (cp. Heb. 9.10,13). As we shall see, it is the rituals of this day that give us the key to understanding the sacrifice of Christ in Mark's Gospel and in the interpretation of the Epistle to the Hebrews.

SACRIFICES AND OFFERINGS

A. THANK OFFERINGS:
Burnt Offering	expression of total self-dedication
Grain Offering	thankful dedication of one's produce
Fellowship Offering	thanksgiving in fellowship with others

B. SIN OFFERINGS:
Sin Offering	forgiveness through the blood of a substitute
Guilt Offering	same, plus compensation for damage
Day of Atonement	same, but for the whole nation

4. THE FESTIVALS

The instructions about the festivals are spread out through the Exodus and Wilderness narrative starting from the moment the Israelites left Egypt and celebrated their first Passover (Exod. 12). They are mentioned in the Book of the Covenant (Exod. 23.14-17; cp. 34.18-26) and discussed in Deuteronomy (ch. 16), but the most detailed instructions are to be found in Lev. 23 and Num. 28–29.

They fall mainly on three occasions in the year and their dates are largely governed by the seasons of cultivation and harvest in the Middle East.

SPRING

Passover (14th Nisan—end of March)
A lamb was slaughtered and its blood smeared on the lintel and door-posts of the house. It then formed part of a meal that was eaten by the people wearing their travelling clothes in memory of the night of the Exodus. This was primarily a household festival, though in New Testament times it was also a pilgrim festival celebrated in the temple. Unleavened bread formed part of the meal, and so Passover began the week of the feast of Unleavened Bread.

Unleavened Bread (14th–21st Nisan)
Throughout this week no leaven was used in baking, in memory of what happened at the Exodus. Later it also commemorated the baking of the first bread from the new corn in the land (Josh. 5.10-12).

Firstfruits
At Passover time, on the day after the Sabbath a sheaf of the first grain harvested was waved before the LORD (Lev. 23.9-14), but the term 'firstfruits' is more frequently associated with the Feast of Weeks (Exod. 23.16; 34.22; Num. 28.26).

MAIN SEASONS AND FESTIVALS

Season	Agricultural	Month	Festival
WET SEASON	Grape harvest	SEPT	Trumpets (New Year) / Day of Atonement / Tabernacles
	First rains	OCT	
	Ploughing and sowing	NOV	
		DEC	Dedication
		JAN	
	Later rains	FEB	Purim
DRY SEASON	Flax harvest	MAR	
	Barley harvest	APR	Passover / Unleavened Bread
	Wheat harvest	MAY	Weeks / Pentecost
		JUN	
	Summer fruit	JUL	
		AUG	
	Grape harvest	SEPT	Trumpets (New Year) / Day of Atonement / Tabernacles
		OCT	

SUMMER

Weeks/Harvest/Firstfruits/Pentecost (7 weeks after the first offering of firstfruits—late May)
This festival celebrated the grain harvest with an offering of two loaves of new flour, accompanied by other sacrifices. It was also a time when the Israelites celebrated God's descent on Sinai and the giving of the law, and therefore a most appropriate occasion for the events described in Acts 2 to take place. The name 'Pentecost' is not found in the Old Testament. It is derived from the Greek word meaning 'fifty' and relates to the dating of the festival, fifty days after Passover (Lev. 23.16).

AUTUMN

New Year/Trumpets (1st Tishri—mid-Sept.)
The new year began with a day of rest and worship on which ram's horn trumpets were sounded (cp. also Num. 10.10).

Day of Atonement (10th Tishri—late Sept.)
This was a day of national confession of sin. The high priest offered a bull for his own and his household's sins. Then for the only time in the year he entered behind the curtain into the Most Holy Place and sprinkled its blood on the atonement cover (the lid of the ark). Next he offered a goat for the people's sin and did the same with its blood. After that a 'scapegoat' was sent into the desert as a sign of the people's sins being carried away, and the festival ended with the high priest pronouncing the Aaronic blessing of Num. 6.24-26 (for full details, see Lev. 16).

Ingathering/Tabernacles (15–21 Tishri—Sept.-Oct.)
This week-long festival marked the final end of the harvest season. The people lived in shelters or tents in memory of Exodus/Wilderness times. It was an occasion of joyous celebration and renewal of covenant (Besides the passages noted above, see Deut. 31.9-13; Neh. 8.14-17).

By New Testament times other festivals were being celebrated besides those commanded to Moses, in particular:

Dedication/Lights (25 Kislev—early Dec.), in commemoration of the rededication of the temple by Judas Maccabaeus in 165 BC (cp. John 10.22), and *Purim* (13-14 Adar—late Feb.), in celebration of the Jewish triumph recorded in the book of Esther (9.26-8).

5. THE ATONING POWER OF THE BLOOD

The priest did different things with the blood in the various sacrifices. Usually it was sprinkled on the altar of burnt offering or poured out at its base, but it was never burnt or eaten. Even when it was not possible to slaughter an animal at an altar the blood had to be poured out on the ground (Deut. 12.16,23f). It was always regarded as specially sacred because it carried the life of the animal.

It was intimately linked with atonement, presumably because it represented a life that was being given in place of or in substitution for the life of the offerer. Lev. 17.11 puts it: 'The life of the creature is in the blood, and I have given it to you to make atonement for yourselves on the altar; it is the blood that makes atonement for one's life.'

Knowing that helps us understand the purpose of the special blood-rituals in the sin offering and the guilt offering. In them the blood is smeared on the horns of the altar of burnt offering, or else taken into the Holy Place to be sprinkled before the curtain and smeared on the horns of the incense altar, at the entrance to the throne-room of God, as it were. On the Day of Atonement this ritual is intensified as the high priest takes the blood behind the curtain and sprinkles it on the atonement cover of the ark, that is at the throne of God in his presence in the sanctuary.

Imagine the high priest on the Day of Atonement as he prepares for the sacrifice. First he washes himself and puts on the clean linen tunic and turban kept for the occasion (Lev. 16.4). He brings forward the bull and the goats (vv. 6-10), slaughters the bull, and proceeds with its blood into the Holy Place. There he fills a censer from the altar of incense and goes behind the curtain amid a cloud of incense that acts as a protecting screen in God's presence (vv. 11-13). With his fingers he sprinkles some of the blood on the atonement cover and then sprinkles more blood seven times before the ark (v. 14). The whole procedure is repeated with the blood of one of the goats (vv. 15-17), and then he goes out to the altar of burnt offering to smear its horns and sprinkle it with the blood of both animals (vv. 18f).

All these blood rituals, we are told, are to make atonement for himself, his household and the whole community of Israel (vv. 11,17,33), but also for the Most Holy Place, the Tent of Meeting and the altar (vv. 20,33). Everyone and everything had to be covered by the blood, for sin contaminates everyone and everything (v. 16), and by God's provision the blood covers all the sin that has caused the contamination, thus making 'at-one-ment' between God and his people.

The ritual of the day continues with the scapegoat symbolically carrying the sins of the community away (vv. 21f) and the burning of the sacrifices (vv. 24f). But before the sacrifices are burnt, the priest has to change out of his special linen clothes into his ordinary sacrificial clothes, for the linen garments are particularly for the work of atonement which is through the blood (vv. 23f,32f).

In Zech. 3 the prophet tells of a vision in which he saw Joshua, the high priest of his day, in filthy clothing and Satan accusing him with thoughts of guilt and inadequacy, so much so that he simply stood there doing nothing, feeling thoroughly helpless. The vision reflects something of the depressed mood among the Jews in Jerusalem after the Exile before the temple was rebuilt, but it also reveals spiritual forces at work seeking to prevent the atonement sacrifices from being resumed. In the vision the LORD himself intervenes, rebukes Satan and commissions his angel to see that Joshua is clothed in his tunic and turban for the work he has to do. The LORD reveals to him that his and his assistants' work is 'symbolic of things to come', for God is going to send his servant 'the Branch' (= Messiah, cp. Isa. 11.1) and then, he declares, 'I will remove the sin of this land in a single day.'

When Jesus came, he offered that final atonement sacrifice in which his blood was shed on the altar of the cross and taken on our behalf before the throne of God in heaven so that our sins might be covered, though this time for eternity. He too lived through Satanic temptation like Joshua's and angels also ministered to him (Mark 1.13), but he donned his robes and entered into the Most Holy Place for us. The Old Testament sacrifices had by then been running for over a thousand years and every Jew well knew the power of the blood—so thoroughly did God prepare his people that they might understand and believe in the atoning power of the blood of his final and eternal sacrifice.

It is important to keep this total perspective in mind as we read some of the hard things the prophets had to say about temple worship from time to time. Sometimes we get the impression they would have been happy to see the whole system abolished altogether, but if we look more closely we shall see that what they condemned was not the system, but the attitudes of those participating in it. For example, Jeremiah says it is pointless trusting in the temple while living in unrepentant sin (Jer. 7.3-15); Amos and Isaiah say that the festivals and sacrifices simply rouse God's anger when they are not coupled with lives lived in justice and righteousness (Amos 5.21-24; Isa. 1.11-17).

By New Testament times the Jews were dispersed through every country of the ancient world, most of them too far from Jerusalem for the laws relating to the temple and its sacrifices to play much of a meaningful part in their daily lives, but many of them still went on pilgrimage to Jerusalem to offer sacrifice. Despite the practical restrictions, the offering of blood remained essential for maintaining good relations with God. So when Christ came, there had to be a blood-sacrifice. But his sacrifice was of a more comprehensive order, and once it was accomplished and the news of it had reached Jews everywhere, the temple was no longer needed. In 70 AD it was removed for ever. But to understand these things more fully we must now move on into the New Testament.

9

Studying the New Testament Sequel

1. A CHRISTIAN APPROACH TO THE PENTATEUCH

Many Christians today think the sacrificial system of the Old Testament has been so fully superseded by the sacrifice of Christ that it is no longer needful even to think about it any more. They regard it as part of an antiquated religious system from which we are now mercifully released and it is therefore best that it be left undisturbed and forgotten in the museums of antiquity. Knowledge of its systems has no value for contemporary faith and daily living.

They would put other religious laws, such as circumcision, food laws, Sabbath observance, and the like, in the same category, again holding them to be outdated and irrelevant. After all, did not Paul say that 'in Christ Jesus neither circumcision nor uncircumcision has any value. The only thing that counts is faith expressing itself through love.' (Gal. 5.6)

The modern inclination of many would also be to regard a lot of the moral and social teachings of the Pentateuch in the same sort of way, so totally surpassed by Christ's great commandment to love that they are now virtually worthless, if not even potentially harmful in their seeming pre-Christian legalism.

Similarly many of the ancient stories about the patriarchs and others in Genesis to Deuteronomy would be considered primeval and of little relevance to the faith of twentieth century man, especially now that we have the Gospels with their more enlightened and less primitive stories.

However, Jesus' own attitude was far from dismissive. In fact any theology that views the law, or indeed any of the writings of the Old Testament, as no longer having relevance for Christian living, is in disharmony with the teaching of Jesus Christ himself, for in the Sermon on the Mount he says:

> *Do not think that I have come to abolish the Law and the Prophets; I have not come to abolish them but to fulfil them. I tell you the truth, until heaven and earth disappear, not the smallest letter, not the least stroke of a pen, will by any means disappear from the Law until everything is accomplished. Anyone who breaks one of the least of these commandments and teaches others to do the same will be called least in the kingdom of heaven, but whoever practices and teaches these commands will be called great in the kingdom of heaven. For I tell you that unless your righteousness surpasses that of the Pharisees and the teachers of the law, you will certainly not enter the kingdom of heaven.'*
>
> (Matt. 5.17-20)

Even Paul, whose teaching so often seems to dismiss the law, actually had the same underlying attitude, for in one of his discussions about the place of the Jews and faith we hear him say, 'Do we, then, nullify the law by this faith? Not at all! Rather, we uphold the law.' (Rom. 3.31)

Certainly our Christian faith does take us beyond the laws God gave to Moses. It would be unthinkable today to offer animal sacrifices at a Christian service, and Jesus did call his disciples to move on beyond the simple requirements of the Ten Commandments (Matt. 5.21-48), but the laws cannot simply have ceased to be of relevance for our faith and our lives. As we pass on to the New Testament our purpose will be to examine what the early Church believed was a proper Christian view of these matters. And we shall discover that the New Testament does have a very positive attitude to the Pentateuch which is still pertinent for our times.

Romans and Hebrews must form the main focus of our attention because they deal specifically with these questions. In both, but particularly in Hebrews, Christ's death is seen as an atonement sacrifice that renders any further sacrifice for sin superfluous. By contrast, John, in his Gospel and

Revelation, speaks of Jesus as the Lamb of God, thereby drawing attention to another aspect of his sacrificial death, to the fact that it also rounds off the salvation work signified by the blood of the Passover lamb. We shall look at this aspect in more detail in another volume, in the context of John's Gospel, but it is worth noting here in passing that Paul, though he says nothing of it in Romans, was by no means ignorant of it. (See 1 Cor. 5.7: 'Christ, our Passover lamb, has been sacrificed.') The fact that in the following pages we concentrate primarily on atonement does not mean that the sacrifice of Christ can only be understood in one way. Jesus also identified the Unleavened Bread with his body given for us (Luke 22.19); he is the 'firstfruits' of those who have fallen asleep (1 Cor. 15.20); the Christian Pentecost is the direct result of his sacrificial death (Acts 2.31-33). Every festival, every sacrifice and every priestly function are gathered into one and brought to perfect completion in his ministry. However, we shall of necessity be concerned here mostly with how his self-offering relates to the sacrifices for the Day of Atonement.

But sacrifice was not the only theme we studied in the Pentateuch. Faith and obedience are both also integral to the teaching of Hebrews and Romans, but before either epistle was written, all three were brought together in sharp focus in the life of Jesus Christ himself. Mark's portrait of Jesus shows that very clearly, and so our starting point will be to review his Gospel.

2. PALESTINE IN JESUS' TIME

The Jews and the Law.
It must be remembered that more than 1,200 years had passed since Moses' day, and during that time a lot had changed. To begin with, the old tabernacle had been replaced by a temple in Solomon's reign. That was destroyed by the Babylonians and another built by the exiles who returned in the Persian era. Its history was far from eventless, but it had now been replaced by a new and much larger edifice commissioned by Herod the Great. Though the

Studying the New Testament Sequel 137

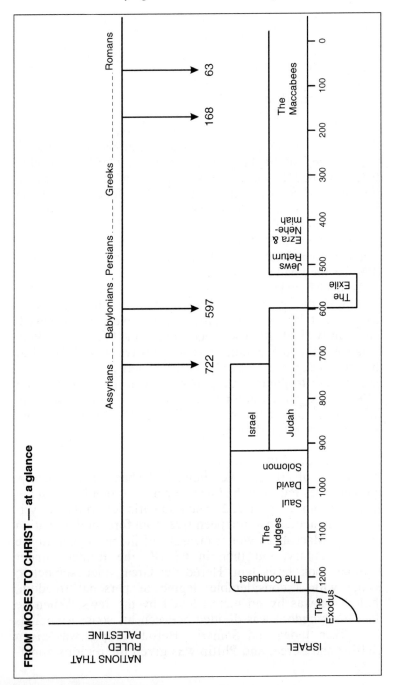

main structure was finished ten years after building started in 19 BC, in Jesus' time the work was still not complete. Many admired its magnificence, but it is one of the ironies of history that six years after its completion it was destroyed by the Romans, as Jesus himself foresaw it would be.

Much had changed also in relation to the religious practices of the Jews. Since most Jews now lived too far from Jerusalem for the temple and its worship to hold much direct meaning for their lives, other religious laws came to prominence, particularly those that seemed to provide distinctive badges for their Jewish faith and identity, such as circumcision, Sabbath observance, tithing, food laws and the like. Indeed some of these observances now played such a large part in the lives of many Jews, in Palestine as well as in the dispersion, that both Jesus and the early Church were to have considerable problems in handling the legalistic attitudes they had engendered.

Another development resulting from the dispersion of the Jews was the synagogue. We know little about its early history, but by New Testament times every local Jewish community had its own one, even in Palestine where distance from the temple was not always a problem. But then the synagogue was only a place where Jews could meet for prayer, teaching and general social intercourse with fellow Jews, not an alternative place of sacrificial worship. Both Jesus and Paul made full use of the evangelistic opportunities offered by the synagogues.

The Political Map in 30 AD.
Politically, of course, everything had changed completely. For centuries Palestine had been a parade ground for foreign armies. From the year 722, when Samaria fell to the Assyrians, the Israelites had not been free from foreign domination until the Maccabees won a measure of independence in the second century, but then in 63 BC the Romans under Pompey took Jerusalem. Herod the Great ruled subject to Rome with a considerable degree of personal freedom, though he was by no means loved by the Jews. When he died his kingdom was divided between his sons: Archelaus was given Judea and Samaria, Herod Antipas was given Galilee and Perea, and Philip was given the regions north-

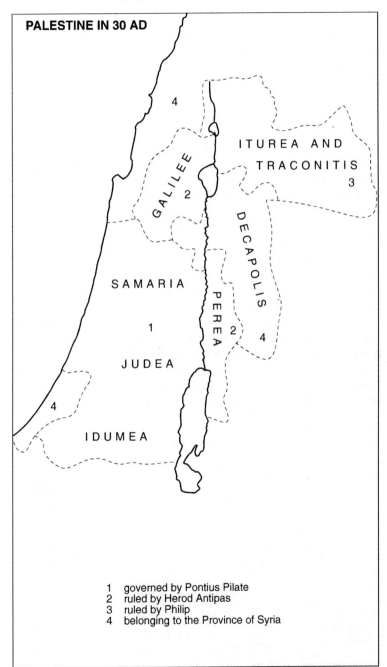

east of Galilee, called Iturea and Traconitis in Luke 3.1. (The region known as Decapolis was never part of Herod the Great's kingdom; it belonged to the Roman province of Syria.) In 6 AD Archelaus was exiled and his lands brought under the direct governorship of Roman procurators, the fifth of whom was Pontius Pilate. And that was roughly how the map looked in Jesus' day.

Shortly after Jesus' death the situation began to change again. Philip died in 34 and his area passed to Herod Agrippa, grandson of Herod the Great. In 39 he added Galilee and Perea to his domains when Antipas was exiled. Then in 41 he was granted Judea and Samaria as well, thus becoming king of the entire territory once ruled by his grandfather. He is remembered in the New Testament as a persecutor of the Church (Acts 12). When he died in 44 the land again came under the direct control of Roman procurators, among whom were to be Felix and Festus (Acts 24–25), then in 53 his son, Agrippa II (Acts 25–26), was made king over Northern Palestine where he ruled until 90 AD.

In 66 revolt broke out in Jerusalem. In 70 the city and its temple were sacked by the Romans. Thereafter Judea was ruled by Roman legates and Jerusalem's story as the religious home of Judaism comes to an end. After a further Jewish uprising in 135 the Jews were expelled from Palestine, not to return again until our own times, in 1948.

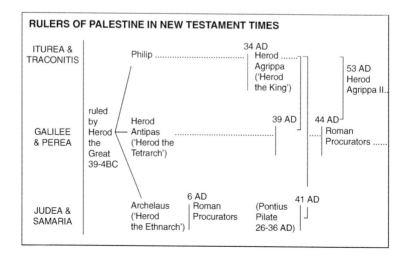

Palestinian Judaism in New Testament Times.

In Jesus' day Judaism in Palestine was split by sectarian divisions. What follows here is only a rough sketch of the various groupings. Our concern is not to trace the history of Judaism, but to understand the purposes of God as he has revealed them to and through men like Abraham, Moses and ultimately Jesus Christ. While the study of Judaism is an interesting subject in its own right, all we need to help us with the New Testament study we shall be doing is a little background information.

1. *The Pharisees* were exclusivists (the name means 'separated'). Ardent believers in holiness and righteousness, their approach to the law was strict, sometimes too strict and legalistic, judging by Jesus' criticisms of them. They were also thoroughly spiritual in their beliefs (Acts 23.8). Many became Christians (including Paul), but some converts found it difficult to abandon their exclusivist attitudes (Acts 15.5). Their origins can be traced back to Ezra the Scribe, but their history is quite complicated, and not unrelated to politics. Because they had an understanding of personal faith, they survived 70 AD and became the leaders of the Jews. By 200 AD Judaism and Pharisaism had become synonymous.

2. *The Sadducees* formed the second main party. Their numbers were fairly small, for they were drawn entirely from priestly and well-to-do families. They were conservative in their religious views, having little time for belief in personal spiritual matters (Matt. 22.23; Acts 23.8). To them religion was very much a matter of what went on at the temple, and so they disappeared from history after 70 AD.

3. *The Herodians* were more a political than a religious group, friends and supporters of Herod Antipas. They always appear in opposition to Jesus, but that was probably for social rather than religious reasons, perhaps because Herod linked Jesus closely with John the Baptist, who dared to criticise him publicly for his immoral ways.

4. *The Zealots* were political militants who believed God, not Caesar, was Israel's true King. They came into existence when Judas the Galilean led a revolt against Rome in 6 AD. They kept his fighting spirit alive thereafter and were active throughout the Jewish revolt of 66–70 AD. Their last strong-

hold, Masada, fell in May, 73. One of Jesus disciples, Simon, was a Zealot (Luke 6.15).

5. *The Essenes*, in contrast with the Zealots, seem to have largely withdrawn themselves from political affairs. They practised a communal life-style, mostly in semi-monastic settlements of which the Qumran Community by the Dead Sea may have been one. They are not mentioned in the New Testament. They also disappeared after 70 AD.

6. *The Samaritans* were descendants of the peoples resettled by the Assyrians around Samaria after 722 BC, but they only properly emerge as a separate religious group in the fourth century, when they built their own temple on Mount Gerizim, opposite Shechem. It was destroyed about 128 BC by John Hyrcanus, one of the Maccabean kings, but Gerizim remained their holy mountain (John 4.20). Their only scripture is their own version of the Pentateuch. We know little about their beliefs in Jesus' time, but many of them responded to the gospel. A tiny community survives today.

3. THE MESSIAH, THE NEW COVENANT AND THE SPIRIT

To help us understand how the portions of the New Testament we are going to study constitute a logical sequel to the Pentateuch, we need to have some sketch of the main spiritual developments that took place in the intervening period, that is, in addition to the religious and political changes we have just noted.

The Covenants of the Old Testament.
The Hebrew word that we translate as 'testament' is also sometimes translated 'covenant'. A covenant is an agreement between two people or two parties. In the theology of the Bible these are, of course, God and a man, or God and his people.

The Treaties of the ancient world were covenants and they often bear some resemblance to Biblical forms. In them the conquering overlord promises to protect his vassals on condition that they offer him total obedience. He sets out various stipulations to which they are required to agree, and pronounces curses on them if they fail to observe these conditions. The pattern is closely followed in Deuteronomy.

The Mosaic/Sinaitic Covenant outlines a relationship similar to that of the ancient treaties. In it God, as overlord, offers his protection and blessing on condition that Israel keeps his laws or stipulations, and he pronounces various curses he will mete out if the laws are not obeyed. The one word that sums up the requirement of the Mosaic Covenant is 'obedience'.

The Abrahamic Covenant is of a different order. In it God lays down no demands, but simply makes promises. Nor are they promises of general blessings, such as long life, health, prosperity, etc., as in the Mosaic Covenant, but particular promises of a land and children and the wider promise of ultimate blessing, not to Abraham himself, but to all mankind through him. Abraham's part in this covenant is almost passive, for there are no stipulations and no curses for failure to observe them. All that is needful on his part is that he believes that God can and will do what he has promised. The one word that covers man's part in the Abrahamic Covenant is 'faith'.

There are other covenants in the Old Testament. One such was *the Davidic Covenant* (2 Sam. 7.5-16). It was like the Abrahamic in that it contained no stipulations, but simply promised the rule over God's people to David and his descendants for ever, thus preparing the way for the coming of Messiah.

The New Covenant.
The prophets foretold a 'New Covenant':
Jeremiah, in 31.31-34, said it would be like the Mosaic Covenant in that it would still have the law at its centre, but different in that it would be written on men's hearts, not on stone tablets. Israel had been unable to keep the Old Covenant, but they would be able to keep this new one, because God would do two things for them:
- firstly, he would forgive and forget the past, thus giving them a fresh start, and
- secondly, he would give them such a personal knowledge of himself within them that obedience would spring, not

from teaching by men, but from inside themselves.

Though Ezekiel does not use the word 'covenant' in 36.25-28, he explains there how it is to work. He too speaks about the heart, the laws, cleansing from the past and a special new relationship with God, but he adds that God is to give men his Spirit within them to enable them to obey in a way they could never do in their own strength.

Thus the New Covenant would not just be a covenant of promise or law like the old, but of promise realised and law fulfilled. The requirement is still faith and obedience, but under the New Covenant the approach is to be radically different. Faith and obedience, so difficult for Old Testament man, are now to be made possible through the gift and power of the Holy Spirit released to the New Covenant people.

The Messiah and the New Covenant.
The old covenants were introduced through the mediation of men like Abraham, Moses and David. The new was also to be introduced through a man, but one who himself bore the Spirit of God in a special way (Isa. 11.1-5). He would come in the anointing of God's Spirit to bring good news, comfort, release, joy and praise (Isa. 61.1-3), would offer his own life as the ultimate sacrifice for our sins (Isa. 53), and in his day God would be pouring out his Spirit on men like water on dry ground (Isa. 44.3). Such was to be the nature of Messiah's kingdom and such the privilege of all who were to become its citizens.

The New Testament.
That man came in Jesus, the Messiah, the Son of God. At his last meal with his disciples he indicated that his death was to be the sacrifice for the sealing of the New Covenant between God and men and that his blood would be sacrificially effective for that forgiveness of sins Jeremiah and Ezekiel had foretold (Matt. 26.28). At that same meal he also spoke much with them about the gift of the Spirit they were to receive once the sacrifice was completed (John 14–16).

That gift was given at Pentecost, seven weeks later, and so Paul is able to write about 'a letter from Christ ... written not with ink but with the Spirit of the living God, not on tablets of stone but on tablets of human hearts ... a new covenant—not of the letter but of the Spirit.' (2 Cor. 3.3-6) It is in this connection that he adds:

> *Even to this day when Moses* (the Pentateuch, or even the whole Old Testament) *is read, a veil covers their* (the people of the Old Covenant's) *hearts. But whenever anyone turns to the Lord, the veil is taken away. Now the Lord is the Spirit, and where the Spirit of the Lord is, there is freedom. And we, who with unveiled faces all reflect the Lord's glory, are being transformed into his likeness with ever increasing glory, which comes from the Lord, who is the Spirit.*
>
> (vv. 15-18)

It is this developing spiritual pattern above all else that makes the New Testament the logical sequel to the Old. At the level of religion, sociology or politics, Judaism has as much claim to be the Old Testament's historical successor as Christianity, but at the level of spiritual development only Christianity offers a sequel. Those Jews who do not accept the gospel are still waiting for Messiah to come and establish his kingdom. They still look for the prophecies about the New Covenant and the Spirit to be fulfilled. The Christian's 'good news'/'gospel' is that Jesus was the Messiah and he has already brought the kingdom; that he has established the New Covenant granting forgiveness of our sins and giving us the Holy Spirit.

Those who appreciate from personal experience the aspect of the Spirit's work Paul describes in 2 Cor. 3 will have little difficulty in recognising the truth of these things, not because of any doctrinal presuppositions, but because of their experience of his working within them. They simply encapsulate the dimension in which Spirit-filled Christians live and therefore need no justification on rational grounds, no more than a man's love for his wife or children needs justification. None the less, it is good to be able to give a reasoned account of one's faith, and in a sense that is all the following pages will try to do.

10

Faith in Action

ST. MARK'S GOSPEL

1. MARK AND HIS PORTRAIT OF JESUS

Mark's is the shortest and earliest of the four Gospels, written probably about 65 AD. In his *Ecclesiastical History*, vol. 3, ch. 39 (early fourth century), Eusebius of Caesarea quotes a second century bishop, called Papias, as having heard a disciple of the Lord called 'John the elder' teach as follows:

> *Mark became Peter's interpreter and wrote accurately, though not in order, as much as he remembered of the things said or done by the Lord. He had neither heard the Lord nor personally been his follower, but later, as I said, he became a follower of Peter, who would use the Lord's teachings, not as though he were putting together an orderly account of his sayings, but according to the need of the moment. Mark therefore did nothing wrong in writing down some things just as he recalled them. Indeed he had one aim in mind, not to leave out any of the things he had heard and not to make any false statements in committing them to writing.*

It is difficult to know how far to trust a third-hand report like this, especially since Eusebius, who quotes it, had no great opinion of Papias' intellectual capabilities. However, a brief glance at Mark's life-story, as far as we know it, suggests there may be more than a germ of truth in it.

John Mark's friendship with Peter probably started towards the end of Jesus' ministry or soon afterwards. At that time he was a teenager living in Jerusalem and may be the youth mentioned in Mark 14.51f who witnessed Jesus' arrest in the Garden of Gethsemane. His home certainly became one of the early Church centres in the city—it was there that Peter went when released from prison (Acts 12.12). He accompanied Paul and his cousin Barnabas on some of the early missionary journeys (Acts 13.5,13; 15.37-39), but lost favour with Paul because he turned back on the first one. Later, when Paul was in prison in Rome, Mark helped to care for him, along with Luke and some others (Col. 4.7-14), and according to later Church tradition, he also ministered to Peter in Rome as his personal assistant, that is until Peter was martyred there along with Paul about 67 AD.

Clearly he was at the very centre of all that was happening in those early days and so must have had plenty of opportunity to listen to the eye-witness accounts of those who had accompanied Jesus on his travels. Some have even thought the Gospel he wrote was more Peter's than his own. Be that as it may, we clearly possess here a book that comes out of the living vibrancy of men who walked and talked with Jesus. It is that sense of thrilled freshness that above all else breathes through this Gospel, much more so than the others where we find more careful editing of the stories, more systematic presentation of the teaching and more theological reflection. Mark actually gives us less of Jesus' teaching than the others; his portrait is essentially of a man of amazing faith and action, before whom people stand in wonder.

That is not to say that Mark simply tells stories without any theological framework or reflection. Not at all, and as we read through the Gospel we shall note some of his dominant themes, such as the hiddenness of Jesus' Messiahship, his charismatic power and authority, the constant amazement of the crowds, his longing to be alone with the disciples, the importance of faith, the intermingling priestly and royal aspects of his last days.

Mark uses the word 'gospel' (literally 'good news', 1.1) to describe what he has written, and that suggests he was like a modern news reporter writing up the story of an exciting piece of good news, all about a man called Jesus who did and said amazing, news-worthy things that people need to hear about since it was news that could change their lives. In some ways his little book is similar to the charismatic biographies we find in Christian bookshops today, telling how an individual is empowered by God's Spirit and has a miraculous ministry that affects many people. Such literature generally creates in the reader a longing for closer fellowship with God and a desire to experience some of the blessings made available by his Spirit. Mark's purpose, as he told his exciting good news, must have been very similar to that.

Basically the story he tells is very simple. Jesus came in the wake of John the Baptist's ministry, preaching the urgency of repentance because of the nearness of God's kingdom. His preaching was with such authority and so attended by miraculous signs and wonders that people everywhere were amazed and crowds flocked to hear him from all over Palestine. He had a few close followers he wanted to teach more intimately, but he could seldom find the peace to do so, for everywhere he went he was mobbed by crowds. Eventually he did manage to withdraw with them for a while. To this point no-one had fully appreciated who he really was (apart from the demons), but now the disciples began to see that he was Messiah. Thereafter he made his way to Jerusalem and others began to realise the same truth. However, the Jewish religious authorities were disturbed and sought to have him silenced. Soon after he entered Jerusalem and claimed it as his royal capital, they had him arrested and crucified, but in his death a sacrificial power was unleashed that took even the centurion supervising the crucifixion by surprise. And in the end death itself could not hold him, for he was the Son of God.

As we follow the story more closely we shall see just how much this Jesus, even though he was God's Son, had to face and overcome the same challenges as we encounter, and how he met them with staunch obedience and unbending faith, proving himself a true successor of his great forerunners in early Old Testament times.

2. 'THE BEGINNING OF THE GOSPEL' (1.1-13)

Mark's introduction is brief compared with the other Gospels. He gives no birth stories, hardly any details about John's ministry and only a bare hint of the dramatic encounters with Satan in the wilderness. His purpose is clearly to get us quickly into the action of Jesus' public ministry.

1.1: The Messianic Secret.
Though this opening verse introduces Jesus bluntly as 'Messiah, the Son of God' (not all manuscripts have 'the Son of God') and though we see Jesus at his baptism being personally affirmed in that truth, we shall soon discover that he discouraged its open proclamation during his ministry, as if he wished to keep it secret (cp. 1.24f,34). It seems he wanted men to look at him without presuppositions based on claims that could be open to wrong interpretations, but simply to see him as a fellow man, and in the encounter let the Spirit draw back the veil and reveal the deeper truth. Mark bids us do the same as we read, namely, lay aside all our presuppositions and simply walk with Jesus on the shores of Galilee, listen to him teach, share in the wonder of his miracles and let the Spirit show us who he is, so that in the end we shall acknowledge with the centurion at the crucifixion, 'Surely this man was the Son of God' (15.39), not because Mark has told us so, nor even because Jesus has argued us into believing it, but because God has revealed it to us in such a profound way that we shall never be able to forget what we have seen, just as he revealed it to Peter and others (8.27-30; 9.2-8).

1.2-8: John the Baptist.
Isaiah had spoken about a voice of one calling to herald the Lord's coming (Isa. 40.3) and at the end of Old Testament times one of Israel's last prophets, Malachi, had again spoken about a messenger who would be sent to prepare the way (Mal. 3.1). Malachi was even able to call him Elijah (4.5). The voice of prophecy then fell silent for over 400 years until John the Baptist came, dressed in Elijah's camel-hair tunic and leather belt (cp. 2 Kings 1.8), or as Luke's

Gospel puts it, going 'on before the Lord, in the spirit and power of Elijah' (Luke 1.17). Jesus taught his disciples that John was Elijah and that he was the last of the old order of prophets (Mark 9.12f; Matt. 11.7-14), though it seems that John was not always too sure about it himself (John 1.21). However, even he agreed that his vocation was to prepare the way for the 'one more powerful than I ... (who) will baptise you with the Holy Spirit.'

1.4,15: *The message of repentance.*

The main way in which John prepared for Jesus' coming was to start preaching the message of repentance that Jesus himself was to preach. Ever since Moses was given the law, Israel had disobeyed it, at some times more than at others. God's response was to raise up prophets to call the people to repent. Moses had foreseen that such a call to repentance would be needed (Deut. 30.1-10), and that call was indeed taken up and repeated generation after generation by men like Samuel (1 Sam. 7.3), Hosea (Hos. 14.1f), Jeremiah (Jer. 4.1f) and almost every other prophet who spoke in the name of the LORD. John revived the call to prepare the way for the preacher whose words were to embrace the message every one of the LORD's prophets had ever given. And the same message has rung down the centuries ever since. It was the call of the first Christian preachers (Acts 2.38) and it was still being loudly proclaimed at the close of the New Testament age (Rev. 2.5,16; 3.3,19). In that respect Jesus' message was not new, but was directly continuous with all the Old Testament preaching relating to the Mosaic Law. The difference was that it was now spoken with a finality and authority unknown before, but that was mainly because of who it was that was now speaking it.

1.8: *'He will baptise you with the Holy Spirit.'*

Moses had longed for this day, prophets had foretold it, John now declared its imminence, and within a few years Peter would be proclaiming its fulfilment (Acts 2). Baptism in the Holy Spirit is not simply a delightful additional bonus available to a few who might like to have it. It is of the very essence of the Bible's message and our Christianity is quite incomplete without it. It is 'what my Father has promised'

(Luke 24.49) and is intimately related to the law, for it is what gives us the power that enables obedience and faith, as Ezekiel for one had realised (see above, pp. 143-5). It is a striking fact that even Jesus did no works the Gospel-writers saw worth recording before the Holy Spirit descended upon him. That enduement enabled his power-ministry to begin, just as baptism in the Holy Spirit later enabled the apostles' ministry (Acts 1.8), and it has had the same dynamic enabling effect on countless Christian lives ever since. It is that without which a biblical-style or Jesus-style Christian life and ministry cannot function. Far from being optional, it is the essential starting point for any Christian ministry.

1.12f: Jesus' temptation.

From Matthew and Luke we learn that Satan tempted Jesus by trying to rob him of the assurance the Holy Spirit had given him about his divine Sonship: If you are the Son of God ... prove it! Mark tells us none of these things, but his picture of Jesus beset by Satan and ministered to by angels reminds us of Zechariah's vision of the high priest having his confidence undermined by Satan, and yet protected and encouraged by the angel. As we shall see later, Jesus, as Mark presents him, is *the* High Priest come to offer God's final atonement sacrifice and, just as Satan tried to stop Joshua, so he also tries to stop Jesus. Had not Zechariah also

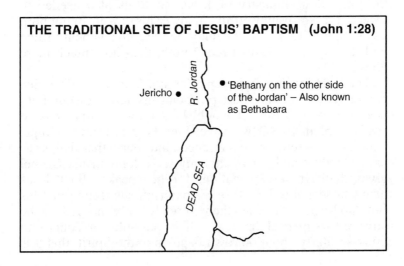

foreseen that Joshua and his assistants were symbolic of things to come? (See above, p.130.)

Jesus' baptism and his humanity.
The question most people ask is, 'If Jesus was the Son of God, why did he need to receive the Holy Spirit in this way?' The answer lies partly in the recognition that Jesus, born of Mary, was a man 'like his brothers in every way' (Heb. 2.17). The only difference is that he did not sin (Heb. 4.15). The logical implication of that is that he had a body like ours, with the same limitations, a mind like ours, a soul like ours, emotions like ours, etc. Therefore he had to grow in wisdom and stature (Luke 2.52) and even had to learn obedience (Heb. 4.8). In other words he was a real man, not a pretend man. That is what Hebrews says, and also what Paul says in Phil. 2.6-11, where he tells how Jesus did not cling on to his 'equality with God', but 'made himself nothing' and 'humbled himself' to become like us, or in 1 Cor. 15 where he likens Jesus to Adam and writes 'since death came through a man, the resurrection of the dead comes also through a man' (v. 21). To be sure, Jesus was born of the Spirit from the start because of the nature of his conception, whereas we get born of the Spirit after our natural birth, but just as born-again Christians need to be filled with or baptised in the Holy Spirit in order to share in the miraculous ministry of Jesus, so Jesus also needed to receive the Spirit himself to empower him for it. Being born of the Spirit (John 3.5-8) cannot be the same as being filled with the Spirit. If Jesus needed both, then how much more do we!

The relationship between Christ's human and divine natures is one of the most profound mysteries of our faith (see also p. 173) and it would be wrong to think it is so easily explained. All we have done here is draw a simple parallel between his experience and ours that helps us understand something of that mystery. John in his Gospel gives a different explanation, for he speaks about Jesus being 'revealed to Israel' in his baptism, suggesting that his full God-ness that was there already only needed to be unveiled to men (John 1.31). It is possible, of course, to think similarly about our own baptism in the Spirit, that it is an experience of drawing out or releasing what is already there from the moment of our conversion and first confession of faith. Luke's Gospel suggests yet another dimension to Jesus' baptism, that it was his commissioning to prophetic ministry, something like the call-experiences of the Old Testament prophets. We shall study these views in greater detail in our other volumes.

Already we have started to speak about Jesus' power ministry, so let us now turn to the Gospel story and see what that was like. Mark lays considerable emphasis on this power dimension, but we shall not appreciate its significance if we start by looking at Jesus as God. We need to remember that Mark invites us to begin by looking at a man, following him around Galilee, going with him to Jerusalem, and in the course of reading his story to become aware of his God-ness by revelation, not by presupposition.

As we go with him we shall see just how real his humanity was. We shall watch him constantly seeking refuge from the crowds, pleading with some of those he healed not to give him any more publicity, a man overtaken in a totally natural way by exhaustion. We shall also see him longing to be alone with his friends, but finding that well nigh impossible because of the crowds that follow him everywhere. He stays away from towns and seeks out lonely places (1.45), he goes up into the hills with his disciples (3.13), he crosses the sea with them in a boat (4.35f), but always the crowds follow him or are already waiting for him wherever he goes. On one occasion, 'because so many people were coming and going that they did not even have a chance to eat, he said to them, "Come with me by yourselves to a quiet place and get some rest."', but even then a crowd of 5,000 followed them (6.31-44). Eventually he does manage to get away with his disciples, but only by taking them well out of the region (8.27). Such is the cost of the popularity that attends power-ministry. We still see it today in the lives of some of our great evangelists, and recognising it helps us to understand better why Jesus wanted to keep his Messiahship secret during the early stages of his mission.

3. EARLY MINISTRY BY THE SEA OF GALILEE (CHS. 1–5)

The structure of Mark's Gospel is quite uncomplicated. Jesus had a very powerful ministry in Galilee where he performed many miracles and where he found open response to his teaching. Then he went up to Jerusalem to face hostility, persecution and death. The turning point is in chs. 8–9, when the disciples began to realise who Jesus truly was. Whilst Mark clearly invites us to enjoy the wonder of the Galilean ministry, Jesus' last week in Jerusalem is so important in his perspective that he devotes a third of his Gospel to it. We need to bear that in mind as we begin to read about our Lord's great exploits of faith.

1.14-34: A dramatic start.
John's ministry is abruptly cut short and Jesus takes over, but, as John had foreseen, in his own style. Galilee, then one of Palestine's busiest and most cosmopolitan areas, is to be his setting, not the desert regions by the Jordan. His message is simple and urgent: 'The time has come. The kingdom of God is near. Repent and believe the good news!' (v. 15) That is, the time you have been waiting for since God first spoke to Abraham about blessing coming through his descendants has arrived at last; the King (Messiah) has come to bring in his kingdom; turn back to God; believe it and you will see it for yourselves!

Almost immediately he attracts followers, some of whom leave everything to be with him. Already we are conscious of a specially dynamic personality.

In the synagogue at Capernaum he startles the congregation with a dramatic act of deliverance and with his very authoritative teaching. The news spreads like wildfire and presently, when Jesus goes to Peter's mother-in-law's house, he finds himself mobbed by crowds of sick people looking for healing. 'The whole town gathered at the door.' (v. 33)

1.35-45: An expanding vision.
Next morning the vision opens wide before him. The crowd wants him to stay, but he knows that his ministry has to be taken throughout Galilee. A man with a vision cannot be held;

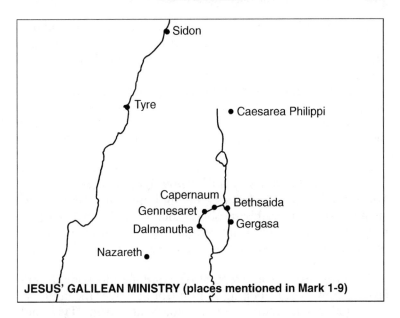

JESUS' GALILEAN MINISTRY (places mentioned in Mark 1-9)

he has to go on.

In this first chapter we see what is to be the continuing pattern of Jesus' ministry. Crowds flock to him, drawn by the dramatic impact of his power. Repeatedly they are 'amazed', but they do not seem to have any clear idea who he is. The demons do, but he silences them. He is a man on fire with a vision that draws him on, but already by the end of the chapter we see an exhaustion factor begin to operate as he pleads with a leper he has healed not to tell anyone about him. Of course the leper does the opposite and the crowds increase, so much so that Jesus is driven to seek refuge in lonely places.

Ch. 2: First stirrings of opposition.
Back in Capernaum the crowds are now larger, and just as amazed as before—'We have never seen anything like this!' (v. 12). But now we encounter the first hint of opposition, not from the crowd, but from other religious teachers. It is neither his miracle ministry, nor his popularity, that bothers them, but his theology! (v. 7)

Criticism continues to mount as the chapter proceeds, coming mainly from Pharisees, who were among the most ardently religious of their day. Three things particularly annoy them—Jesus' popularity with 'sinners' (v. 16), the festival atmosphere among his disciples (v. 18), and his apparently lax attitude to the Sabbath (v. 24).

The theologians were bothered by his doctrinal stance, the pious were disturbed by his religious attitudes, but he had an answer for everyone and none yet dared challenge the authority of his miracles, though that too was to come soon (3.22).

Ch. 3: Growing ministry and growing opposition.
Jesus emphasises the priority of his kingdom mission over such matters as Sabbath-observance (2.27f), but narrow religious minds cannot appreciate that and, after a healing on the Sabbath, opposition becomes self-consciously organised (vv. 1-6).

Nevertheless, Jesus' reputation continues to spread, and crowds now begin flocking to him from all over the country, from Judea and Idumea in the south and from Tyre and Sidon in the north (vv. 7-12). Note how Jesus still wants his identity to be kept secret (v. 11).

With the work now spreading, Jesus sees the need to build up a support team, so he chooses twelve from 'those he wanted' to train them: 'that they might be with him and that he might send them out to preach and to have authority to drive out demons,' that is to learn to do his ministry for themselves (vv. 13-19).

The crowds love him, his own family think he has gone mad, the theologians say he is possessed, but Jesus acknowledges those that are prepared to recognise and do the will of God (vv. 20-35).

4.1-34: A sample of Jesus' teaching.
Crowds again! Jesus has to preach from a boat. So far we have heard about the impact of Jesus' teaching, but have actually heard little of its content. Here we see him teaching in parables, which was apparently his usual method, except when with his own disciples to whom he explained everything in detail (v. 34). The parables issued the challenge of his kingdom: Will Jesus' word be received and allowed to take root (vv. 3-20)? Will it be received but then hidden

away (vv. 21-25)? Or will it be allowed to grow (vv. 26-29)? And will it grow enough to bless others (vv. 30-32)?

Like Isaiah long before him, Jesus had no illusions about the effect his teaching would have on his hearers (vv. 11f). It is a sad fact all evangelists have to live with, that their preaching, while it will bring some to salvation, will also have the effect of driving others away from it.

4.35 – 5.20: An encounter with the powers of evil.
Perhaps it was just to get away from the crowds that Jesus sailed over the Sea of Galilee, but if so, the very elements did not seem to want him to rest. Or perhaps it was specifically to help a lost soul, and, foreseeing what would happen on the other side, they tried to stop him from getting there.

Note how the disciples still do not recognise who Jesus is, even after his astounding display of authority in calming the storm, but at least now they begin to ask the question (4.35-41).

The healing of the demoniac gives an equally astounding revelation of Jesus' authority and another crowd is left amazed (5.20). Contrary to his custom, Jesus bids this man tell his family what the Lord has done for him (v. 19). That was maybe to prepare for his return. This was a mainly Gentile region, not Jesus' regular field of ministry, but when he returned, he found that his reputation had indeed spread in the area and he ministered to a crowd of 4,000 (8.9).

5.21-43: Even raising the dead!
Back on the other side, a crowd flocks round him again, and once more we hear him ask that his healing ministry should not be given any additional publicity (v. 43). His miracle this time leaves everyone 'completely astonished' (v. 42).

4. WIDER MINISTRY IN GALILEE AND BEYOND (CHS. 6–9)

6.1-6: The absolute necessity for faith.
Jesus, now a man all Galilee longs to meet, returns home, but to a very mixed reception and now it is his turn to be amazed—'at their lack of faith.'

Jesus' ministry caused the crowds to wonder at the 'authority' (*exousia*) of his teaching (cp. 1.22) and the 'power' (*dunamis*) behind his miracles (2.10; 5.30). But from time to time Mark is careful to remind us that Jesus was no wizard using magical powers, no mere wonder-worker or novelty-preacher. He makes it clear that Jesus' power and authority are those of the Spirit and the Word of God, and that they only operate in accordance with faith. Thus it is faith that releases the paralytic let down from the roof (2.5), that heals the woman with the issue of blood (5.34), and that restores sight to blind Bartimaeus (10.52). On several occasions we see Jesus encouraging faith before ministering to a sick person. He assures the leper that he *is* willing to heal him (1.41), he bids the synagogue ruler believe so that his daughter can be restored to life (5.36), and he rouses another father to have faith for his son's deliverance (9.23f). We also hear him encourage faith in his disciples in a very different way, by upbraiding them, like a teacher would, for their lack of it during the storm on the lake (4.40) and for their failure to use it in a case requiring deliverance (9.18f).

Here, back home in Nazareth we see for the first time just how essential faith is for releasing God's working and how impossible it is for God to work where it is absent (cp. 9.18f). Yet equally, Jesus teaches about the immensity of the power available through faith, not only to himself, but to us as well: 'Everything is possible for him who believes' (9.23); 'whatever you ask for in prayer, believe that you have received it, and it will be yours' (11.24); 'these signs will accompany those who believe ...' (16.17).

6.6-30: The Twelve are sent out on mission.
Out and about, Jesus' mission is expanding and the time has come for him to get the Twelve actively involved in its work. This was, of course, all part of their discipleship training, for in the not too distant future they were going to have to continue the work themselves (6.6-13,30).

John the Baptist is beheaded about this time (vv. 14-29). Perhaps the timing is significant, for he had come to prepare the way for Jesus' ministry and he now dies at the point where it is fully established and others are being made ready to take over from Jesus.

Luke 10.17-24, though relating the outcome of a different mission, gives us some idea of the excitement such trial missions generated among the disciples, and in Jesus himself.

6.31-56: Jesus desires to be alone with his disciples.
After the disciples return from their mission, Jesus feels a need to be alone with them, but the crowds will not leave them and Jesus finds himself ministering to 5,000 instead (vv. 30-44).

He then sends the disciples across the lake, presumably to find somewhere they can be by themselves, but again the crowds gather. Everywhere they go it is the same—crowds, crowds, crowds (vv. 45-56).

The reason why Jesus wanted to withdraw with the disciples becomes clear as we read on. They have accompanied him on his missions, heard him teaching, observed him healing and casting out demons, and have learned the basics of doing it themselves. Now he needs to introduce them to the deeper challenges of sacrificial service and Messianic calling. They need to learn who Jesus really is and be prepared for his coming passion. However, it is to be some time yet before he is able to do that properly.

7.1-23: The problem of religion.
In the meantime Jesus continues with his ministry, some of it very tricky. He has to relate basically to three groups: the religious (Pharisees and teachers of the law, v. 1), the crowd (v. 14), and his disciples (v. 17). He speaks differently to each group: to the first with hard-hitting criticism, to the second with challenging preaching, to the third with deeper teaching and explanation.

In this passage we see clearly Jesus' attitude to the law. He has no patience with legalistic religiosity, but like Moses in Deuteronomy, takes his hearers to the heart of the law. In essence what he says here is the same as we shall see Paul teaching in Romans.

7.24 – 8.9: Jesus goes further afield, into Gentile territory.
Still desiring to be alone he crosses the border into Syrian Phoenicia and then into Decapolis in Transjordan, but in both places his reputation has gone before him. By the Sea

of Galilee a crowd gathers around him again and he feeds 4,000, this time perhaps mainly Gentiles (cp. Matt. 15:31), since he is still on the east side of the Sea, in the Decapolis.

8.10-26: *The culmination of his Galilean ministry.*
Back in Galilee we see the unbelieving reactions of the Pharisees again (v. 11) and, while making a further sea crossing, the lack of understanding among the disciples (v. 14).

The healing of a blind man at Bethsaida brings Jesus' ministry by the shores of Galilee to an end (vv. 22-26). His last miracle before entering Jerusalem is also to be the opening of blind eyes (10. 46-52). Both stories are immediately followed by acknowledgment of Jesus as Messiah. It is as if the opening of physical eyes is symbolic of the opening of spiritual eyes to see who Jesus is. Here it is the disciples that see, later it is the crowd in Jerusalem.

8.27 – 9.13: *The opening of the disciples eyes.*
Caesarea Philippi represents the turning point in Jesus' ministry. As he takes them up north, still seeking refuge from the crowds, the disciples now for the first time acknowledge him as Messiah. Immediately he begins to speak of his suffering, death and resurrection, but he still asks for secrecy (8.27-38).

Six days later he at last manages to get alone with some of his disciples by going up a high mountain. There God reveals to them the truth of what they began to realise at Caesarea Philippi. They now hear for themselves what Jesus had heard at his baptism (cp. 2 Pet. 1.16-18).

The Transfiguration brings together three of history's greatest revivalists and saviours of God's people, as we have already noted (p. 107). Luke tells us they spoke with Jesus 'about his departure, which he was about to bring to fulfilment at Jerusalem' (Luke 9.31). Clearly what happened was not just for the disciples' benefit, but also to strengthen Jesus for what lay ahead. No man living could have encouraged Jesus at this point for his coming trial because no-one yet understood the nature of his mission, not even his closest disciples, who had themselves only just realised he was Messiah, and even then had been quite unable to cope with what that was to mean for him (8.29-33). Only the Father could encourage him now, which he did by allowing him to commune in this wondrous way with two giants of faith who had been privileged to share profoundly in the vision and work of salvation.

The role of the man of vision called by God is always a lonely one. There is seldom anyone he can discuss his call with, because those he is called to lead will not have gone his way before him. Like Moses, Elijah and Jesus, he will always have to have recourse to the Father and have to be strengthened by spiritual means.

5. ON TO JERUSALEM (9.14 – 10.52)

Immediately they return the crowds are around him again and there is more ministry (9.14-29). But Jesus moves on. The time for his evangelistic missions is now past and there is urgent need for him to spend more time alone with his disciples, to prepare them for what lies ahead (vv. 30-32) and to teach them more about the ways of the kingdom (vv. 33-50).

As Jesus makes his way south, the miracles and the ministry to the crowd gradually tail off, but the teaching intensifies, though most of it now presents a challenge about where people stand in relation to Christ and about the cost of following him (10.1-45).

Jesus takes the road through Transjordan, thus avoiding Samaria (v. 1). At Jericho, as he begins the last leg of his journey, he meets blind Bartimaeus, who follows him with his sight restored (vv. 46-52). He is the first, apart from the disciples, to acknowledge Jesus' Messiahship ('Son of David'; cp. on 8.22-26). The revelation of the truth is now beginning to dawn more widely as Jesus' ministry draws to its close, and that without him having taught it openly to anyone. Presently the crowd will proclaim it throughout Jerusalem.

Obedient unto death.
In Jesus himself something deeper was at work: the challenge of obedience and faith. In a remarkable prophecy Isaiah had

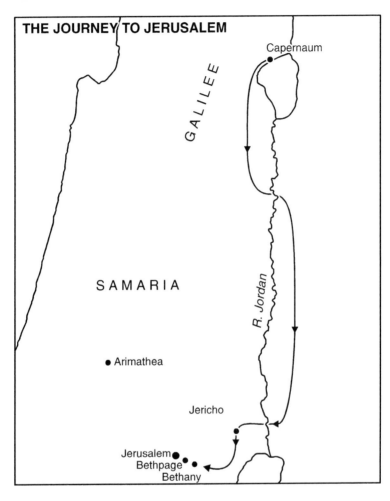

foreseen, not only that Jesus would have to give his life as a sacrifice for sin, but that afterwards he would again see the light of life (Isa. 53). Jesus believed his Father's word and so went resolutely to death, trusting there would indeed be a resurrection. Nevertheless, the challenge was immense. Already his disciples had tried to stop him and presently the burden of it all would become nigh unbearable. Today we know his faith was vindicated; he could only trust it would be.

6. JESUS' LAST WEEK (CHS. 11–16)

Mark's account of Jesus' last week is more of a factual record than we find in the other Gospels, in keeping with the action-packed style of the earlier chapters. But the importance of the events in Mark's thinking is clearly shown by the fact that it takes up more than a third of his whole book.

The Sacrifice of Christ.
In chs. 11–15 we shall see Jesus come as Messiah to his kingdom's capital to be enthroned as king. But he also comes to die, as he himself well knows and as Isa. 53 said he would—'to give his life as a ransom for many' (10.45). The key to understanding the relationship between these two facets of his story lies in Ps. 110, which Jesus himself quotes in his last address to the crowd (12.36). There the Davidic king is also called a priest (the theology is explained in Hebrews; see pp. 175-9). Jesus is both Priest and King. His palace is the temple (11.11-17), his throne is the altar (= the cross), and his coronation is to be his sacrifice on that altar. The Jewish Atonement sacrifice had granted the high priest access through the veil into God's throne-room in the Most Holy Place, but Jesus' high-priestly sacrifice now causes that veil to be torn asunder creating open access for the new people of God.

The rending of the veil is a declaration that it and the whole system of atonement sacrifices associated with it are no longer needed, since Jesus has now offered the ultimate atonement sacrifice, for which they were but a preparation, and has entered with his own blood behind the veil of heaven into the very presence of God himself. The reality of what he achieved by his sacrificial death on the cross is clearly demonstrated in the reaction of the first person to benefit from it, namely the man who stood directly facing him at his death, the centurion in charge of the execution (15.38f).

The Priest-King comes for his sacrifice/coronation and by it establishes a New Covenant in his blood, the constitution of his kingdom, which from that date forward we now recall every time we celebrate the Lord's Supper (14.24).

11.1-11: Sunday.

The Messiah triumphantly enters Jerusalem. Jesus is the King come to claim back territory for God. Galilee was a place of friendship, where he had prepared his heralds and troops; Jerusalem is a place of hostility, and yet it is his throne city (the 'City of David'), where he now comes with his entourage to claim his inheritance (cp. 12.1-12). Today he simply enters his capital, surveys his palace (the temple), and then retires to Bethany.

11.12-19: Monday.

The King's first reforming act is to reclaim his palace.

11.20 – 13.37: Tuesday.

His third day is largely taken up with giving audience to his subjects:

• The religious leaders (chief priests, teachers of the law and elders), who cannot accept his authority, that he is the rightful heir to the vineyard of which they are the tenants (11.27 – 12.12). They are the ones that will eventually have him killed (12.12).

• The pious and the politicians (Pharisees and Herodians), who are concerned about God and Caesar (12.13-17). Jesus challenges them to get their allegiance right.

• The social churchmen (Sadducees), whom he declares to be simply mistaken, because their faith is not scripturally based (12.18-27).

• The theologian (teacher of the law), who is so near to the truth, and yet not near enough (12.28-34).

• The general populace (the crowd), who are simply delighted about all their King is saying (12.35-40) and from whom comes a beautiful example of true kingdom commitment and devotion (12.41-44).

• His own courtiers (the disciples), to whom he unfolds the future strategy of the kingdom. He emphasises their need to be strong and faithful in the gospel work, and exhorts them, because of the urgency of the times, to wake up out of complacency, to 'be alert' and to 'watch' (ch. 13).

Jesus' prophecy in Mark 13 found dramatic fulfilment in the outcome of the Jewish War of 66–70 AD. Thousands of Jews were killed, hundreds of villages were destroyed and many areas were denuded of trees. Temple, priests and sacrifices all disappeared, as did most of the religious parties. Life changed radically for the Jews and neither Palestine nor Judaism were ever to be the same again. While Jesus foretells these things here, his words also carry an eternal prophetic value that transports us far beyond New Testament times, for he also sees that the approaching crisis will be like a foretaste of some far greater drama that will

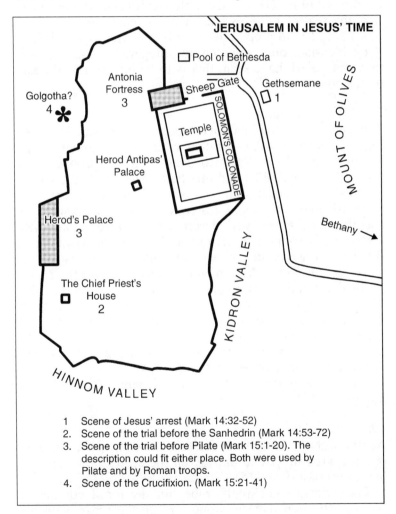

1. Scene of Jesus' arrest (Mark 14:32-52)
2. Scene of the trial before the Sanhedrin (Mark 14:53-72)
3. Scene of the trial before Pilate (Mark 15:1-20). The description could fit either place. Both were used by Pilate and by Roman troops.
4. Scene of the Crucifixion. (Mark 15:21-41)

only be fully played out at the end of history, just before he returns to bring to completion this kingdom work that he has started and that his disciples will have to continue in the interim.

14.1-11: Wednesday.
Jesus has retired again to be with his friends in Bethany where he is dramatically anointed before going to Jerusalem for the last time. There is a double significance in this event. It is the seal of his Messiahship (*messiah* means 'anointed one') and it is to prepare him for burial. He goes as Priest-King Messiah, duly anointed and prepared for his coronation, but, as we have seen, that is to be his sacrificial death on the cross.

14.12-72: Thursday.
The account of the Passover meal is dominated by the forthcoming betrayal, but in that setting Jesus announces the inauguration of the New Covenant that the prophets had foretold (see pp. 143f) and that he as Messiah had come to establish as the constitution of his kingdom (vv. 12-26).

Jesus' own faith is now tested to the limit. He knows his friends, even Peter, will desert him, and so, alone with Father, he is tempted to give up at this last crucial moment. But he emerges with renewed strength and the rest of the story becomes one of fast moving drama (vv. 27-42).

Suddenly the storm breaks and Jesus is arrested (vv. 43-52). He is brought before the Sanhedrin whose false charges he refuses to acknowledge—Messiah does not come for such a thing! But to the question 'Are you the Christ?' he openly and firmly declares, 'I am', whereupon he is condemned, insulted and beaten (vv. 53-65).

Meanwhile Peter, his closest friend, denies that he knows him (vv. 66-72).

Ch. 15: Friday.
At first light he is taken to Pilate who seems to be the only one prepared to defend him. Even the crowd now calls for his crucifixion (vv. 1-15).

The soldiers mockingly robe him as for a coronation (vv. 16-20), then they enthrone him on the cross, with his heraldic title pinned over his head for all his subjects to see (vv. 21-32).

What should have been his most joyful moment, when he appeared before his subjects as King, turns out to be Jesus' darkest hour. Abandoned by all men, he now feels totally forsaken, even by his Father. But then comes the most startling moment of breakthrough as the coronation/sacrifice takes effect. The temple's veil is torn in two granting access to God and 'the centurion who stood there in front of Jesus' sees clearly that this man is even more than 'King of the Jews', but is indeed 'Son of God' (vv. 33-39).

The focus now shifts to Jesus' friends who begin to creep out of the shadows and show their true colours as they ask for the body of Jesus (vv. 40-47).

16.1-8: Sunday.
Resurrection, the vindication of faith! Note the 'and Peter' in v. 7—this, after all, is traditionally Peter's Gospel presented by the pen of Mark. Galilee was the place of first preparation, ministry and friendship; it is to be the place where Jesus will now prepare his friends for the next phase.

16.9-20: Conclusion.
These verses are not included in some of the best manuscripts of Mark's Gospel, and so many biblical scholars feel they should be omitted from the text of the New Testament. But whether original or not, at least they summarise the Easter stories found elsewhere and give us a fair impression of how the early disciples were to continue the kingdom-ministry Jesus had taught and prepared them to do.

Mark started by telling us his book was to be good news about Jesus—Messiah and Son of God. Through a dramatic and fast-moving narrative we have seen these claims substantiated as eyes of faith have been opened, first among the disciples, then among the Jews, and ultimately among the heathen. Mark has invited us to watch a play, a drama presenting a man and his claims. We have seen him proclaim first the coming of the kingdom, demonstrating its arrival with power and authority among the crowd in Galilee, then taking us on to Jerusalem to watch Christ claim his inheritance and finally be granted a mockery of a coronation. Truly this kingdom does not operate as the world's kingdoms do (10.35-45). The portrait of this charismatic figure who drew the crowds and yet gave his life as a ransom for many is essentially a portrait of a man of faith in God, of obedience to his Father's will, and of sacrifice for the redemption of all who will believe in him.

What the great men of the Pentateuch glimpsed and longed to become, namely people of true faith and obedience, Jesus lived to the full. He stepped into history like a second Adam with all the flavour of the Garden of Eden enfolding him. Just as his presence brought stirrings of wonder, expectancy and hope into many Galilean hearts, the encounter with him through the pages of this little Gospel has continued to do the same in countless other hearts down the centuries ever since it was first written. He brought a touch of Paradise back among men and showed them it was certainly not lost for ever. Even now, by joining his kingdom, its benefits can already be enjoyed. And surely that is indeed 'good news'—for today as well as for Mark's time!

PART FIVE

CHRISTIAN INTERPRETATION

Up to this point we have been following a story. Because it tells of God's saving purposes for his world, we have inevitably encountered a fair amount of interpretation on the way, but our main concern has been to plot the course of the drama. Before we round off the story with a brief glance at the course of events since Christ's death, we must pause for a while and consider how his earliest followers viewed the records of God's grace that we have been studying.

While other New Testament writings also comment on the Pentateuchal stories and laws (e.g., Corinthians and Galatians), the most comprehensive treatments of the subject are found in Romans and Hebrews. We shall therefore restrict our study to these two letters only.

11

The Shadow and the Reality

THE EPISTLE TO THE HEBREWS

Hebrews gives us the Christian answer to the question, 'What should my attitude be to the laws of sacrifice and priesthood in the Old Testament?' But more than that, with its comments about faith (chs. 11–12), about rebellion in the wilderness and about entry into God's promised rest (chs. 3–4), it gives a fairly complete outline of what our attitude should be to the whole story of God's dealings with his people from the beginning of Genesis down to the time of Joshua.

We have no idea (though there have been many guesses) who wrote Hebrews, or to whom it was written, or when. It is not even a letter in the proper sense, but someone's sermon ('my word of exhortation', 13.22) sent to a church or group of churches somewhere (13.24), with a little note added to the end of it ('only a short letter', 13.22-25 or 18-25) recommending that they read it and expressing his hope that he will be able to visit them soon. Though we cannot tell exactly when it was written, it probably predates 70 AD, because it never betrays any recognition that the temple has been destroyed, which would have been a clinching proof of its argument that Jesus' sacrifice supersedes those of the Old Covenant system, if the letter were written later.

As a sermon it contains both teaching and exhortation. The pattern is very simple: teaching + exhortation, teaching + exhortation, teaching + exhortation, and so on.

The teaching theme is also quite simple and straightforward: that Christ and his work are superior to everything we read about in the Pentateuch, indeed in the whole of the Old Testament.

The exhortation theme is to keep going forward in Christian faith and obedience. It seems that part of the problem in the church the letter was sent to was that its Jewish members (Hebrews) were tempted to revert to their old religion. He warns them that to turn back is to be finished.

The argument falls into five clearly definable parts.

1. THE SON IS SUPERIOR TO ANGELS (1.1 – 3.1)

a. Because of his divinity, for he is the very 'radiance of God's glory and the exact representation of his being.' (1.1-4)
b. Because the Old Testament attests to his superiority (1.5-14).

Therefore
we must pay more careful attention to what has come to us through him than to what came to us through angels before him (2.1-4).

c. Because of his humanity, which gives him the right to reign over the world of men and to become the author of our salvation through his obedience, suffering, and death as a sympathetic high priest (2.5-18).

Therefore
'fix your thoughts on Jesus …' (3.1)

In Old Testament times God had used angels, as well as prophets, to carry his word to Israel. Angels and prophets would continue to mediate God's word in Christian times, but in Jesus God had spoken in a new and far superior way. Angels may attend God in heaven (Rev. 5.11), but they are only 'ministering spirits' whose function is to go at God's command and 'serve those who will inherit salvation' (Heb. 1.14), whereas Jesus is God's Son to whom he gives the sceptre and crown of his kingdom and who therefore rules over all angels.

In ch. 1 we have one of the highest statements of Jesus' divinity in the New Testament. In discussing the creation story in Gen. 1 we noted how God acts through his Spirit and his Word (p. 16). Here, in Heb. 1.1-3, Jesus is virtually identified with that creative Word of God (cp. John 1.1-14): God spoke formerly through prophets, but now in Jesus he has spoken 'by his Son ... through whom he made the universe.'

By contrast, in ch. 2 we have one of the strongest statements of his humanity. We read that this Jesus 'was made a little lower than the angels', had to 'taste death', had to be made 'perfect through suffering', and 'shared in their humanity', and 'had to be made like his brothers in every way'.

The author makes no attempt to explain how both statements can be true together. He simply states them and leaves us with the paradox, which rationally we cannot resolve. However, both have to be true to make sense of the gospel. If Jesus were not of God and higher than the angels, then God has not visited his people and we are still no better off than they were in Old Testament times. Equally, if Jesus were not a real man like us in every way, then we have been conned by some supernatural being into believing that a man can live the kind of life Jesus lived and in the end can conquer death. Faith needs both statements to be true and neither must cancel out the other. He who died on the cross was a man, a totally real man. He had had to suffer temptation (2.18), learn obedience (5.8), receive the Spirit (see p. 152), and in every respect share our weaknesses, though without sinning (4.15). But equally, if he was no more than a man, then his story is merely a tragic tale that offers us no hope of anything more than the possibility of living a better life if we try to emulate him.

Faith needs both the complete humanity and the complete divinity of Jesus. No human mind can logically or scientifically explain the paradox, but faith knows it to be true and knows the power of it to transform and heal lives. And therein lies Jesus' superiority over any angel or other being created by God.

2. THE SON IS SUPERIOR TO MOSES (3.2 – 4.2)

a. Because, whilst Moses was faithful, he was no more than a servant in God's house, whereas Jesus, who was also faithful, was the son and heir of the Builder himself (3.2-6).

Therefore
see to it that none of you has a sinful, unbelieving heart that turns away from God in disobedience, like the followers of Moses who rebelled in the wilderness and so failed to enter into their promised rest (3.7 – 4.2).

b. Because his successor, Joshua was never able to lead the people into God's 'rest' (4.3-10).

Therefore
let us make every effort to enter that rest—and don't think that you can hide your disobedience from God! (4.11-13)

The failure of the wilderness generation is put down to unbelief and disobedience, just as in Numbers (cp. pp. 85, 87): 'those who disobeyed ... were not able to enter, because of their unbelief' (3.18f), '... because of their disobedience' (4.6). They heard God's call and his promise, but they 'did not combine it with faith' (4.2). The lesson for today is obvious, and even more urgent than it was in Moses' time because of who Jesus is.

This section can only be properly understood in the light of the whole drama we have been following, relating to the restoring of Paradise. The quality of life after the six days of creation was to be 'rest'. God rested on the seventh day himself, and the portrait of the Garden of Eden has nothing unrestful about it. After Adam's sin, God's desire was to restore that rest. He revealed his plan to Abraham and later to Moses, promising the blessings of Eden to all who would live in faith and obedience. Yes, Joshua successfully led the Israelites into the land, but they never obtained that promised, Paradisal rest because they continued in disobedience. However, God has not withdrawn his promise, but has renewed it even more powerfully through Jesus, and so the call to enter his rest remains open for us today.

3. JESUS IS THE *GREAT* HIGH PRIEST (4.14 – 6.20)

a. Because, though he is the Son of God who has passed through the heavens, yet he is totally sympathetic with us in our weaknesses, having been tempted as we are (4.14-16).
b. Because he perfectly fulfils the qualifications necessary for a true high priest: chosen as a man to represent men before God, pastorally sympathetic, and called by God, not self-appointed (5.1-6).
c. Because he fulfilled his calling in total obedience (5.7-10).
(5.11 – 6.3 is a kind of aside: This subject of Jesus' priesthood needs further explanation, especially if you have found it difficult to cope with what you have read so far, but we will return to that presently, in chs. 7–10.)
Therefore
we must beware of falling away from the blessings he has won for us (6.4-8), and we must press on in faith, taking comfort and hope from God's own promise and oath, for it gives us a hope that is sure and certain, one that will not fail us, but will take us to where he has gone ahead as our high priest into the inner sanctuary of heaven itself to prepare the way for us (6.9-20).

The key to understanding this section is again the recognition that Jesus, though he was the Son of God and has gone through the heavens, was also a fully human person. Without that primary qualification he could never have been a priest on our behalf.

The statements that Jesus had to learn obedience and be made perfect may look enigmatic at first, because they seem to imply that there was a time when he was not obedient and not perfect. But that was never so. There are two ways to be made perfect. When a potter works with clay he may shape it imperfectly and so have to reshape it until it is perfect; or he may shape the clay gradually and perfectly through each stage until it ends up as the perfect vessel he wants it to be. Either way he cannot finally say it is perfect until its formation is completed. Jesus attained his perfection the second way.

Similarly, there are two ways to learn obedience: either by discovering the painful consequences of disobedience, or by learning the joyous results of obedience. Again Jesus' way was the second one. At each stage in the moulding of his life, Jesus had to face the challenges of temptation and in them learn obedience. That process continued right up to the moment of his death; only then was his perfection secure. Before that point he could have sinned—such was the risk God took on our behalf when Jesus was born into this world as a man! It was only with his dying breath that Jesus could finally utter the words, 'It is finished' (John 19.30).

The refusal of second repentance implied in 6.4-8 has also troubled many Christians. Perhaps the best way to view these verses is in the light of those that follow: 'Even though we speak like this, dear friends, we are confident of better things in your case.' It should be remembered that we are reading a sermon and that it is the job of a preacher to warn his people about the seriousness of reverting to old ways and securities, even though he believes better things for them. Just as Jesus could have sinned, so we too can fall away. If Jesus could only say, 'It is finished,' right at the end of his life, dare we say it any earlier? Yet we also should live as those 'confident of better things', for our call is to live in faith, not fear.

It should also be noted that the warning in vv. 4-6 relates to being restored to repentance, not salvation. The difference is that salvation is God's work and repentance is ours. It is always God's desire that we be saved, that we should repent and live (Ezek. 18:30-32). That was what Jesus died for and that can never change. We can ourselves, however, reject or ignore the salvation he offers (cp. 2:3), and even reach a point where we cannot bring ourselves to repentance and accept it any more. The salvation will always be there for us, but we must return to receive it. The prodigal's father was always waiting for him, but he had to return home himself (Luke 15:11-24). The potential danger was that he would sink to a point where he could not do so.

4. JESUS' PRIESTHOOD IS SUPERIOR TO AARON'S (7.1 – 10.39)

a. Because it belongs to the order, not of Levi, but of Melchizedek, whose superiority is seen in the fact that he was himself pre-existent and remains a priest for ever (7.1-3), and that even Abraham, from whose descendants Levi was to come, paid him tithes and received his blessing (7.4-10).
b. Because, being of this different order, it is not dependant on Levitical ancestry, but on its own inherent spiritual power and on the word of God (7.11-19), on the very oath of God himself (7.20-22).
c. Because it has a permanence and perfection that other priests could never attain—his sacrifice only had to be offered once, not every year (7.23-28).
d. Because he serves in the true, heavenly tabernacle made by God, not by men. The Israelite tabernacle was but a copy of that heavenly tabernacle whose pattern was revealed to Moses at Sinai (8.1-5).
e. Because the New Covenant, of which he is the priestly mediator, is, by admission of the Old Testament itself, superior to that of Moses (8.6-13).
f. Because he offered his sacrifice in the eternal tabernacle of heaven, not the earthly, which was only a place of ceremonial rituals and 'external regulations applying until the time of the new order' (9.1-10).
g. Because he offered the perfect atonement sacrifice of his own blood that works total cleansing, not that of animals that works only outward, ceremonial cleansing (9.11-22).
h. Because he offered the complete, perfect, all-sufficient sacrifice that does not have to be repeated yearly, as those in Old Testament times had to be (9.23-28).
i. Because the Old Testament scheme of things in the law was only a foreshadowing of the better things that were yet to come, a copy of the realities, not the realities themselves. Now that the realities have come, there is no longer any need for the copies (10.1-18).

These verses round off the discussion about the superiority of Christ's priesthood by recapitulating the main arguments of chs. 7–9.

Therefore
> let us draw near to God with faith in the effectiveness of Christ's sacrificial work, encouraging one another to faith (10.19-25); let us beware of falling back into sin and hence into judgment (10.26-31); stand firm and do not shrink back lest you be destroyed (10.32-39).

Some of the arguments in these chapters may sound a little strange to modern ears, but they are quite logical and are soundly based in Scripture.

We know very little about Melchizedek from the Old Testament. We first meet him in Gen. 14.18-20, where we discover that he was king of pre-Israelite Jerusalem, but also that he had the additional role of being its priest. Abraham, on his return from rescuing Lot and the men of Sodom, comes to Jerusalem where he receives hospitality from Melchizedek, is blessed by him and gives him a tenth of his booty. The author of Hebrews notes that his name suitably means 'King of Righteousness' and that the old name of Jerusalem, Salem, is the Hebrew word for 'peace' (7.2), but it is the fact that no record of his genealogy is given that he finds most striking, and that suggests to him overtones of pre-existence and eternity. Certainly he is not a Levite, for Levi himself was still not born, and if anything was now paying tithes to Melchizedek through his forefather Abraham, thus acknowledging Melchizedek's priestly superiority (7.4-10).

We find his name again only in Ps. 110.4. This is the Messianic psalm quoted by Jesus in his last address to the crowd in Jerusalem (Mark 12.36). It celebrates the fact that God has appointed his Messiah to be both king (vv. 1f) and priest (v. 4), but significantly the order of his priesthood is that of this primeval king of Salem, not that of Levi. That fits, of course, because Jesus was of the tribe of Judah, not Levi. But more than that, by linking Messiah with Melchizedek God was by-passing an order of priests that had never had the capability of dealing finally with sin, and tapping a more primitive source of priesthood, the roots of which seemed to go back into God himself, that is, rather than to any patriarchal ancestor. For the offering of that final sacrifice that would reach heaven as well as earth, something like that was indeed essential (7.11-28).

But not only did the priesthood have to be of a different, more spiritual order, so also did the tabernacle, the altar and the sacrifice. As we have already noted, while the pattern of the tabernacle was given by God himself, it was only 'a copy and shadow of what is in heaven' (8.5; cp. pp. 121f). While Jesus qualified to be High Priest by his full humanity, he was also a priest sent from heaven so that his sacrifice could be offered in the very tabernacle of heaven itself (8.1-5).

Similarly, the sacrifice Christ offered had to be of a superior order. When we studied the atonement sacrifices of the Old Testament, we saw that they had only limited power to deal with sin and did not readily cover sins that were other than external or ceremonial (see also 9.1-10; cp. pp. 125-7). By contrast, the atonement sacrifice Jesus offered was with his own blood and penetrated the Most Holy Place of heaven itself—once for all and to deal with all sin (9.11-28).

Having studied the sacrificial laws of the Old Testament as we did earlier, these things should not be too difficult to understand. The clue to interpreting them from a historical perspective is given in summary in 10.1-18: 'The law is only a shadow of the good things that are coming—not the realities themselves' (v. 1). The tabernacle Moses made was only 'a copy of the true one' (9.24) and its priestly rituals were only intended to foreshadow or prepare the way for the real thing that was coming in Messiah's day. It taught God's people the meaning of sacrifice and the purpose of it, and so by the time Jesus was crucified they were well prepared for understanding the deeper significance of his death and its effectiveness in dealing with sin. The old Levitical system was God's gift to his people, but it was not much more than a model given to educate and prepare them for coping with the reality, rather like a flight-simulator is to a pilot, to train and prepare him for coping with the real aeroplane. It was not a mere trivial play-thing, but a powerful educational instrument, but once the real thing is in operation, classroom copies are no longer needed. It was therefore right that the temple should have been destroyed when it was, in 70 AD, by which time the gospel had been carried to God's ancient people, the Jews, everywhere throughout the world.

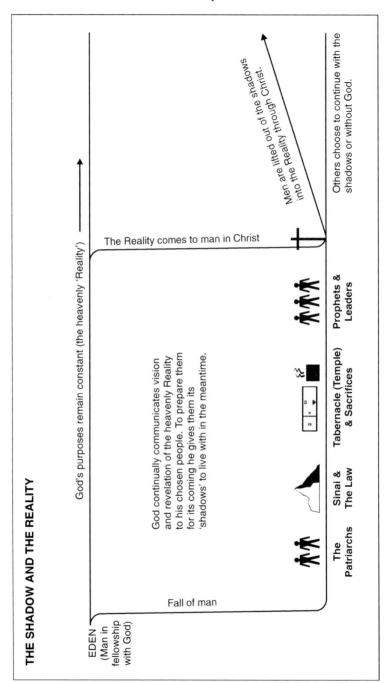

5. JESUS IS THE AUTHOR AND PERFECTER OF OUR FAITH (CHS. 11–12)

The stories in the Pentateuch and beyond tell of many outstanding deeds of faith. We learn an immense amount about faith by studying them (11.1-38). The men of old were commended for their faith, but God did not give them the promised eternal inheritance; that comes only with Jesus and is now offered to us (11.39 – 12.3).
Therefore
   Stand firm and do not lose heart (12.1-3). If the going gets hard, regard it as discipline that will strengthen you (12.4-13). Live in peace, holiness and gratitude, for God has brought you to a wonderful inheritance that you must not view lightly, 'for our God is a consuming fire.' (12.14-29)

What better climax than this exhortation to faith and obedience, because that's what it is all about, as we have seen repeatedly from the beginning of Old Testament history. The difference for New Testament man is that, because of Jesus' work that releases us from the burden of sin and gives us access to God and because of his example that encourages us in faith in a way no Old Testament hero ever could, obedience is eminently more possible today than it was in Abraham's or Moses' time.

The contrast is finally highlighted in the comparison of Mount Sinai with the heavenly Jerusalem (12.18-24). The one inspired fear, the other lifts us up 'to thousands upon thousands of angels in joyful assembly, to the church of the first-born, whose names are written in heaven' and brings us 'to God, the judge of all men, to the spirits of righteous men made perfect, to Jesus the mediator of a new covenant, and to the sprinkled blood that speaks a better word than the blood of Abel.' Clearly the reality we have in Christ is indeed far superior to the interim copy God gave to Moses. What we have now is eternal, and it cannot be shaken (12.25-29).

6. CONCLUSION

Finally, be loving and holy in your dealings with each other (13.1-6). Be faithful to your leaders, their teaching and above all to Jesus (13.7-17). Pray for us—and may God bless you all (13.18-21).

Please take my sermon seriously. This is only a short note, but I hope to see you all soon.

Greetings to everyone from all of us here! (13.22-25)

In the final analysis the theme of Hebrews is that all that is found in the Pentateuch is very much part of the total plan of God's purposes for Christians, but only by way of preparation for the greater and more perfect work of Christ. In the Old Testament we see clear, God-given teaching about priesthood and sacrifice, but all of it is in the nature of a foreshadowing of Christ's priesthood and sacrifice. The tabernacle in the Old Testament is a copy of the heavenly tabernacle revealed to Moses on Mount Sinai. The priesthood and all the other sacrificial institutions were also of the same nature: reflections, shadows or copies of heavenly reality. And that reality came to us in Jesus Christ, thus rendering the old Jewish system obsolete. (The destruction of the temple in 70 AD was a clear confirmation of the truth of the epistle's argument.) None the less, it was God-given and preparatory for Christ, and the more we understand it, the more we can appreciate all that Jesus' life and sacrifice should mean for us.

In the same way there are wonderful examples of faith and tremendous lessons about obedience that can be learned from the Old Testament, and they are not at all to be despised. Indeed the contrary is the case, but again they pale in the light of Christ whose perfect faith and obedience achieved what theirs was never able to do. The lessons to be learned from the Pentateuch are vital and powerful for Christian living, but they must always find their focus and fulfilment in Jesus Christ.

12

Faith and the Righteousness from God

PAUL'S GOSPEL IN ROMANS

Hebrews gave us a Christian interpretation of many aspects of the Pentateuch, but not all of them. Whilst it covered the sacrificial systems and the stories of disobedience and faith, it had little to say about the moral and social laws, those that speak of justice and righteousness. It also said nothing about a proper Christian attitude to the Jewish cultural or religious laws, such as circumcision, Sabbath observance and the food laws. It is with these aspects that Romans is mainly concerned, and so between them Romans and Hebrews give us a fairly comprehensive review of most of the Pentateuch from a Christian standpoint.

Paul wrote Romans in 58 AD, towards the end of his third missionary journey, before he left Corinth to return to Jerusalem for the feast of Pentecost at which he was finally arrested (during the three month period mentioned in Acts 20.3). At that point he was planning a fourth mission trip, this time to Spain, and he wrote his letter to the Roman Christians to ask for their help, that he might stop over with them and use their church as a base for the next leg of his journey west (15.14-33). It seems, however, that he also wanted to stay in Rome for a while, both to encourage the congregation there and to receive some encouragement from them himself (1.8-15).

But there was a problem. Paul had had a lot of opposition during his missions from Jewish Christians who held that Gentile converts should be circumcised and required to keep the laws of Moses, just as they did themselves. Paul had met with the apostles in Jerusalem to discuss this matter in 48 AD (Acts 15; Gal. 2) and had received their approval of his Gentile mission, but the trouble still continued and because of it Paul had to write his letter to the Galatians. Perhaps the news of their opposition in the East had unsettled the church in Rome about him, or perhaps his critics were already in Rome exerting pressure not to support him, but for some reason now unknown to us Paul felt he had to write this long theological treatise explaining to them his position in relation to the law and Christ. The result is a fairly full statement of Paul's Gospel, of how he saw and presented the good news of Jesus, and as such has been treasured by countless millions of Christians down through the ages.

1. INTRODUCTORY SUMMARY OF PAUL'S GOSPEL (1.16-17)

Paul introduces his account of the gospel with two summary sentences:

- The first indicates the effect it has on people's lives, whoever they be: 'it is the power of God for the salvation of everyone who believes ...'
- The second summarises its teaching: 'in the gospel a righteousness from God is revealed, a righteousness that is by faith from first to last ...'

In the rest of his letter he tries to show what that means in detail, working through his theme in five main stages to which the remaining divisions of this chapter will correspond:

- Firstly, he argues that all men are in need of salvation.
- Secondly, he shows how salvation is made available in Christ.
- Thirdly, he gives a brief description of its benefits.
- Fourthly, he explains how it all fits together in history.
- Fifthly, he describes the new quality of life it requires.

The two key words in his gospel are 'faith' and 'righteousness', but Paul's teaching about both has often been grossly misunderstood and misinterpreted—even in his own day (3.3-8, 27-31; cp. 2 Pet. 3.15f).

Some seem to have thought he was teaching that neither the law nor good works were necessary any more, since all that was now needful was faith in Christ. Paul strenuously refutes such thinking, but he does also maintain that it is only by faith we receive our salvation. Of course the man of true faith will actually uphold the law and do plenty of good works, but it is only faith that will make his salvation secure. Salvation can never be earned or attained by human means, otherwise it would have been attainable by Old Testament man and Christ need never have come. Only God can save, and faith is man's response to what God has done to save him, his acceptance of the salvation God offers him in Christ.

Righteousness must also be understood in the same way. It is not something man achieves, but something God gives him. That is why Paul calls it 'a righteousness from God.' In his usage it is almost synonymous with salvation, for it describes what God has done for man through Christ: he has put him 'right', or brought him into a 'right' relationship with himself. In some ways righteousness is more like an activity than a condition—the activity of God putting us right with himself, and that is much the same as salvation.

We could therefore paraphrase Paul's summary thus: 'The gospel has the power to save everyone who believes it, because it tells how God puts us right with him and how we can receive the good of that for ourselves by simply trusting or having faith in what the gospel tells us about it.'

These verses have had a powerful influence on the lives of many of God's saints down the centuries, one of the most notable being Martin Luther who first discovered the truth of the gospel as he read them. It is a striking witness to the unchanging nature of God's word that already, more than 600 years before Paul's day, the prophet Habakkuk had also found enlightenment and life as he came to realise something of the same truth (Hab. 2.4).

2. THE WRATH OF GOD (1.18 – 3.20)

— is revealed from heaven against all the godlessness and wickedness of men ...

1.18-32: The sin of the Gentiles.
Gentiles should be able to recognise God through creation, because he has left his imprint on it everywhere (vv. 18-20), but sadly they have worshipped the creation rather than the Creator, making idols for themselves, etc. (vv. 21-23), and the result of their spiritual decline has been a corresponding decline in morals and social conduct, ending in all sorts of perversion and depravity (vv. 24-32). We see the truth of what Paul says here in our own time, for morals are always higher where there is living faith in God and always decline when idolatrous, atheistic and occult practices increase.

2.1 – 3.8: The sin of the Jews.
Jews should have an advantage over the Gentiles because they have the law to help them (3.1f), but they fail to keep it and so bring themselves under judgment. If anything their sin is worse than the Gentiles' because they should know better. They have been taught God's law and they have approved his teaching, so when they fail to live by it they actually dishonour God and make his name a mockery among the Gentiles (2.17-24). The law is only a blessing if it is obeyed; otherwise it earns condemnation (2.25-27).

3.9-20: All have sinned.
Paul's conclusion is simple and logical: no-one is righteous and so all men are subject to judgment. But that is nothing new, for it is the story of man from Adam to Christ, as several Old Testament writers clearly pointed out.

Sin is in control everywhere and all men, whether Jews or Gentiles, are inescapably and helplessly under its power. The law shows the potential, but is powerless to save by itself. So what is needed, it seems, is for God to stretch out his hand and do something else apart from the law. And that is what he did in Christ.

3. THE RIGHTEOUSNESS FROM GOD (3.21 – 7.25)

— is revealed in Jesus Christ.

3.21-31: Introductory definition of the righteousness from God.

a. It is quite independent of the law, though we can read about it in the Old Testament. It is powerful in its own right (v. 21).
b. It came with Jesus Christ (v. 24).
c. It is received by faith in him (v. 22).
d. It is for *anyone* who believes, Jew or Gentile (v. 22).
e. It is freely given, an act of God's grace (v. 24).
f. It is completed in the sacrifice of the cross, which is therefore the focal point for faith (v. 25).
g. It deals completely with all sin, past or present, and so demonstrates God's justice totally (vv. 25f).

Most of these points will be elaborated on in chs. 4–7, but two of them call for comment here. Paul's first point, that the righteousness from God is 'apart from law' is basic to our understanding of his presentation of the gospel. For Paul the law is only the content of a book. Yes it is a unique book, it is 'holy, righteous and good' (7.12), it is given by God and expresses his will, it can have a powerful effect in highlighting sin (7.7), and it testifies to God's coming salvation (3.21). But it remains a book and has therefore of itself no power to save, only to point out the need for and the way to salvation. The power to save resides in God, not in any book, and that power came in Jesus, God's Messiah, as the Law and the Prophets had foretold it would.

It is for that reason Paul can immediately pass on to say that:

a. Jews therefore have no reason for boasting because they have the law, since salvation is not by the law, but by faith in Jesus (v. 27f).
b. This salvation is available to both Jews who have the law and Gentiles who have not (v. 29), and for both it requires the same faith, simple faith in Jesus (v. 30).
c. The law does not, however, become worthless, something

displaced by faith. Far from it, for since it testifies to this salvation that is by faith, its worth is now proved, not discredited (v. 31).

The second matter that merits some comment here is Paul's three-fold description of Christ's saving work in vv. 24f in terms of justification, redemption and atonement. We discussed atonement so fully in the context of our study of Old Testament sacrifice, Mark and Hebrews that no further explanation of it should be necessary, but we do need to say something about the other two. (See pp. 131f, 163, 179.)

Justification is a legal term. When the court pronounces an accused person 'not guilty', that person has been justified; it has been shown that his case is a just one and that he is innocent. The 'good news' about the salvation available in Jesus is that, since he has paid the penalty on our behalf by his death as a condemned man, God now freely pronounces us 'not guilty'. That is why our righteousness is 'from God', because it is his gift to us, freely given, not something we can obtain by ourselves. All we are asked is to accept it, and doing so is faith.

Redemption suggests a different metaphor. When a man pawns his goods, he can redeem them with a price. In olden times men sometimes were forced to sell their children into slavery because of poverty and often these children could be redeemed or bought back, again for a price. People could become slaves under other circumstances besides poverty, for example, by being taken prisoner in time of war, or by being sentenced in a court of law, and again could sometimes be redeemed by a relative at a cost. We have been in slavery to sin from the day Adam fell, but Jesus has bought our freedom, redeemed us from our bondage, at the cost of his own life.

Justification, redemption and atonement are three different ways of looking at what God did for us in Jesus. It is best to think of them as different and not to try explaining one in terms of the other, but alongside each other they do add up to a fairly comprehensive description of the power of salvation through the cross.

Ch. 4: Abraham's faith and ours.

This righteousness, or justification, that is received by faith was already known to Abraham and is thus a much more ancient and fundamental principle of God's operation than the law.

Paul's argument here is ever so simple and thoroughly logical (cp. Gal. 3). When God renewed his promise to Abraham and sealed it by covenant in Gen. 15, Abraham still knew nothing about circumcision, nor indeed about anything else that was to become part of Jewish law. In other words, he was still a Gentile, and yet it was at that moment, as he simply believed God's promise, that God credited his faith to him as righteousness. It was therefore faith, and faith alone, that put him in the right relationship with God.

Two chapters later he and his son Ishmael were circumcised and then he became, as it were, father of the Jewish race. But the circumcision was only something like a badge or token declaring that he was already right with God, for his justification still rested in his faith, not in the circumcision. We see how true that was as we follow his story through and watch how he still had to go on in faith that God would do what he had promised.

It was never intended that faith should be replaced by the law, for it is the fundamental principle on which all God's activity among men depends. We saw a clear illustration of the truth of that in Jesus' ministry (see pp. 157f). Truth does not change, and so these words in Genesis about faith and righteousness were not only for Abraham's benefit, but also for ours today (vv. 23f). Although Abraham's faith looked forward to Christ, whereas ours looks back to him, the two are essentially the same (vv. 24f).

5.1-11: Peace and joy in believing.

Here Paul simply delights in the benefits made available to us through the blood of Christ. Note the words he uses: justified, peace, access to this grace, rejoice, hope of glory (vv. 1-2). Even in suffering we see God's faithfulness as the Holy Spirit shows us hope (vv. 3-5). He continues by telling of God's love for us, and how we are saved from God's wrath and reconciled to God, all because of the blood of

Christ (vv. 6-11). Today we can know an inner peace and joy because, when we accept by faith the salvation/justification God offers us in Jesus, we lose all fear of death, wrath and judgment; we simply know we have been reconciled with God, restored to that loving, non-judgmental relationship Adam had with him in the Garden of Eden.

5.12-21: Adam and Christ.
Jesus is like a second Adam, but come to reverse the damage caused by the first! Adam was put in the Garden of Eden but spoiled it by his sin; Jesus was put into a corrupt world and redeemed it by his sinlessness. The law came during the time between, but all it did was highlight the sinful condition of the sons of Adam and their need for a Saviour.

Paul contrasts Adam and Christ again in 1 Cor. 15. In both passages he speaks much about death resulting from Adam's sin and new life or resurrection coming with Christ. Death is man's last enemy, so no matter how much peace or joy we may experience in our faith, no matter how many miracles we may see, no matter how much our churches grow, if in the end there is only death, the curse of Adam remains. The good news is, however, that Jesus broke every aspect of that curse and 'as in Adam all die, so in Christ all will be made alive' (1 Cor. 15.22). Paul does not discuss the return of Christ and the general resurrection in Romans, but, when we couple what he says here with his teaching in 1 Cor. 15, the picture is well nigh complete. Jesus has opened the door again to Eden. We receive that by faith now and know the first benefits of it in the peace and joy we experience (vv. 1-11). That, however, is only a foretaste of the fuller glory that will finally be ours in the resurrection. We shall say more about this in connection with ch. 8.

Ch. 6: In Christ we are set free from sin.
Firstly, we are set free by death and resurrection, for by identifying with Christ's death and resurrection in our baptism we ourselves die to sin and rise to new life in Jesus (vv. 1-14).

However, there is nothing magical about baptism. Its benefits, like everything else in Christianity, are appropriated only by faith and so Paul still has to say, 'count yourselves dead' (v. 11), 'do not let sin reign' (v. 12), etc. The difference between that and self-persuasion is that by faith in Christ it all becomes a lightsome and joyous affair, but by self-persuasion it is an impossible, heart-rending trial, just the same as being under the law. In other words, faith in Christ really works, but we must go on living in that faith for it to continue to work.

Secondly, we experience a transference of ownership and service, for we cease being slaves to sin, receiving its deadly wages, and become 'slaves' to God, freely receiving his gift of eternal life (vv. 15-23).

Paul admits the expression is awkward (v. 19), but at least it makes the point clearly, just as Jesus made it rather bluntly when he warned that no man could serve two masters (Matt. 6.24). Roman slaves were sometimes paid pocket-money which some of them would save up in the hope of one day buying their freedom, but usually the only last reward a slave could look forward to was death in service. That is also man's only hope in his bondage to sin. Transference to Christ's service means an end to all that, for God does not pay wages. He only gives free gifts, and that even before we begin working for him. Right at the start he will give us his Holy Spirit, fill our lives with joy and hope, and in the end give us eternal life. Christians with a living faith have also discovered that God freely gives them the more physically tangible blessings promised in the law of Moses as well, such as good health, material provision and happy family life. The point is that it is good to serve God, for he is a loving and generous Master.

Ch. 7: In Christ we are set free from the law.
Paul continues with the theme of the generosity of God as our Master. Not only are we set free from death at the end of our lives, but even now we are set free from the cramping restrictions that the law puts on our lives, released to serve God with freedom, 'in the new way of the Spirit, and not in the old way of the written code' (v. 6).

In secular life it takes a death to break the bondage of law. Thus a woman is only free from the law of marriage when her husband dies. Similarly in Christ it is a death that sets us free from the law, namely our death in him (vv. 1-6).

Though experience shows that the law can be a terrible tyrant, the fault lies not with the law, which is God-given, but with sin in man (or Sin, virtually a personalised being in this chapter; cp. Gen. 4.7). Sin uses the law to stir up guilt feelings in us and to make us think we are not really spiritual enough and not really free. It stands there accusing us, just as Satan accused both Joshua the high priest and Jesus (pp. 132, 151f), seeking to undermine our confidence, and as we listen to his nagging voice, we begin to feel helpless failures, pulled down towards death just as before. The only way to break out of such a downward spiral is to turn to Christ again in faith and cry with Paul, 'Thanks be to God—through Jesus Christ our Lord!' By that cry of faith the accusing spell is shattered and we emerge once more into the light of God's freedom (vv. 7-25).

Scholars have debated about these verses, whether they describe man's state before coming to Christ, or are Paul's account of his own conversion, or were written to remind us that there is a struggle involved in living a Christian life. Considering the progression of Paul's argument, which has already covered the processes associated with conversion, it seems clear that what he is describing is the turmoil that ensues at any time in our lives when we turn our eyes off Christ and listen to other voices that would seek to undermine our faith. The need to continue in faith does not stop at conversion. As we have already noted, even Jesus could only cry, 'It is finished,' with his dying breath.

Sin's subtlety is clearly demonstrated when Paul points out how its negative voice can take even the good things of God and use them to undermine our faith. That, he says, is what has happened with the law. Of itself it is holy, righteous and good (v. 12), but sin twists its teaching to suggest condemnation and thus produce death (vv. 11,13). The lesson is a salutary one and applies to other things besides the law. Today sin's voice still distorts the good things of God, turning churches into shrines, preachers into gurus, sacraments into idols, prayer into a technique, the Bible into another law-book, and so forth. All of these distortions stifle the voice of the Spirit and undermine our faith, ultimately working that same death as sin did among the Jews through the old law of Moses.

Paul's theme in chs. 4–7 can be summarised with a simple illustration (see following page). Before conversion we are bound, chained, as it were like a prisoner, to sin/Satan and are being pulled down by it/him to death. Such is the curse of Adam, but as we look to Christ in faith that chain is broken by the power of his sacrifice and we find ourselves being drawn up out of its bondage into a new life of freedom that ends in eternal life with God. That is how we receive the righteousness that is from God, or are brought into a right relationship with him.

The law was given to Moses as an interim measure. It foreshadowed and testified to this coming salvation and it prepared men for it by making them conscious of their sin and their need for salvation, but of itself it could not give that salvation. The law is good and Christ's life has proved its worth, but sin has turned its governance into a bondage from which God wants to set us free in Christ. God calls us to move on to a new life, not to die in the old.

4. NEW LIFE IN THE SPIRIT, AND THE HOPE OF GLORY (CH. 8)

— that is still to be revealed.

Here we have one of the happiest chapters in the New Testament. Its theme is basically that the freedom from sin and law, that comes as Christ's Spirit fills us and makes us aware of his new life within us and of his love for us as adopted children of God, is only a foretaste of the far greater glory we are yet to receive. Meantime we have the Spirit of God himself within us and, despite our weakness, have a strength that will keep us in God's love through anything.

This is a chapter all Christians love, but unfortunately one whose blessings not all enjoy very fully. That is mainly because they read it as if it were outlining a philosophy of life, rather than describing the richness of the life a Christian should be experiencing with the help of God's Spirit. Paul has mentioned the Spirit a couple of times already (5.5; 7.6), and in both places he speaks about matters of experience, not philosophy—God's love poured into our hearts and

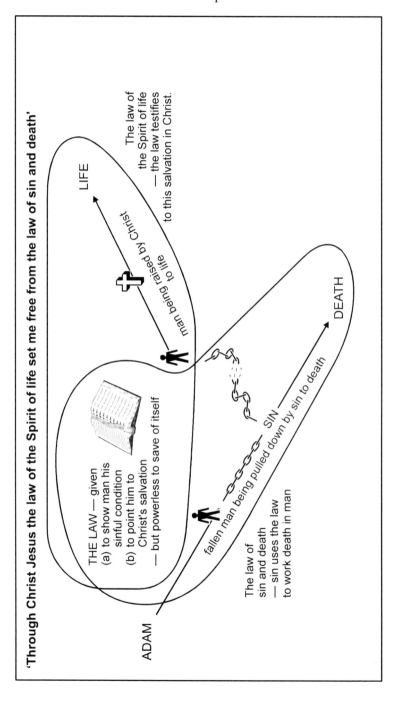

the new way of serving in the Spirit.

When Paul speaks about the relationship between the mind and the Spirit here in ch. 8 it is the same. He is not writing advice for philosophers. Basically what he says is: You have a choice between letting your mind be governed by your sinful human nature (literally 'your flesh') or by the Spirit of God (vv. 1-8). There is a vast difference in the quality of life resulting from the choice, because our sinful human nature and the Spirit of God have nothing in common, indeed they are opposed to each other. That means if we are refusing to let God's Spirit have his way in us we cannot possibly please him. Indeed we are not even Christians if we have not received the Spirit (vv. 7-9). But if the Spirit of Christ is in us, it is totally different, for then we know the intimacy of being sons of God.

In v. 15 and in Gal. 4.5 the Greek word Paul uses for sonship signifies adoption, which correctly defines our status as people he has accepted by his grace. However, once adopted he then gives us his own Spirit, and that makes us more than adopted sons, but, as it is said in John's Gospel, sons 'born of the Spirit', 'born again', or 'born of God' (John 1.11; 3.3-8). We thus become those in whose body lives the very Spirit of his own Son, Jesus, so that we can confidently cry *'Abba'* (Daddy), not because someone has taught us to say the word, but from hearts overflowing with the love of a son, through the Spirit of Jesus who now lives in us (vv. 10-16).

Now if we are sons, then we are heirs, co-heirs with Jesus (v. 17). His inheritance was the throne of God's kingdom, the dominion over all God's creation. But that was also the original inheritance of Adam, whom God made to 'rule over ... all the earth' (Gen. 1.26). Recovering that inheritance is all part of what Paul refers to in the next paragraph when he speaks about creation eagerly waiting for the sons of God to be revealed.

From v. 18 on Paul's mind turns forward to the future, to the third stage of gospel revelation. First it was wrath that was revealed, that is to man without Christ (1.18), then it was righteousness, bringing him into the right relationship with God (3.21), but in the end it will be glory. And that will be not just for men, but for all creation, for the breaking of the curse of Adam in men must ultimately lead to the restoring of Paradise for the earth, and so creation waits eagerly in the meantime for the liberation of the children of God to be brought to completion (vv. 18-21). This vision of Eden restored on earth in the end time is not new. It is, as we have seen repeatedly, what the whole Bible story is all about and it was expressed in words from time to time by the prophets (e.g. Isa. 11.1-9; Ezek. 47.1-12).

In the meantime the gift of God's Spirit is like firstfruits of that fuller glory, like an early foretaste of what it will fully mean in the end. That builds hope into us while we wait (vv. 22-25).

But more than just giving us hope for the future, the Spirit gives us real, living contact with the mind and the will of God now (vv. 26f) and so we have a strength built into us that surpasses anything humanly natural, together with a knowledge that nothing can separate us from God's love and that nothing can finally defeat us (vv. 28-39).

That is not a new philosophy of life; it is a new way of living—made possible by the sacrifice of Christ and the gift of the Holy Spirit within us. If we do not know the truth of ch. 8 from living experience, then our Christianity is sorely deficient.

5. GOD'S PLAN AND PURPOSE IN HISTORY (CHS. 9–11)

Hitherto Paul has been dealing almost exclusively with the personal aspects of salvation. Now he turns to the broader perspective of history, and in particular to the place of God's chosen people in it. But the focus of his attention remains in the Pentateuch.

9.1-29: Israel's history has been governed by God's sovereign choice.
Paul's heart concern is that the Jewish people, his own kinsmen, have for the most part rejected the gospel, despite everything God has done for them (vv. 1-5). But there are reasons for that happening, the first of which lies in God's

own sovereign control of history.

When God set out to redeem mankind, he chose Abraham and a certain line of his descendants to be the people through whom he would work out his salvation. He made the choice of his own free will; nothing of it depended on their desire, effort or merit. We see that clearly in the story of Jacob, for there was no obvious human reason why he should have been chosen in preference to Esau. He became heir of the promises simply because God chose him to be so (vv. 6-13).

The same truth must also apply in a converse sort of way to people like Pharaoh. His opposition to the Exodus was not simply a matter of his own will, for God had chosen him for that very purpose, that he might display his power in him and that his name might be proclaimed in all the earth, as Moses himself realised (v. 17, cp. Exod. 9.16). That may seem a more awkward statement to justify, but then, even a potter makes pots for different purposes (vv. 14-21). Note, however, that God never hardened the heart of anyone who did not first harden his own heart. God is not capricious in his sovereignty (see pp. 59-61).

And the final purpose of all God's choices in history has been that his glory could now be made known to us Christians, a people drawn from both Jews and Gentiles—and none of that is merited either, because it is something God planned long ago and already foretold through the prophets (vv. 22-29).

9.30 – 10.21: *Israel failed to trust God's programme.*

The second reason for the Jewish rejection of Christianity is their own failure to trust in the ancient promises of God. God's sovereignty does not cancel out man's freedom and the people of Israel were always free to co-operate with God or not. They would have received the full benefits of God's promise, if they had but accepted it in faith and not tried to work out a salvation of their own, even if based on his law (9.30-33).

In ch. 10 Paul launches into an extended argument to show that that ancient way of promise is still available, now in even greater fullness in Christ, and the principle is still the same, that it be received by faith—but never in a stubborn exercise of human free will, in seeking to work out 'my own righteousness', as the Jews did, and did ever so zealously at that. Too many Christians today still want to 'do it my own way', and that is never God's way, for his way is always by simple faith (10.1-13).

However, the fault does not always lie with the do-it-yourself Christians, but often with those who have discovered the power of faith for themselves and have not told others about it, for faith is only kindled by hearing the word of God, and if people do not hear, how can they believe? Yet equally, it is not the preaching alone that gives salvation, but only the faith of the hearer, and not all who have heard have accepted the good news. That too was foreseen by God and foretold by the prophets (vv. 14-21).

Ch. 11: In the end God's purposes will reach fulfilment.
God has not rejected the Jews. It has always been the case, and will continue to be so, that only a proportion of God's people (a remnant) will live by faith and according to his promises. The faith in Old Testament times was always kept alive by such a remnant, and so today it is only a remnant of the Jews that have chosen the way of faith (vv. 1-10). But God in his mercy has now grafted the Gentiles into that Jewish remnant—though that is no reason for the Gentiles to start boasting, because they are only there by God's grace and can easily be lopped off again. Part of the purpose in grafting them in anyway is to provoke the Jews to jealousy and thus to repentance (vv. 11-24), for once 'the full number of the Gentiles has come in ... all Israel will be saved' (v. 25f). God has not forgotten his ancient promises to the patriarchs (vv. 26-29). Just as the Pentateuchal law is not nullified by the gospel, but rather fulfilled by it (3.31), so the history of God's purposes in the Pentateuch is not brushed aside by the arrival of Christianity, but brought nearer to fulfilment by it. In the end God's aim is still to bless all peoples on earth (Gen. 12.3), or as Paul puts it here, to 'have mercy on them all' (v. 32).

Christianity is the historical sequel to the Pentateuchal stories in a most wonderful way, just as its faith is the spiritual sequel to its law.

Faith and the Righteousness from God

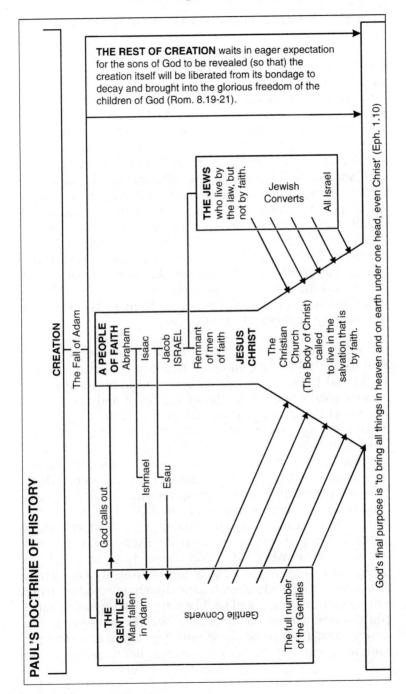

6. THE HEART OF THE NEW LAW IS LOVE (CHS. 12–15)

Just as our survey of the Pentateuch ended with Moses uncovering the heart of the law to Israel, so it is apt that our New Testament survey should end here with Paul laying bare the heart of the new law to the Church. In 10.6-8 he took the words of Moses in Deut. 30.11-14 about how the law is not something distant, but intimately near, 'in your mouth and in your heart,' and reapplied them to the word of faith about Christ. The new law, like the old, has a warm, homely, personal heart, and that is summed up in one word, 'love' (13.10). Jesus said the same when he was asked which was the most important of all the commandments (Mark 12.28-31) and when he said to his disciples, 'A new command I give you: Love one another. As I have loved you, so you must love one another. All men will know that you are my disciples if you love one another.' (John 13.34f) Paul's teaching in this last section of Romans is virtually a commentary on these words of Christ.

Ch. 12: In the Body of Christ 'love must be sincere.'
Paul speaks about the Church as the Body of Christ in 1 Cor. 12–14 and Ephes. 4 as well as here, and in all three places he also speaks about the gifts of the Spirit and about love. The list of the gifts differs in each place. 1 Cor. 12 gives the list of seemingly more miraculous gifts that Pentecostals and Charismatics love to cite, in Rom. 12 the gifts are more of homely service, and in Ephes. 4 they are leadership ministries. But in each place the general theme is the same. These gifts are not natural endowments, but gifts of God's grace. (The word 'charismatic' comes from a Greek word, *charismata*, which means 'things or gifts of grace'—*charis* means 'grace'.) They therefore need to be exercised with faith (v. 3). Faith, as we have already seen, is as essential for living the Christian life as it is for entering it. The fact is that Jesus himself had a supernaturally empowered ministry that operated by faith, and so, if we are to share in that same ministry, we need to have faith in him for salvation to get started, next faith to be filled with his Spirit, and then the continuing exercise of faith to perform his ministry. At no

stage will it be possible to step down from that spiritual, faith dimension and return to the level of operating in our own strength if we are truly to be his disciples. We may not be able to exercise all the gifts he had, but each of us is called to exercise what gifts he does receive 'in proportion to his faith' (vv. 1-8).

When we probe beneath the layers of spiritual gifts and ministries to find the heart that beats inside them, we discover love. That has to be so, for the gifts and ministries are Christ's, and he is of God, and God is love (cp. 1 John 4.7-12). The gifts without love, as Paul says in 1 Cor. 13.1-3, are nothing more than noise and emptiness. So in every aspect of Christian living and ministry 'love must be sincere' (vv. 9-21).

Ch. 13: 'Love is the fulfilment of the law.'

Love is not sentimentality, but relates to very practical matters, even to our relationship with governmental authorities. Paul does not actually use the word love in discussing the Christian's attitude to the state, but the words 'respect' and 'honour' are close approximations given the context. His advice is basically to regard the authorities as God's servants and do what is right by them (vv. 1-7).

Then comes Paul's great statement that every commandment is summed up in the command to love, but again he immediately reminds us that love is not something sentimental by urging us to express it in wise attitudes and in decent living. Furthermore, to live by the law of love is to 'clothe yourselves with the Lord Jesus Christ', to have his style of life, to have his heart control our hearts, to be led by his Spirit, not 'the desires of the sinful nature' (vv. 8-14).

Love and Jesus Christ are virtually synonymous. 'Love is the fulfilment of the law' (v. 10) and 'Christ is the end of the law' (10.4) are to all intents and purposes identical statements.

Ch. 14: Love your weaker brother.

Christians who criticise other Christians for their religious practices are not acting in love. What if someone has views about food, or about religious festivals, or about similar matters, that you do not approve of? Your calling is not to criticise and so pull that person apart, but to build him or her up in Christ, to edify in true faith, for 'the kingdom of God is not a matter of eating and drinking, but of righteousness, peace and joy in the Holy Spirit' (v. 17). The question is: What are you aiming to do as a Christian, share the good news about salvation in Christ and lead others into the fullness of life in his Spirit, or promote a system of religious doctrines and rituals, which is really not much different from pursuing the old legalism of the Jewish religion?

Ch. 15: Aim to be like Jesus Christ.
In the end this is our calling. Jesus did not put his own interests first, but lived for others. Aim to do the same (vv. 1-12). Then:

> *May the God of hope fill you with all joy and peace as you trust in him, so that you may overflow with hope by the power of the Holy Spirit.*
>
> (v. 13)

The rest of the epistle is occupied with personal greetings and discussion of Paul's travel plans, some of which we reviewed at the beginning (1.1-15; 15.14 – 16.27) .

CONCLUSION

Paul's attitude to the law in Romans is very similar to the attitude to the priestly laws found in Hebrews. It was given by God to teach the Israelites and to prepare them for what was coming in Christ, but it has now been overtaken by the fullness of life in the Spirit that he brought. His approach is summed up beautifully in one Greek word he uses in Gal. 3.24, *paidagogos*, which means something like 'tutor' (NIV translates 'put in charge to lead us'). It was used of the educated slave in a wealthy family who had the responsibility of providing the children with an elementary education, and then later of conducting them to a school for further tuition. His job was to lay a preparatory groundwork, and in due course to hand over to the properly qualified teacher. To

Paul the law was like that, 'a *paidagogos* (leading) to Christ', an interim tutor preparing us for The Tutor, who is Christ.

In saying that, he does not deny the value of the law. On the contrary, he upholds it—but only as a preliminary to the fuller ministry of Christ; that is, in the same way as further education does not deny the value of primary teaching, but reinforces it—again only in as much as it is a preliminary to the fuller education following. The law has much to teach us, but Christ has much more. Also Christ has a power that the law does not. The law could only show us our need for salvation; Jesus gives us that salvation.

PART SIX

CONCLUSION

13

Faith Means Forward in Obedience

TO PARADISE AND TO GOD

The history of redemption began when God called Abraham to step forward and follow the vision he set before him. Others down the centuries heard the call, caught the vision and went forward out of their securities to follow. For some the challenges involved were greater than for others. Isaac's path was very different from Joseph's, Jacob's very different from Moses', but all of them had to learn two basic attitudes that were to prove essential for fulfilling the call: faith and obedience—faith in God's purposes and promises, obedience to his call and command.

'All these people were still living by faith when they died. They did not receive the things promised; they only saw them and welcomed them from a distance' (Heb. 11.13), but they discovered the blessing of the Lord as they went forward in obedience to their call—and equally the curse of disobedience when they went astray from it. The temptation was always to turn back, to return to Egypt, to revert to known securities, or else simply to give up and stop, to sit down in despair. But time and again they learned that faith called them onward and they found the reward of faith as they obeyed. The Red Sea only opened before the Israelites when they went forward, and the border of Canaan only closed behind them when they turned back.

The call of faith remains the same today. Of course, many things have changed, the most significant being that our focus of faith now lies in the past as much as in the future because Christ has come. Abraham's faith was almost entirely prospective, looking forward to what God was going to do to work the salvation of mankind, whereas our faith is strongly retrospective, looking back to what God has done for our salvation in Jesus Christ. Similarly, the obedience asked of Moses in the law was something prospective in that its purpose was to train the people of God in ways of holiness and so prepare them for the way of life their Messiah would institute, whereas our obedience is retrospective in as much as it is lived out in grateful response to the love of the One who first 'loved us and sent his Son as an atoning sacrifice for our sins.' (1 John 4.10)

Nevertheless, the nature of faith has not changed, and it still summons us onward. Or as Paul writes in Phil. 3.12-15:

Not that I have already obtained all this, or have already been made perfect, but I press on to take hold of that for which Christ Jesus took hold of me. Brothers, I do not consider myself yet to have taken hold of it. But one thing I do: Forgetting what is behind and straining towards what is ahead, I press on towards the goal to win the prize for which God has called me heavenwards in Christ Jesus. All of us who are mature should take such a view of things.

Those in New Testament times who were faithful and did take such a view of things discovered for themselves the richness of the fruit of their obedience. We only need to glance through the Acts of the Apostles to discover the truth of that. There we read of men and women who lived their lives in a different dimension, whom the Spirit filled and led with hearts full of praise, for whom the world became a place of mystery and wonder, who saw the sick healed, the lame walk, the dead raised up, who witnessed lives transformed by the name of Jesus and the power of the Holy Spirit, and who at life's end saw not death, but 'the glory of God ... heaven open ... Jesus standing at the right hand of God' (Acts 7.55f).

The forward call of faith now has its focus on the return of the same Christ whose coming was its first focus. Already, by the blood of Jesus and baptism with the Holy Spirit, we enter into a life that has the flavour of Eden about it. But Paradise is still not fully ours. We live today at the intersection of two ages. The twilight of the old age is past, for the birth of Jesus heralded the dawn of the new. Already we live in its dawning light, but the full splendour of Paradise's day is not yet ours, not until the sons of God are 'revealed' (Rom. 8.19) and Christ returns to usher in the full reign of his end-time kingdom, where there will be no more death or mourning or crying or pain, where once more we shall know the joy of Eden's Garden and find ourselves by its life-giving stream with its tree of life, where there is no longer any more curse, and where finally we shall see God's face (Rev. 21.1-4; 22.1-5).

Our age is therefore like an in-between time, in which we live life in a double dimension. With Christ's first coming heaven touched earth, eternity entered time, God came to man. Abraham saw it all coming and he rejoiced at the thought of seeing Jesus' day (John 8.56); Moses was shown how to prepare for it and was given the law that was to be our tutor to lead us to Christ (Gal. 4.24). But these men of old could only live with the foreshadowings of its coming in the promise, the law and the sacrifices. With Christ came the heavenly, eternal, divine reality. And 'Christ is the mediator of a new covenant, that those who are called may receive the promised eternal inheritance' (Heb. 10.15), not just look forward to it.

Almost 2,000 years have passed since the sacrifice of Christ made it possible for us to live in the foretaste of this final vision. Today Christians are numbered in millions and millions and daily the number increases, in some places with amazing rapidity. In this century we have seen God pouring out his Spirit in ways scarcely heard of since New Testament times. The Pentecostal gifts flow freely in the churches, we witness an outpouring of power in miraculous signs and wonders, men report visions of God and conversations with angels, the gospel is reaching new people all over the earth with a power unheard of before, millions are flocking into the kingdom. Our age today has a feel about it that was also known in Bible times in the days of Moses, Elijah and Jesus. But then 'our salvation is nearer now than when we first believed ... the day is almost here' (Rom. 13.11f). One wonders just how near!

AMEN. COME, LORD JESUS.

Chronology

The dates given to Biblical events are often approximations, some of them open to a great deal of debate.

In the Old Testament, for example, some prefer to date the Exodus in the fifteenth century, or place Joel in pre-exilic times. Dates for the kings of Israel and Judah are notoriously difficult to pin down.

In the New Testament there are also many problems: There are several views about dating Jesus' birth, the crucifixion can be placed any time between 29 and 33 AD, dates for Paul's life are subject to a lot of discussion, and so forth, but the discrepancies seldom amount to more than two or three years.

The dates used here are widely accepted ones and, despite the uncertainties, they provide a convenient framework for tracing the Bible stories. Fortunately precise dating of Biblical events seldom affects our appreciation of spiritual truths much.

The dates given to extra-Biblical events are also generally open to discussion. Different scholars use different systems for the history of the second millennium BC, though the discrepancies are seldom much more than 10 or 20 years either way. Dating becomes more precise the nearer we approach Christian times, though plenty of uncertainties remain.

Chronology

THE SECOND MILLENNIUM B.C.

	PALESTINE	EGYPT	MESOPOTAMIA
3000		26-25th c.: The Pyramids	Sumerian City States 2360-2180: Empire of Akkad
2000	The Patriarchs		Fall of Ur 1950 Rise of City States: Mari, Babylon, etc. Emergence of Assyria
1720	Hebrews go down to Egypt.	Hyksos ('Foreign Kings') come to power.	
1570		Hyksos expelled	Ascendancy of Assyria
1400	The Exodus ? The Conquest ?	1400-1350: Amarna Period	
1290	The Exodus ? The Conquest ?	1290-24: Rameses II	
1224	The Judges Philistines settle	1224-11 Merniptah - battles with Sea Peoples 1183-52 Rameses III – battles with Sea Peoples	[Fall of the Hittite Empire] Period
1100		End of Egyptian Empire	of
	Fall of Shiloh Samuel		weakness
1050	Saul		in
			Mesopotamia
1010	David		

THE DIVIDED KINGDOM

	JUDAH	ISRAEL	INTERNATIONAL
970	Solomon		
931	Rehoboam 931-14 Abijah 914-11 Asa 911-870	Jeroboam I 931-10 Nadab 910-09 Baasha 909-886 Elah 886-85 Omri 885-74 Ahab 874-53	 Expansion of Assyria begins
	Jehoshaphat 870-48	*Elijah* Ahaziah 853-52	Assyrian advance halted at Qarqar 853
850	Jehoram 848-41 Ahaziah 841 (Athaliah 841-35) Joash 835-796	Jehoram 852-41 *Elisha* Jehu 841-14	 Jehu pays tribute to Shalmaneser III 841
800	 Amaziah 796-67 Uzziah 767-42	Jehoahaz 814-798 Jehoash 798-82 Jeroboam II 782-53 *Amos* Zechariah 753-52 Shallum 752	
750	*Isaiah* Jotham 742-35 *Micah* Ahaz 735-15	Menahem 752-42 *Hosea* Pekahiah 742-40 Pekah 740-32 Hoshea 732-22 -------------------722	 Tiglath-Pileser III Takes Damascus 732 Sargon II deports the people of Samaria 722
700	Hezekiah 715-687 Manasseh 687-42		Sennacherib besieges Jerusalem 701
650	Amon 642-40 Josiah 640-09 *Jeremiah* *Zephaniah* *Nahum* *Habakkuk* Jehoahaz 609 Jehoiakim 609-597		 Rise of Babylon Fall of Nineveh 612
600			

	JUDAH	ISRAEL	INTERNATIONAL
550	Jehoiachin 597 Zedekiah 597-87 *Ezekiel* -------------------587 *Obadiah* *Isaiah 40-55*		Nebuchadnezzar takes Jerusalem 597

THE POST-EXILIC PERIOD

	PALESTINE	INTERNATIONAL
	THE PERSIAN PERIOD	
539		Cyrus takes Babylon
538		Cyrus' Edict allows exiles to return
537	Exiles start to return and Sheshbazzar is made Governor	
535(?)	Zerubbabel is appointed Governor	
520-15	The Temple is rebuilt *Haggai & Zechariah*	
522-486		Darius I
486-465	*Joel ?*	Xerxes I
465-424	*Malachi*	Artaxerxes I
458	Ezra arrives with more exiles	
445	Nehemiah is made Governor	
423		Xerxes II
423-404		Darius II
404-358		Artaxerxes II
	THE GREEK PERIOD	
336-323		Alexander the Great conquers and establishes his Greek Empire
323		After his death, the Empire is divided between his generals
	Palestine is taken under the rule of the Egyptian Ptolemies	

	PALESTINE	INTERNATIONAL
200	The Seleucids take Palestine	Antiochus IV Epiphanes (175-63)
168	The Temple is profaned and the Maccabean Revolt begins	
164	The Temple is rededicated and Judas Maccabeus establishes the Hasmonean Dynasty	

THE ROMAN PERIOD

	PALESTINE	INTERNATIONAL
63	Pompey takes Jerusalem	
39-4	Herod the Great rules Palestine	
27		Augustus Emperor (–14 AD)
5	Birth of Jesus Christ	
4	Palestine divided between Herod's sons: Archelaus (*Judea & Samaria*) Herod Antipas (*Galilee & Perea*) Philip (*Iturea & Traconitis*)	

THE EARLY CHURCH

	BIBLICAL		IMPERIAL
27	Jesus begins his ministry	14-37	Tiberius Emperor
30/31	The Crucifixion	26-36	Pilate Procurator of Judea
35	Paul's Conversion		
38	Paul visits Jerusalem	37-41	Gaius (Caligula) Emperor
38-45	Paul in Syria and Cilicia	41-54	Claudius Emperor
43	Herod's Persecution (Acts 12)	41-44	Herod Agrippa I, King of Judea
45	Paul & Barnabas in Antioch		

	BIBLICAL		IMPERIAL
45-46	Famine relief taken to Jerusalem		
46-47	First Missionary Journey		
48	Jerusalem Conference *Galatians*?		
48-51	Second Missionary Journey *1 & 2 Thessalonians*	49	Claudius expels Jews from Rome
51-53	Paul back in Antioch	51-52	Gallio Proconsul of Achaia
	Galatians?	52-60	Felix Procurator of Judea
53-59	Third Missionary Journey *1 & 2 Corinthians* *Romans*	53-90	Agrippa II, King of Northern Palestine
		54-68	Nero Emperor
59	Paul arrested in Jerusalem		
59-61	Paul held at Caesarea		
61	Paul sails for Rome	60-62	Festus Procurator of Judea
62-64	Paul held in Rome *Philippians* *Colossians* *Philemon* *Ephesians*		
64-7	Paul freed & goes to Spain? *Mark's Gospel* Paul returns to Asia? *1 & 2 Timothy* and *Titus*	64	Neronian persecution
67	Paul & Peter martyred in Rome? Jerusalem Church moves to Pella *Matthew* and *Luke-Acts*?		
70	Fall of Jerusalem	70-79	Vespasian Emperor
73	Fall of Masada		
		81-96	Domitian Emperor
85+	*John's Gospel* and *Epistles*		
95	*Revelation* Clement of Rome's letters *To the Corinthians*	95	Domitian's persecution

Glossary and Index

(REFERENCES TO MAPS ARE IN ITALICS)

People

Aaron, Moses' brother and Israel's first High Priest 171
Abel, son of Adam, brother of Cain 19, 24, 47f, 181
Abraham, first patriarch (Gen. 12-25) 4, 7f, 12-14, 21, 26-50, 66, 70f, 105-7, 141-4, 154, 174, 177-9, 181, 207, 209
Adam, first man (his name is also the common Hebrew word for mankind) 18, 21, 23, 107, 119, 152, 168, 174, 186, 188, 190, 193-5, 199
Akhenaten, mid-fourteenth century Pharaoh, who promoted a kind of monotheism in Egypt, by making Aten, the Sun-god, his only god 30
Amos, eighth century prophet 134
Amosis, mid-sixteenth century Pharaoh who expelled the Hyksos 30
Archelaus, son of Herod, ruler of Judea during Jesus' childhood 138, 140
Balaam, fourteenth century pagan prophet summoned to curse Israel 89, 91f
Balak, king of Moab in Moses' time 89, 91
Barnabas, Mark's cousin, early Christian evangelist 147
Bartimaeus, blind man healed by Jesus at Jericho 158, 161
Benjamin, Jacob's youngest son, tribe 33, 46, 80, 82, *93*
Bezalel and Oholiab, craftsmen of the wilderness tabernacle 52, 83
Bilhah, maid in Jacob's house, mother of Dan and Naphtali 33, 46
Cain, son of Adam, brother of Abel 14, 19, 20, 47, 66, 85
Caleb, spy, who with Joshua recommended entering Canaan 52, 85, 92
Cyrus, Persian king who overthrew Babylon in 539 BC 6
David, king of Israel, early tenth century 5, 12, 31, 66, 91, 137, 143, 161, 163f
Eleazer, Aaron's son and successor as High Priest 89
Eliezer of Damascus, Abraham's slave 36
Elijah, ninth century prophet who appeared with Jesus at the Transfiguration 107, 149f 160f, 209
Elisha, Elijah's disciple 66
Enoch, descendant of Seth 19f

Esau, Jacob's brother 33, 41-7, 197
Eusebius, Bishop of Caesarea, Church historian, third to fourth century AD 146
Ezekiel, sixth century prophet 143f, 151
Ezra, fifth century priest 115, 137, 141, 211
Felix, Procurator of Judea, 52-60 AD 140
Festus, Procurator of Judea, 60-62 AD 140
Gideon, one of the Judges 66
Habakkuk, seventh century prophet 185
Hagar, Sarah's servant, mother of Ishmael 36
Haggai, sixth century prophet 6
Ham, Son of Noah, father of North African and Arabian peoples 21, *22*
Herod the Great, ruler of Palestine, 39-4 BC 136, 138, 140, 165
Herod Antipas (the Tetrarch), ruler of Galilee till 39 AD 138, 140f, 165
Herod Agrippa I, ruler of Iturea and Traconitis 34-44 AD 140
Herod Agrippa II, ruler of Palestine after 53 AD 140
Hobab, Moses' brother-in-law 52, 66, 82f
Hosea, eighth century prophet 152
Hur, one of Moses' assistants 52, 65, 74
Isaac, second patriarch (Gen. 21-35) 28, 30, 32f, 39-43, 46, 50, 52, 199, 207
Isaiah, eighth century prophet 112, 121, 133, 149, 157
Ishmael, son of Abraham and Hagar 36, 39, 189
Jacob, third patriarch (Gen. 25-50) 28, 30, 32f, 40-50, 52, 56, 85, 91, 105, 197, 199, 207
Japheth, Son of Noah, father of Indo-European tribes 21, *22*
Jeremiah, seventh to sixth century prophet 66, 133, 143f, 150
Jesus Christ (see also **Messiah**) xiii-xviii, 7f, 15, 17f, 27f, 39, 51, 62, 74, 82, 84, 95, 97, 107, 112, 114, 116, 121, 127, 132f, 134-209
Jethro, Midianite priest, Moses' father-in-law 52, 56, 65-7, 82
Jezebel, pagan Queen of Israel in Elijah's time 109
Joel, fifth century prophet 84, 211
John, author of fourth Gospel 135f, 152
John the Baptist, forerunner of Jesus as Messiah 141, 148-51, 154, 158
John the Elder, first to second century churchman 146

219

Glossary and Index

John Hyrcanus, Maccabean king, 135-104 BC 142

Joseph, son of Jacob, became vizier of Egypt 30, 33, 47-50, 52f, 56, 86, 94, 207

Joshua, Moses' assistant and successor 5, 30, 52, 66, 84f, 89, 91, 98, 106f, 115, 171, 174

Joshua, High Priest after the exile 132f, 152, 192

Judah, son of Jacob, tribe 33, 48, 80, 82, 93, 178

Judas the Galilean, probable founder of the Zealot movement 141

Judas Maccabaeus, 167-61 BC, founder of the Maccabean dynasty 131

Kedorlaomer, foreign king defeated by Abraham 36

Korah, Levite who led a rebellion against Moses and Aaron 87

Laban, father of Leah and Rachel, Jacob's employer for twenty years 33, 43f

Lamech, descendant of Cain 19f

Lamech, father of Noah 19f

Leah, Jacob's wife 33, 43, 50

Levi, son of Jacob, father of the Levites 33, 123, 177f

Lot, Abraham's nephew 33, 35-7, 177

Luke, author of the third Gospel and Acts 147, 151, 153, 160

Martin Luther, German Church reformer, sixteenth century 185

The Maccabees, Jewish rulers after Judas Maccabaeus in second to first centuries BC 129, 137f, 142

Malachi, fifth century prophet 6, 149

Manasseh, son of Joseph, tribe 33, 50, 80, 82, 92, *93*, 98

Mark, author of second Gospel 136, 146-8, 151, 154, 158, 161f, 167f

Mary, mother of Jesus 152

Matthew, author of first Gospel 151

Melchizedek, king of (Jeru-)Salem in Abraham's day 36, 177-8

Merniptah, thirteenth century Pharaoh 30, 53f

Methuselah, descendant of Seth, longest-living man 19f

Miriam, Moses' sister 52, 88

Moses, chosen by God to lead the Israelites from Egypt 5, 7, 10, 48, 52-124, 135-7, 141, 143, 145, 150, 159-61, 174, 177, 181, 193, 197, 200, 207f

Nadab & Abihu, sons of Aaron who died offering 'unauthorised fire' 77, 83

Nehemiah, fifth century governor of Jerusalem 137

Noah, the ark-builder, saved from the great flood 14, 19-21, 24

Og, thirteenth century king of Bashan in N. Transjordan 89, 98

Papias, second century bishop of Hierapolis in Asia Minor 146

Paul, apostle xv, 27, 96, 112f, 116, 134-8, 141, 144f, 147, 152, 159, 183-203, 208, 211

Peter, apostle 84, 146f, 149f, 154, 166f

Pharaoh, title of king of Egypt 30, 35, 48, 52, 56-63, 75, 83, 197

Philip, Tetrarch of Iturea and Traconitis, 4 BC - 34 AD 138, 140

Pontius Pilate, Procurator of Judea, 26-36 AD 139f, 165f

Pompey, first century BC Roman general 138

Rachel, Jacob's wife 33, 43, 46

Rameses II, thirteenth century Pharaoh ruling at the time of the Exodus 30, 32, 53f

Rebekah, Isaac's wife 33, 39, 41, 43, 50

Reuben, Jacob's oldest son, tribe 33, 46, 80, 82, 92, *93*, 98

Reuel (= Jethro), Moses' father-in-law 56

Samuel, prophet and judge, eleventh century BC 6, 150

Sarah, Abraham's wife 33, 35-7, 39, 50

Saul, first king of Israel, eleventh century BC 5, 66, 137

Seth, son of Adam 19f, 24, 47

Sethos I, fourteenth to thirteenth century Pharaoh 53f, 57

Shem, son of Noah, father of Semitic peoples 21, *22*

Sihon, thirteenth century king of the Amorites in S. Transjordan 89, 98

Simon the Zealot, one of Jesus' twelve Apostles 142

Solomon, David's son, third king of Israel, tenth century 6, 54, 136f

Terah, Abraham's father 24, 28, 33

Tutenkamen, fourteenth century Egyptian boy-king whose tomb and its treasures were discovered in 1922 30

Zechariah, sixth century prophet 6, 149f

Zipporah, Moses' wife 56, 58

Places and Nations

Akhetaten, Akhenaten's capital, see Tel el-Amarna 29
Akkad(ian), major S. Mesopotamian city, empire at end of third mil. BC 28, 30
Amalek(ite), desert tribe south of Canaan 52, 65, 91
Amarna, see Tel el-Amarna
Ammon(ite), kingdom in eastern Transjordan 30, 52, 88, *90*, 98, 93
Amorites, people living in hills of Canaan, controlled Transjordan in Moses' day *31*, 52, 66, 89
Antonia Fortress, Roman garrison headquarters in Jerusalem *165*
Aperu, Egyptian name for kinsmen of the early Hebrews 30
Aqaba, Gulf of *55*, 86
Arabia, the whole peninsula between the Red Sea and the Persian Gulf 21, *22*, 29
Arad, in the Negev, first town to fall to the Israelites *55*, *86*, 89, *90*
Aram (Paddan Aram, Gen. 28.2), region in N. Syria & Mesopotamia 21, *22*, 28, *29*
Arimathea, home of Joseph who provided Jesus' tomb *162*
R. Arnon, seasonal river in N. Moab *90*
Assyria(n), kingdom in N. Mesopotamia, empire ninth to seventh century BC 6, *22*, 28, *29*, 32, 91, 137f, 142
Baal-Peor, see Peor
Babel, city in ancient Shinar (Sumer), possibly near the site where Babylon later stood 4, 11, 14, 23, 27
Babylonia(n), kingdom in S. Mesopotamia, empire seventh to sixth century BC 6, 17, 21, *22*, 23, 28, *29*, 32, *35*, 136f
Bashan, fertile area in N. Transjordan 89, *90*
Beersheba, city in south Canaan where Abraham and Isaac both stayed *38*, 39
Bethany, village near Jerusalem where Jesus stayed in his last week *162*, 164, *165*, 166
Bethany, village in Transjordan near where John baptised *151*
Bethel, sanctuary town north of Jerusalem 35, *38*, 43, *45*, 45, 49
Bethlehem, village near Jerusalem, birth-place of David and Jesus *38*, 45
Bethphage, village beside Bethany near Jerusalem *162*

Bethsaida, town by Sea of Galilee *155*, 160
Bitter Lakes, possible site of crossing of the Sea at the Exodus *63*, 64
Caesarea Philippi, town in N. Palestine where Peter recognised Jesus' Messiahship *155*, 160
Calvary, site of Jesus' crucifixion 7
Canaan(ite), land taken by Israel 5, 13, *22*, 24, 28, *29*, 30-2, *35*, 50, 52, 64, 66, 71, 82, 88, 91f, 97, 99, 105
Capernaum, Jesus' ministry base by Sea of Galilee 154, *155*, 155, *162*
Corinth, trading city in Greece 183
Dalmanutha, district by Sea of Galilee *155*
Dead Sea, also called the Salt Sea (Gen. 14.3) 30, *38*, *45*, *86*, *90*, 142, *151*, *162*
Decapolis, region south of the Sea of Galilee in NT times, mainly in Transjordan *139*, 140, 159
Dothan, fertile plain where Joseph's brothers grazed their sheep 38
Mount Ebal, overlooking Shechem 105
Eden, location of God's primeval garden and symbol of his end-time Paradise 4f, 11, 14, 17, 23, 27, 34, 41, 51, 79, 85, 105, 119, 121, 168, 174, 180, 190, 196, 208f
Edom(ite), kingdom south-east of Canaan 30, 45, 52, 66, 88-91, *90*, 98
Edrei, Og's capital in Bashan *90*
Egypt, empire included Canaan until driven back by the Sea Peoples in the thirteenth century BC 5, 10-12, 21, *22*, 28-32, *29*, *31*, *35*, 35-7, 41, 46-67, 82-5, 88, 91, 96, 107, 207
Elam(ite), kingdom east of Babylonia 21, *22*, 28, *29*
Emmaus, village seven miles from Jerusalem xiii
Ephraim, son of Joseph, tribal area in N. Israel 6, 33, 50, 80, 82, *93*
Ephrath, ancient name of Bethlehem, site of Rachel's tomb *38*, 45
Etham, Egyptian border town on Exodus route *55*, *63*, 63
R. Euphrates, one of the two main rivers of Mesopotamia *29*, *35*
Gad, son of Jacob, tribal area in Transjordan 33, 80, 82, 92, *93*, 98
Galilee, region west of Sea of Galilee xvii, 89, 138, *139*, 140, 149, 153-63, *162*, 167f
Gennesaret, town by Sea of Galilee *155*

221

Glossary and Index

Gerar, home of Abimelech in Abraham's and Isaac's day 37, *38*, 41
Gergasa, town by Sea of Galilee *155*
Mount Gerizim, site of the Samaritan temple, opposite Mount Ebal 107, 142
Gethsemane, garden outside Jerusalem 82, 147, *165*
Gilead, region of Transjordan *90*
Golgotha, place of crucifixion *165*
Goshen, region in Nile Delta where the Hebrews settled *55*, *63*
Greece (Greeks), empire fourth to first century BC, won by Alexander the Great 6, 137
Haran, Abraham's home in N. Mesopotamia 24, 28, *29*, 33, *35*, 43f, 50
Hebrews (OT), name of Israelite ancestors and sometimes of the early Israelites themselves 30, 56, 101
Hebrews (NT), Jewish Christians, particularly Hebrew-speakers 172
Hebron, Abraham's home in Canaan *38*, 39, *45*
Heshbon, Sihon's capital in S. Transjordan *90*
Hinnom Valley, on south side of Jerusalem *165*
Hittites, people of Hatti in Asia Minor, empire eighteenth to thirteenth century BC *29*, *31*, 52
Hivites, people living in central and north Canaan 52
Mount Horeb (= Mount Sinai) *55*, 57, *86*, 97-100
Hormah, town near Arad in the Negev *55*, *86*, *90*
Hyksos ('Foreign Kings'), Semitic rulers of Egypt c. 1720-1570 BC 30, 32, 47, 53f
Idumea (Greek name for Edom), region south of Judea in NT times *139*, 156
Israel, God's chosen people 8, 11f, 30, 32, 40, 44, 53-133, 137f, 150, 199, 202, 207
Israel, the Northern Kingdom 6, 137, 211
Iturea and Traconitis, name given by Luke to Philip's tetrarchy, east of Galilee (Luke 3.1) 138, *139*
R. Jabbok, tributary of the Jordan, where Jacob wrestled with God *38*, 44, *45*, 90
Jahaz, site of battle against Sihon *90*
Jebusites, pre-Israelite inhabitants of Jerusalem 52
Jericho, first city to be taken in Canaan, passed through by Jesus on his last journey to Jerusalem 89, *90*, *152*, 161, *162*
Jerusalem, Jebusite city taken by David and made Israel's capital 6f, *38*, 89, 132f, 138, 140, 147f, 153f, 160f, *162*, 163f, *165*, 167, 177, 183
Jews, name given to descendants of Israel after the Exile xvii, 6f, 116, 132-42, 145, 148, 164, 167, 172, 179, 182-9, 196-9
R. Jordan, border of Canaan and region where John the Baptist baptised 11, *38*, *45*, 89, *90*, *151*, 154, 162
Judah, main southern tribal area 66, 83, *93*
Judah, the Southern Kingdom 6, 137, 211
Judea, Greek and Roman name for the land of Judah 138, *139*, 140, 156
Kadesh or **Kadesh-Barnea**, last wilderness stopping-place *38*, *55*, 65, 81, 85, *86*, 87-9, *90*
Kenites, a tribe of Midianites 66
Kidron Valley, on east side of Jerusalem 165
Mahanaim, in Gilead, where Jacob saw angels before meeting Esau *38*, *45*
Makir, son of Manasseh and part of tribe of Manasseh in Gilead 92
Masada, fortress built by Herod west of the Dead Sea, site of the Zealots' last stand against the Romans 142
Mediterranean Sea 30, *31*, 64, 88
Meribah, name for both Rephidim and Kadesh (= place of quarrelling) 65, *86*, *90*
Mesopotamia, the land 'Between the Rivers' Tigris and Euphrates 12, 20f, 24, 28, *29*, 30, 32, 41
Midian(ite), region south of Edom *29*, 52, *55*, 56, 66, *86*, 91f
Minoans, early inhabitants of Crete *31*
Moab(ite), kingdom east of the Dead Sea 30,, 52, 66, 88f, *90*, 91, 93f, *93*, 98
Mount Moriah, site of the 'sacrifice' of Isaac and of Solomon's temple 39f
Myceneans, early inhabitants of Greece *31*
Nazareth, Jesus' home town *155*, 158
Mount Nebo, in Moab, where Moses died after seeing Canaan *90*, 106
The Negev, southern part of Judah merging with Sinai *38*, *55*, 66
River Nile, turned to blood by Moses *55*, 59
Oboth, wilderness stopping-place (Num. 21.10) *90*
Mount of Olives, east of Jerusalem *165*
Palestine name for Canaan in Roman times 7, 30, 137-41, 148, 154, 164
Paran, wilderness region on east side of Sinai Peninsula *55*, *86*
Penuel, place where Jacob crossed the Jabbok *38*, *45*
Peor, place in Moab where Israelites worshipped Baal 91, 98
Perea, name given to Gilead in Roman times, = 'the region across the Jordan' (Mark 3.8; 10.1) 138, *139*, 140
Perizzites, a people in pre-Israelite Canaan 52
Persia(ns), kingdom east of Babylon, world empire sixth to fourth century BC 6, 136f
Philistines, Sea Peoples who settled in south-west Canaan 5, 30, *55*, *63*, *86*, 88, *90*, *93*
Phoenicia, coastal strip west of Syria 159

Places and Nations

Pi-Hahiroth, unidentified place on Egyptian border 63
Pithom, Egyptian city where Hebrew slaves worked 53, 55, *63*
Qumran, site of the community of the Dead Sea Scrolls, NW of the Sea 142
Rameses (= Avaris, Zoan), Rameses II's capital, where Hebrew slaves worked 53f, *55*, 62, *63*
Red Sea, crossed by Moses at the Exodus *29, 55*, 64, 66, *86*, 207
Rephidim, last stopping-place before Sinai, where Israel fought the Amalekites 65, 89, 91
Rome, Roman(s), rulers of the ancient world in Christian times 6f, 137-41, 191
Rome, the empire or the imperial capital 138, 141, 147, 183f
Samaria, N. Israelite capital and the region surrounding it 138, *139*, 140, 142, 162, *162*
Samaritans, people of Samaria, region between Judea and Galilee 105, 142
Sea of Galilee, main centre of Jesus' early ministry 157, 159f
Sea Peoples, fourteenth century migrants from the Aegean 30, *31*, 32, 88
Seir, mountain region of Edom *38, 45*
Semites (Semitic), descendants of Shem, Noah's son 21, 30
Shechem, at the foot of Mount Ebal & Mount Gerizim in central Palestine 35, *38*, 44f, *45*, 105, 142
Shinar, land where Babylon was later built, see Sumer 22, 23
Shittim, last stopping-place before crossing the Jordan 90
Shur, Desert of, region in NW Sinai *55*, *63*, *86*
Sidon, Phoenician port north of Tyre *155*, 156
Sin, Desert of, in south of Sinai Peninsula *55, 86*
Sinai Peninsula, region of Israelite wilderness wanderings *29, 55, 86*
Mount Sinai (= Mount Horeb), mountain of God in south of Sinai Peninsula 5, 11, *29*, 54, *55*, 57, 65, 67, 70-82, 85, *86*, 91, 93, 97, 107, 119, 130, 177, 180-2
Sodom & Gomorrah, towns beside Dead Sea destroyed in Abraham's time 36f, *38*, 177
Spain, Paul's proposed destination on his fourth missionary journey 183
Succoth, first stopping-place after coming out of Egypt *55*, 62, *63*
Succoth, in Gilead *38, 45*
Gulf of Suez *55*, *63*, 64
Sumer(ian), early S. Mesopotamian civilisation 28, 32
Syria, kingdom founded by Greeks in late fourth century BC, a Roman province after first century, in area called Aram in the OT 21, 28, 139f, 159
Tel el-Amarna, modern name of site of Akhetaten *29*, 30, 32
R. Tigris, one of the two main rivers of Mesopotamia *29, 35*
Timnah, Danite/Philistine border town *38*
Transjordan, mainly Gilead in OT and Perea in NT times 30, 66, 89f, 92, 98, 159, 161
Troy, important city overlooking the entrance to the Black Sea, destroyed in thirteenth century BC *31*
Tyre, principal seaport of the Phoenicians, south of Sidon *155*, 156
Ur, Sumerian city in S. Mesopotamia, Abraham's original family home 24, 28, *29*, 32, *35*
R. Yarmuk, tributary of the Jordan *90*
R. Zered, seasonal river in S. Moab *90*
Zin, Desert of, wilderness region on borders of Canaan *55, 86*
Zoar, city SW of Dead Sea to which Lot fled *38*

Theological and Historical Titles and Themes

Alienation, of man from God and man from man 4, 27

Angels, God's messengers, and other spiritual beings 37, 40, 75, 91, 119, 121, 132f, 151, 172f, 181, 209

Apostles, 'the ones sent out', the Twelve xiii, 151, 157f, 183

Ark of the Covenant, box containing the Covenant Tablets and symbol of God's throne in the temple 82, 120-2, 130-2

Atonement (Day of, Sacrifice of), autumn festival for cancelling sin to restore one-ness between man and God 78, 120-33, 135f, 151, 163, 177f, 188

Baptism, in water, in the Spirit xiv, xvii, 149-53, 160, 190, 208

Blessing, particularly God's 27, 34, 42f, 46, 49f, 73, 75, 78f, 91, 96, 100, 104f, 114, 120, 143, 154, 175, 191, 193, 198, 207

Blood, offered in sacrifices to 'make atonement for one's life' (Lev. 17.11) 21, 59, 62, 74, 78, 101, 120, 124-33, 136, 144, 158, 163, 177f, 181, 189, 208

Caesar, title of the Roman Emperors 141, 164

Charismatic(s), endowed with gifts of the Holy Spirit xv, 6, 9, 107, 147f, 167, 200

Cherubim, heavenly attendants of God, represented in the temple 121f

The Church, the whole body of Christian believers xvi, 8, 48, 85, 88, 102, 107, 135, 138, 140, 147, 171f, 181, 183f, 190, 192, 199f, 209

The Conquest, of Canaan led by Joshua 5, 53f, 137

Covenant 142-45
  Abrahamic (Gen. 12 & 15) 36, 143
  Mosaic (Exod. 20 & 24) 72-6, 100, 104-6, 110, 113, 126, 130, 143, 171, 189
  Davidic (2 Sam. 7) 143
  New Covenant (cp. Jer. 31.31 & Mark 14.24) 6, 74, 142-5, 163, 166, 177, 181, 209
  Book of the Covenant (Exod. 20-23) 72-4, 109, 128
  The Covenant Tablets, or The Tables of the Testimony, on which were inscribed the Ten Commandments 72-6, 97, 110, 122

Creation 4, 11, 14-18, 20f, 23, 51, 95, 105, 115, 172-4, 186, 195f, 199

The Crucifixion, the Cross 28, 39, 117, 132, 148f, 163, 165-7, 173, 179f, 187f, 211

Curse, particularly God's 15, 18f, 27, 89, 91, 96, 100, 104-6, 110, 114, 120, 143, 190, 193, 195, 207

Decalogue, see Ten Commandments

The Dispersion, or **Diaspora**, of Jews scattered abroad after the Exile 6, 133, 138

Elders, tribal leaders in OT, church leaders in NT 52, 58, 72, 84, 91f, 97f, 164

Election, God's choice of men, in the OT particularly of Abraham and his descendants, in the NT, of Christians 47f, 196-9

The End, of history, the eschaton 7, 15, 17, 165, 196, 209

Essenes, semi-monastic sect of Judaism 142

Eucharist, Lord's Supper, Holy Communion 62, 74, 163

The Exile, of the Jews after the fall of Jerusalem in 597 BC 6, 132, 136f

The Exodus, from Egypt 32, 52-67, 70f, 81, 85, 128, 130, 137, 197, 211

Faith (main passages only) xvf, 3-8, 12f, 26, 28, 33, 39f, 46, 49-51, 58-64, 70, 85-8, 92-4, 136, 143f, 147f, 150, 157f, 166-203, 207f

The Fall, of man in Eden 4, 14, 18, 180, 188, 199

Festivals 62, 73, 78, 81, 101f, 115, 127-33, 136

Firstfruits, festival for offering first sheaves and fruits of the harvest 56, 79, 104, 128, 136, 196

The Flood, in Noah's time 11, 14, 20f

Galatians, Paul's letter to the churches in central Asia Minor 184

Gentiles, nations other than the Jews 112, 183-9, 197-9

Glory of God, the manifestation of his presence in the tabernacle and the richness of his blessing that still awaits men in Christ 72, 75f, 189f, 193, 195-7

Gods (pagan) 12f, 28, 40, 91f, 98-102, 106, 126, 186

Gospel, 'good news' about Messiah coming in Jesus 7, 26, 134-6, 142, 145, 147f, 154, 164, 174, 179, 183f, 187, 195f, 198, 209

Theological and Historical Titles and Themes

Herodians, supporters of Herod Antipas 141, 164
History (God's plan in it) xvi, 3f, 7, 11f, 14, 27, 31-3, 79, 97, 179, 184, 196-9
Holiness, Holy, God's nature as the totally other 71, 73, 77f, 88, 96, 99, 101f, 104, 109f, 112f, 116, 120f, 126, 141, 181
Holiness Code (Lev. 17-26) 78f, 109
The Holy Place and **The Most Holy Place**, the main hall and inner sanctuary in the tabernacle and temple xviii, 112, 119-23, 130-33, 163, 178f
Homer's *Iliad*, a Greek epic poem celebrating the fall of Troy 31
Humanity of Christ, essential to the full work of salvation 152f, 172f, 175f, 178
The New Jerusalem, at the end of time 18, 181
Judaism, the faith and culture of Jews after the Exile 116, 136-42, 145, 164
Judges, leaders in Israel in thirteenth to eleventh century BC 3, 5, 66, 102, 137
Justification, act of being declared and made righteous before God 188-90
Kingdom (of God), God's rule over this world xvf, 135, 144f, 154, 156, 161, 163-8, 172, 195, 201, 209
Kings/the King, of Judah, Israel, God's kingdom 3, 5-7, 91, 102, 115, 141, 154, 163-7, 198, 211
Kohathites, Gershonites & Merarites, the three divisions of the Levites who cared for the tabernacle 80, 82, 123
Law, the Law of Moses 4-13, 57, 70-81, 87, 95-131, 99-106, 109, 121, 124, 130, 134-8, 141-45, 150f, 159, 164, 177, 180, 183-203, 208f
Levites, the tribe from which priests and temple servants were drawn 56, 75, 79-81, 91f, 101f, 106, 115, 123f, 178f
Love (of God) 27, 96-100, 104, 111-13, 134, 189, 193, 196, 200f, 208
Mana (& Quails), the Israelites' wilderness food 64, 83
Messiah, Hebrew for 'the Anointed One', 'Christ' in Greek xv, 6f, 111, 132, 142-9, 153f, 159-63, 166f, 178f, 187, 208
Miracles and other supernatural wonders xvi, 9, 49, 57, 59f, 62, 64, 81, 107, 148f, 152, 154-61, 190, 200, 208f
Nazirite, one who has taken a special vow to God 80
Obedience, response called for by the Law and by faith xvf, 3, 7f, 11, 13, 26, 39, 41, 58, 85-8, 91, 96-100, 105, 113f, 136, 143f, 148, 151f, 167f, 172-6, 181f, 207f
Paradise, the garden of God (in Eden) to be restored to man one day (the word is also used in a general way of a place or condition of spiritual blessing) 8, 14, 18, 24, 51, 168, 174, 196, 207-9

Passover, spring-time festival commemorating the Exodus salvation 59, 62, 80, 128f, 136, 166, 183
Patriarchs, forefathers of Israel 11f, 18, 28, 51, 58, 105, 178, 180, 198
Pentateuch, 'the Five Books' of the Law, Genesis to Deuteronomy xv, 4, 9-13, 82, 95, 109-11, 116, 134-6, 142, 145, 168-71, 179-83, 196, 198, 200
Pentecost, 'Fifty Days', festival seven weeks after Passover, commemorating God's coming on Sinai 7, 84, 129f, 136, 144
Pentecostal(ism), of the present-day Pentecostal Movement xv, 200, 209
Pharisees, largest party in Judaism in Jesus' day 116, 135, 141, 156, 159f, 164
Priests, Levites, sons of Aaron, whose main function was to offer the sacrifices and teach the law 3, 6f, 10, 65, 72-80, 102, 114, 117-33, 141, 147, 163-7, 171, 175-82
High Priest, or Chief Priest 120, 130, 132, 151, 163, 165, 172, 175, 178
Procurator, title of Roman provincial governors 140
Promise (see also Covenant):
  to Abraham 5f, 13, 28, 33-7, 40-6, 49-51, 79, 84, 98, 100, 105, 143, 189, 197f
  to Moses 58f, 61f, 75, 93, 100, 174
Prophecy, visions, messages from God through his people on earth xv, 9, 50, 84f, 145, 164f
Prophet(s), men moved by God's Spirit to speak his message xiii-xvi, 3, 6f, 9, 18, 84, 89, 101-3, 107, 124, 133, 135, 150, 172f, 180, 187, 196-8
Purity, moral and ritual 77, 80, 104, 113, 125
Rebellion and grumbling against God 3, 5, 18, 37, 40, 70f, 75f, 81, 85, 87, 95, 105f, 126, 171, 174
Rechabites, descendants of Jonadab son of Rechab, who faithfully kept his ascetic rules 66
Reconciliation, restoration of harmony between man and God and between man and man 27, 189f
Redemption, act of buying back from slavery and from bondage to sin 3f, 13, 79, 168, 188, 196, 206
Remnant, the faithful few who survive God's judgment and continue to work out his purposes on earth 49, 198f
Repentance, turning back to God 5, 75, 98, 104, 106, 127, 148, 150, 154, 176, 198
Righteousness, being, or being made, right with God 7, 71, 110-13, 133, 141, 178, 181, 183-9, 193-7, 202
Sacrifice(s), offerings to God for various purposes, primarily to atone for sin xvf, 7f, 39, 49, 74, 77, 100-5, 113, 117-36, 144, 148, 159, 163f, 167f, 171, 176-83, 187f, 193, 209

Glossary and Index

Sadducees, upper-class party of Judaism 141, 164

Salvation, from Egypt, from enemy oppression and from sin 7, 27, 42, 52, 62, 70, 96, 99, 107, 136, 157, 160, 172, 184-98, 202f, 208f

Sanctuary, building set apart for the worship of God 56, 73, 100f, 119, 127, 131

The Sanhedrin, ruling Jewish council in Jerusalem 165f

Satan, 'the Accuser' (not a proper name), title for the devil describing his activity of bringing accusations against men 17, 19, 23, 132f, 149, 151, 192f

The Settlement, the process of tribal settlement after the Conquest 5

Sin, the cause of alienation 4, 7, 15, 18-24, 46, 88, 107, 113, 124-7, 130-33, 144f, 152, 156, 174, 176-82, 190-95

The Spirit, regularly 'the Holy Spirit' in the NT, generally just 'the Spirit' in the OT xiii-xviii, 3-9, 16, 18, 27, 51, 76f, 84, 91f, 97, 107, 109, 113, 116, 142-53, 158, 173, 189-96, 200-202, 208f

Synagogue, local Jewish meeting places apart from the temple 138, 154, 158

The Tabernacle, the place of worship in the wilderness 52, 72, 74, 76-80, 112, 119-27, 136, 176-92

Tabernacles (Feast of), autumn festival for harvest thanksgiving and for reading the law 102, 129f

The Temple, place of sacrificial worship in Jerusalem 6f, 39, 54, 77, 112f, 121-23, 128, 132f, 136, 138, 141, 163f, *165*, 167, 171, 179f, 182 (Samaritan temple 105, 142)

Ten Commandments, The Decalogue (Exod. 20; Deut. 5) 72f, 99, 109-11, 122, 126, 135

Tent of Meeting, the sanctuary in the wilderness tabernacle 73, 75-7, 80, 82, 84, 91, 132

Tetrarch, title used by Herod the Great's sons 140

Tongues, prayer language, given to Christians after Jesus' ascension 27, 84

Transfiguration, occasion when Jesus was transformed in vision before the eyes of some of his disciples 107, 160

Tree of Life, source of life and healing in the Garden of Eden and in the New Jerusalem 18, 51, 85, 209

Tribes, twelve divisions of Israel, descendants of twelve sons of Jacob 33, 80, 82, *93*, 106

Unleavened Bread, seven day feast following Passover 128f, 136

Weeks (= Pentecost), festival celebrated 7 weeks after Passover 102, 128-30

Wilderness/Desert, of Sinai, place of Israel's wandering 5, 11, 40, 52, 56, 61-4, 87, 91-3, 95, 97f, 123, 128, 130, 171, 174

Wisdom, unusual understanding granted by God 114f, 152

Word (of God), primary means of God's communication with men xv, xvii, 3, 6, 9, 16, 18, 51, 58, 76, 110, 114, 116, 158, 172f, 176, 198

Wrath (of God), God's attitude to sin 21, 72, 75, 83, 85, 92, 100, 133, 190, 195

Zealots, militant party of Judaism in NT times 141f

Summary Outline and Reading Guide

The following pages serve a double purpose:

1. They show at a glance the contents of the main Biblical books covered in this volume.
2. They divide these books up in such a way that reading them can be spread evenly over a period of about six months.

As you read your Bible, keep your mind open to hear what the Holy Spirit has to tell you. Allow him to speak to you personally through its pages.

Watch carefully for what God does and says, and for how the men of Old and New Testament times respond to him, because that is what the Way of the Spirit is all about.

And don't forget to keep asking yourself what lessons you should be learning from their experience, so that you can apply them to your own life as a Christian.

(The reading scheme outlined here forms the basis of the home study course advertised on p. 235.)

Week 1

The Bible's Story
Gen. 1–3: Creation and the Fall.
Gen. 12.1-9 & ch. 15: God's covenant with Abraham.
Exod. 20 & Lev. 19: God's covenant with Moses.
2 Sam. 7: God's covenant with David.
Jer. 31.31-34; Ezek. 36.24-29: A new covenant.
Isa. 9.2-7; 11.1-5; ch. 53; Mark 1 & 14-15: The Messiah.
Acts 1–2: The promise of the Father.

Week 2

Paradise Lost (Genesis 1–11)
Ch. 1: Creation.
Chs. 2–3: Eden and the Fall.
Chs. 4–5: Cain, Abel and Seth.
Chs. 6–8: The Flood.
Chs. 9–10: Noah and his sons.
Ch. 11: From Babel to Abraham.

Week 3

Abraham (Genesis 12–25)
Ch. 12: Call and first challenge.
Chs. 13–14: Continuing challenges.
Chs. 15–16: Faith credited as righteousness.
17.1 – 18.15: God waits for faith.
18.16 – 20.18: Sodom and Canaan.
Chs. 21–22: Isaac, child of promise.
Chs. 23–25: The reward of faith.

Week 4

Jacob (Genesis 25–36)
Chs. 25–26: Jacob's childhood.
Chs. 27–28: Jacob's flight and 'conversion'.
Chs. 29–30: Jacob at Laban's farm.
Ch. 31: Jacob leaves Laban.
Chs. 32–33: Jacob meets God, then Esau.
Chs. 34–35: Settling back in the land.
46.1-7: Jacob goes to Egypt.

Week 5

Joseph (Genesis 37–50)
Chs. 37–38: The brothers in Canaan.
Chs. 39–40: Joseph in prison.
Ch. 41: Joseph over Egypt.
Chs. 42–45: Family reunion.
Chs. 46–47: The descent to Egypt.
Chs. 48–50: Looking forward in faith.

Week 6

Moses and the Exodus (Exodus 1–18)
Chs. 1–2: Moses in Egypt.
Chs. 3–4: The Call of Moses.
Chs. 5–7: First confrontations.
Chs. 8–11: The Plagues.
Chs. 12–13: The Exodus.
Chs. 14–15: Crossing the Red Sea.
Chs. 16–18: On to Sinai.

Week 7

At Mount Sinai (Exodus 19 – Numbers 9)
Exod. 19: God comes to Sinai.
Exod. 20–24: The Covenant.
Exod. 25–31: The Pattern of the Tabernacle.
Exod. 32–34: The golden calf.
Exod. 35–40: The Tabernacle.
Lev. 8–10: Worship at the tabernacle begins.
Num. 1–2 & 7–9: Organising the camp.

Week 8

From Sinai to the Plains of Moab (Numbers 10–36)
Chs. 10–12: On to Canaan.
Chs. 13–14: Turning back at the borders.
Chs. 15–19: Forty years of wandering.
Chs. 20–21: From Kadesh to Moab.
Chs. 22–24: Balak and Balaam.
Chs. 25 & 31: Sin and its consequences.
Chs. 26–27 & 32–37: Final preparations.

Week 9

Moses Preaches Faith and Obedience (Deuteronomy 1–16)
Chs. 1–3: A review of history.
Chs. 4–5: Obedience and the Law.
Chs. 6–8: Hold fast to God.
Chs. 9–11: It is all God's gift.
Chs. 12–14: Be wholly for God.
14.22 – 16.20: Care for the poor.

Week 10

A Challenge to Obedience (Deuteronomy 17–34)
16.18 – 18.22: The nation's leaders.
Chs. 19–21: In war and peace.
Chs. 22–25: Miscellaneous laws.
Ch. 26: Remember and obey.
Chs. 27–28: Blessing and curse.
Chs. 29–30: Choose life.
Chs. 31–34: Moses' last days.

Week 11

The Law
• The Decalogue (Exodus 20.1-17) • The Book of the Covenant (Exod. 20.22 – 23.33) • The Holiness Code (Lev. 17–27) • Ceremonial and Physical Purity (Lev. 11–15; Num.5).
Exod. 20.1-17: The Ten Commandments.
Exod. 21.1 – 22.17: Various civil laws.
Exod. 22.18 – 23.33: Mixed social, moral, religious laws.
Lev. 18–20: Be holy!
Lev. 24–25: Love God and your neighbour.
Lev. 26–27: Obey God and pay your vows.
Lev. 11–15: Ceremonial Purity and Physical Cleanliness.

Week 12

The Tabernacle and its Priests
• The Tabernacle (Exod. 25–27, 30–31, 35–40) • The Priests (Exod. 28–29, 39; Lev. 8–10, 21) • The Levites (Num. 1, 3–4, 8, 16–18, 35; Deut. 18, 27, 31).
Exod. 25–27,30–31: The plan of the tabernacle.
Exod. 35–40: Making the tabernacle.
Exod. 28–29,39; Lev. 8: Ordaining the priests.

Summary Outline and Reading Guide 231

Lev. 9–10 & 21–22: Priests must be holy.
Num. 1.47-53; 3–4; 8.5-26: The Levites.
Num. 18 & 35: Rights and duties of priests and Levites.

Week 13

Sacrifices and Festivals
• *Sacrifices (Lev. 1–7, 17, 22; Num. 15; Deut. 12)* • *Festivals (Exod. 12, 23, 34; Lev.16, 23; Num. 9, 28–29; Deut. 16)*
Lev. 1–3: Thank offerings.
Lev. 4–7; Num. 15.22-31: Sin offerings.
Lev. 16–17: Blood's atoning power.
Lev. 22: Holy offerings.
Exod. 23.14-17; Lev. 23; Num. 28–29: The Festivals.
Deut. 16: Joy and love.

Week 14

Jesus in the Power of the Spirit (Mark 1–5)
1.1-13: Jesus and the Spirit.
1.14-45: First ministry.
Ch. 2: First opposition.
Ch. 3: Growing popularity and opposition.
4.1-34: Declaring the kingdom.
4.35 – 5.20: Jesus at war.
5.21-43: Raising the dead.

Week 15

Jesus, Man of Faith, Messiah (Mark 6–10)
Ch. 6: Who is this Jesus?
Ch. 7: Strangers acknowledge him, but not Jewish leaders.
8.1-26: Culmination of the Galilean ministry.
8.27 – 9.13: Opening the disciples' eyes.
9.14-50: The challenge of following Jesus.
10.1-31: On the way to Jerusalem.
10.32-52: Son of David.

Week 16

The Sacrifice of Christ (Mark 11–16)
11.1-11: Sunday.
11.12-19: Monday.

11.20 – 12.44: Tuesday.
Ch. 13: Tuesday evening.
14.1-11: Wednesday.
14.12-72: Thursday.
Ch. 15: Friday.
Ch. 16: Sunday.

Week 17

The Superiority of Jesus (Hebrews 1–4)
1.1-4: Jesus' divinity.
1.5 – 2.4: A superior revelation.
2.5 – 3.1: Jesus' humanity.
3.2-6: Servant and Son.
3.7 – 4.2: Faith and obedience today.
4.3-13: Enter God's rest now.

Week 18

Jesus our Great High Priest (Hebrews 5–10)
4.14 – 5.10: Jesus' qualifications to be priest.
5.11 – 6.20: Don't turn back.
Ch. 7: Jesus and Melchizedek.
Ch. 8: Priest of the New Covenant.
9.1-10: In the old tabernacle.
9.11-28: In the new tabernacle.
10.1-18: Recapitulation.

Week 19

Persevering Faith (Hebrews 10–13)
10.19-39: You need to persevere.
11.1-16: Commended for faith.
11.17 – 12.3: Faith down the ages.
12.3-13: Training in faith.
12.14-29: We have come to eternal reality.
13.1-17: Live in faith and love.
13.18-25: Final greetings.

Week 20

Wrath and Righteousness (Romans 1–4)
1.1-17: Introduction.
1.18-32: The sin of the Gentiles.
Ch. 2: Don't Jews have an advantage?
3.1-20: All have sinned.
3.21-31: Righteousness and faith.
Ch. 4: Abraham's faith and yours.

Week 21

New Life in Christ (Romans 5–8)
5.1-11: Summary of benefits available in Christ.
5.12-21: Adam and Christ.
6.1-14: Dead to sin.
6.15 – 7.6: Change of allegiance.
7.7-25: Victory over sin
8.1-17: New life in the Spirit.
8.18-39: Hope and victory.

Week 22

Christ and History (Romans 9–11)
8.18-25: The creation waits.
9.1-13: God's people of promise.
9.14-29: Is God unjust?
9.30 – 10.13: A people of faith.
10.14-21: So the gospel must be preached.
11.1-10: The remnant.
11.11-36: The Gentiles and the Jews.

Week 23

The Heart of the New Law of the Spirit (Romans 12–16)
12.1-8: Living the Christian life.
12.9-21: Love.
13.1-7: State authorities.
13.8-14: Love again.
Ch. 14: Love your weaker brethren.
15.1-13: Encourage one another.
15.14-33: Paul's future travel plans.
Ch. 16: Final greetings.

Home and Further Study Courses

The present book can be used as the working manual for a six-month home study course suitable for use by groups or individuals. The additional materials available are: a book of weekly work sheets and a set of six tapes, each with four 20-minute talks relating to the week's reading. Assistance by correspondence can also be arranged if required.

Six levels of study and training are now available through The Way of the Spirit:

1. SHORT BIBLE READING COURSES
 • 4-6 weeks • on certain Biblical themes • for home or group study.

2. THE FULL BIBLE READING COURSE
 • 4 six-month parts • giving complete coverage of the Bible • for home, correspondence, group, church, or college use.

3. BIBLICAL COMMENTARIES
 • 8 weeks • more detailed studies of single books of the Bible • for home or group study.

4. BIBLICAL AND PROPHETIC FAITH (CERTIFICATE)
 • 2 years • full Bible course plus discipleship and ministry training • local group, class and seminar teaching.

5. PROPHETIC BIBLE TEACHING (DIPLOMA)
 • 1 year • part-time training for local church or group Bible teaching • three short residential schools and monitored home study.

6. PROPHETIC BIBLE TEACHING (FULL-TIME TRAINING)
 • variable duration depending on qualifications and experience • a course for training Bible teachers for more long-term works • full-time residential training.

For details of any of these courses please write to:
The Way of the Spirit, Lamplugh House, Thwing,
Driffield, East Yorkshire YO25 3DY